Where Texts and Children Meet

It is impossible to reflect upon children's books without considering the children who read them. *Where Texts and Children Meet* explores the ways in which children make meaning of the various texts they meet both in and out of school.

Eve Bearne and Victor Watson have brought together chapters on all the major issues associated with the nature and history of children's literature, including:

- the meaning and relevance of terms such as 'literature' for children
- an analysis of new genres including picture books and CD-ROMs
- moral dilemmas and cultural concerns in children's texts.

Where Texts and Children Meet shows how the understanding of children's books is changing, informing teachers' knowledge of popular and classic texts.

Eve Bearne is an Assistant Director in Research at Homerton College, Cambridge. She was a project officer for the National Writing Project and taught English in schools for over thirty years. She has written several books for Routledge, including *Making Progress in English*, *Use of Language Across the Primary Curriculum* and *Use of Language Across the Secondary Curriculum*.

Victor Watson is an Assistant Director in Research at Homerton College, Cambridge, and was previously a Senior Lecturer in English at Homerton. He has edited and contributed to a number of publications in this field, including *Opening the Nursery Door* for Routledge and texts such as *Voices Off* for other publishers.

Where Texts and Children Meet

Edited by Eve Bearne and
Victor Watson

London and New York

First published 2000
by Routledge
11 New Fetter Lane, London EC4P 4EE

Simultaneously published in the USA and Canada
by Routledge
29 West 35th Street, New York, NY 10001

Routledge is an imprint of the Taylor & Francis Group

© 2000 selection and editorial matter, Eve Bearne and Victor
Watson; individual chapters, the contributors

Typeset in Goudy by Routledge
Printed and bound in Great Britain by TJ International Ltd,
Padstow, Cornwall

British Library Cataloguing in Publication Data
A catalogue record for this book is available from the British
Library

Library of Congress Cataloging-in-Publication Data
Where texts and children meet / [edited by] Eve Bearne and
Victor Watson.
        p.   cm.
Includes bibliographical references and index.
1. Children's literature, English–History and criticism. 2. Children's
literature, American–History and criticism 3. Children–Books and
reading. I. Bearne, Eve. II. Watson, Victor.
PR990.W47   2000   99-36160
820.9'9282–dc21   CIP

ISBN 0–415–20662–6 (hbk)
ISBN 0–415–20663–4 (pbk)

Contents

PART II
Crossing boundaries: where cultures meet

PART III
In the picture: the meeting place for authors, illustrators and readers

PART IV
Meetings in imaginative spaces

Illustrations

Figures

Plates (between pp. 112 and 113)

Notes on contributors

Eve Bearne has taught English, drama and education in schools and colleges for over thirty years. She was a project officer for the National Writing Project and editor of a number of their publications. She is co-editor of a series of books about children's literature (for Cassell) and has written and edited several books about language and literacy for Routledge. She is currently Assistant Director in Research at Homerton College, Cambridge, dividing her time between teaching, running in-service courses, researching and writing.

Janet Bottoms teaches in the English Department at Homerton College, Cambridge. She has written several articles on aspects of the use of Shakespeare with children, and also on Mary Lamb's other book for children, *Mrs Leicester's School*. At present she is working on a critical history of Shakespeare in schools from the mid-eighteenth century to the present day.

Formerly Head of English in a Cambridgeshire comprehensive school, **Gabrielle Cliff Hodges** is Secondary Team Leader at Homerton College, Cambridge. She jointly coordinates the secondary English and Drama PGCE course and lectures in English, language, children's literature and core studies on post-graduate and undergraduate courses. She has contributed chapters to several books about English teaching and is co-editor and contributor to *Critical Narratives: Tales, Tellers and Texts* (Cassell, 1999). From 1996–8 she was Chair of the National Association for the Teaching of English.

Jenny Daniels is a Senior Lecturer in Language and Literature at the University of Central England in Birmingham. She has taught in a variety of contexts, most recently in teacher education. She has contributed to several books on children's literature, particularly looking at girls' reading preferences. She is currently developing literature courses for undergraduate students training for primary teaching. The role of literature for children is central to these.

Trained as an art historian, **Jane Doonan** now writes and teaches about illustrative art in picture books, combining aesthetic and semiotic approaches as described in *Looking at Pictures in Picture Books* (The Thimble Press, 1992). Her studies of the work of picture-book makers and illustrators appear in major journals about children's books. She is an invited contributor to the *International Companion Encyclopedia of Children's Literature* (ed. Peter Hunt, Routledge, 1996) and to the forthcoming *Cambridge Guide to Children's Books* (ed. Victor Watson, Cambridge University Press). She is a member of the International Research Society for Children's Literature.

Elizabeth Grugeon is a Senior Lecturer in English in Primary Education at the School of Education, De Montfort University (Bedford). She has co-authored *Teaching, Speaking and Listening in the Primary School* (David Fulton, 1998). Her continuing research into children's playground language and oral culture has recently appeared as an article in the United Kingdom Reading Association's journal *Reading* (vol. 33, no. 1). She is continuing to look at how children's language experience out of the classroom feeds into their developing literacy and learning.

Jacqueline Kirk has been teaching Reception children in Hertfordshire for two years after graduating from Homerton College, Cambridge in 1997. Whilst at college she developed an interest in children's literature, particularly picture books, and is herself writing one which she aims to publish. Her chapter for this book developed from an assignment she wrote for the Education Tripos at Cambridge University. She is shortly to begin teaching in Suffolk and plans to follow an MA in Children's Literature.

Margaret Meek Spencer is Reader Emeritus at the Institute of Education, University of London. She has written many books on children's literacy and literature, several of them – *On Being Literate* (The Bodley Head, fourth reprint, 1998), *How Texts Teach What Children Learn* (The Thimble Press, 1988) and *The Cool Web: The Pattern of Children's Reading* (co-edited with Griselda Barton and Aidan Warlow, The Bodley Head, 1977) – now considered classic texts. She is a member of the Executive Committee of the National Literacy Trust. Her chapter is based on the final, challenging and inspirational keynote address which she gave at the 1997 Conference from which this book has developed.

Helen Nicholson is Director of Drama Studies at Homerton College, Cambridge, where she teaches undergraduate courses in contemporary theatre practice and postgraduate courses in drama education. Before that she taught drama and English in secondary schools in Bristol for eleven years. She has contributed to several international conferences in drama, most recently in Kenya, and has published articles on different aspects of drama education, including a chapter in *On the Subject of Drama* (ed. David Hornbrook, Routledge, 1998) and has researched into arts education.

Now retired from primary teaching and lecturing, **Anne Rowe** continues to work on aspects of children's literature. She was headteacher in two

Berkshire primary schools and for some years worked with the Reading Centre based at Reading University. Her particular interests lie in picture books and she has contributed chapters on this subject to several collections on children's literature. Following her current research, she is becoming increasingly interested in nineteenth-century illustrators.

Lisa Sainsbury is a Lecturer in Children's Literature at the National Centre for Research in Children's Literature at Roehampton Institute, London. She teaches on both undergraduate and postgraduate courses. She has written several articles on children's multimedia and has recently completed her Ph.D. on the postmodern play of textual forms and structures in children's literature.

Morag Styles is a Principal Lecturer and Reader in Children's Literature at Homerton College, Cambridge. She has compiled many anthologies of poetry for children and co-edited a range of books on children's literacy and literature, including the three books from previous Homerton Conferences. She is also co-editor of *Opening the Nursery Door* (with Mary Hilton and Victor Watson, Routledge, 1997) and *Talking Pictures* (with Victor Watson, Hodder, 1997). One of her recent books, however, is devoted to her continuing studies of poetry for children: *From the Garden to the Street: An Introduction to 300 Years of Poetry for Children* (Routledge, 1998). With Holly Anderson she has just edited the companion book from the Homerton conference, *Teaching through Texts* (Routledge, 1999).

Nicholas Tucker is a Lecturer in Child Psychology and Children's Literature at the University of Sussex. Formerly a teacher, then an educational psychologist, he has written widely for both adults and children. His best-known work is *The Child and the Book: A Literary and Psychological Exploration* (reprinted by Cambridge University Press in the Canto 'Classics' series). Recent works have included *Enid Blyton: A Celebration and Reappraisal* (1997, co-edited with Kimberley Reynolds in NCRCL Papers 2, National Centre for Research into Children's Literature, Roehampton Institute, London SW15 4HT) and an edited collection, *School Stories from Bunter to Buckeridge* (1999, NCRCL Papers 4). He also writes and reviews for the *Independent*, the *New Statesman* and for all three *Times* supplements.

Victor Watson is Associate Director in Research at Homerton College, Cambridge. He has written and lectured widely in children's literature, contributes to international conferences and is co-editor of a range of books about children and their reading. He has a special interest in the history and nature of children's books and their relationship both with adult literature and the changing nature of childhood. He has made a close study of books for children in the eighteenth and nineteenth centuries, having a particular interest in William Blake, Lewis Carroll and Arthur Ransome. He has just completed the major task of editing the *Cambridge Guide to Children's Books*.

David Whitley is a Senior Lecturer in English at Homerton College, Cambridge, where he teaches literature, largely from the earlier periods, as well as film studies and children's literature. His research interests include the development of Aesop's fables, on which he has published a number of articles. He is currently working on a book about forms of medieval narratives in children's literature.

Preface

In September 1997 Homerton College, Cambridge, held a conference called 'Where Texts and Children Meet'. This was the fourth of a series of biennial conferences about the texts that children read, watch and enjoy. The separate chapters of this book explore the texts themselves in detail for the complexities they offer to readers who are growing in experience. These texts may be spoken, written or visual; young readers may meet them at home, in the playground, in the classroom, in bookshops, at the cinema, or in their own imaginations as they make sense of existing texts or make their own texts by drawing on the models they are familiar with.

In each section the chapters are grouped around common themes relating to the overall theme of 'where texts and children meet'. Part I draws together contributions about established, older texts and their relevance to young people who will be the readers of the twenty-first century. This historical perspective leads to a cross-cultural view in Part II of meetings between poets, dramatists, novelists from around the world and children who are making their own texts – oral and written – within their own cultures of home and peer groups. Part III brings authors, illustrators and readers together, examining a variety of aspects of pictorial text. Part IV uses the spatial concepts of pictorial text to move into the imaginative places where texts and children meet, exploring the relationship between realism and fantasy. The book closes with a chapter by Margaret Meek Spencer who considers the challenge of new texts alongside the history of make believe.

Encounters between texts and readers raise some complex issues about the value given to traditional types of literature in comparison with what new genres offer. The different contributors tackle the paradoxes and problems associated with the mediation of texts in a changing reading culture. This is not a book about how to use texts in teaching children, although of course we hope it will help in doing just that. It is, rather, a reflective book about the meeting places between texts and children which we hope will add to the debate about what is considered valuable and why. Traditional stories, well-loved favourites which have stood the test of time, literature which has long been accepted as part of children's 'cultural heritage' mingle with newly popular genres and literacies.

Pictorial texts and children's oral culture add to the rich mixture. In looking at literature from the past and turning towards texts of the future, this book examines some of the complexities associated with young readers and texts in a changing literary environment.

Eve Bearne and Victor Watson
Homerton College, Cambridge

Permissions acknowledgements

Plate 9 is from Martin Waddell (1992) *Rosie's Babies*, illustrated by Penny Dale, and published in London by Walker Books.

Thanks also to Iona Opie for permission to quote in chapter 7 the rhyme 'We are the Barbie Girls', from I. Opie and P. Opie (1985), *The Singing Game*, Oxford: Oxford University Press, p. 478; to Great Ormond Street Hospital for permission to quote in chapter 12 several lines from J.M. Barrie (1988; first published 1906) *Peter Pan*, London: Viking Kestrel, p. 11; and to Michael Rosen for permission to quote in the Afterword his poem 'On the Question of Whether It's Possible to Sleep on a Train', from Michael Rosen (1997) 'A Materialist and Intertextual Examination of the Process of Writing a Work of Children's Literature', PhD thesis, University of North London.

Introduction

Children's literature is dead: long live children's reading

Victor Watson

The term 'children's literature' is now widely used as a generic label covering all texts published for children. This practice has the advantage of side-stepping those ideological complications implicit in the word 'literature'. However, if you call everything 'literature', you have effectively done away with literary distinctiveness. At the same time the study of children's literature in universities all over the world is often entirely divorced from an interest in its intended readership. If one approach ignores the notion of *literature* and the other is uninterested in *children*, one wonders if a scholarly interest in their relatedness might disappear altogether. But that is, in fact, a melodramatic way of putting it. It would be misleading to suggest that there are two camps separated by an unbridgeable philosophical division. It is true that a wide range of different critical perspectives exists, but scholars concerned with children's books are remarkably eclectic, pragmatic and tolerant of one another, happily allowing themselves new insights deriving from critical theories that they do not themselves embrace. And there are some whose critical practices bear little relationship to the critical theory they espouse The differences between the two disappear almost completely in the area of history, where the evidence of children's responses is more sketchy anyway. Insofar as there is any difficulty in this apparently divided situation, the most hopeful way forward is probably to be found in Peter Hollindale's concept of 'childness' (Hollindale 1997), a critical theory which sees a coherence uniting childhood, adulthood and narrative. However, for any scholar with a professional commitment to teaching, it is impossible to reflect upon children's books without considering the children who read them. In my case, it is not so much a critical position as a deeply ingrained professional habit of thought that goes back to September 1962, when I took up my first teaching post and faced the dispiriting contents of the English stock cupboard. It is precisely that relatedness – that *meeting* – which is the central concern of *Where Texts and Children Meet* and which has broadly characterised the Homerton approach to children's books for more than a decade.

What has distinguished most approaches to children's reading in recent years has been the development of new and more refined critical languages. As I have said, if we describe all children's texts as *children's literature*, we have effectively abolished literary distinction. This might not be a bad thing – it is not a quality that interests most young readers, and adults cannot agree what they mean by it. But that does not mean that issues of excellence and questions of value have become irrelevant, and at the heart of *Where Texts and Children Meet* lies a concern for quality. Judgements are explicitly or implicitly made – not in sweeping literary or heritage terms, but in the form of detailed and discriminating comments upon provision. In recent years, the analysis of picture books – largely through the work of David Lewis, Jane Doonan and Judith Graham – has developed a new and liberating terminology and new kinds of discourse. But the new technologies also need new critical languages: you cannot helpfully apply the old literary criticism to film, video games, CD-ROMs and electronic books. Lisa Sainsbury's chapter is a model of how such an enterprise might develop. Although there are no references to *literary* quality, almost every contributor to this volume addresses issues of quality, excellence and good value. As Gabrielle Cliff Hodges shows in her chapter, much of the best criticism emerges from the various ways teachers make possible new ways of arranging the meetings between texts and children, and become attentive to the developing critical responses of young readers.

While new critical languages need to be developed and refined, terms such as 'children's literature' and 'the classics' have lost their sharpness, their ability to illuminate and inspire new understandings. Although they are brought back into play when some aspect of children and their reading is given prominence in political or journalistic controversy, it is an unsatisfactory business – these superannuated critical weapons cannot be drawn cleanly from the rock. They are rusty and dented, and cannot be used with precision.

Nevertheless, the concept of 'children's literature' has its own honourable history and awaits its researchers. It was once an Excalibur – sharp, challenging and inspirational. It came into being in the United Kingdom associated with a wish to raise the status of children's writers, and of the teachers, librarians and academics interested in the books that children read – and particularly to acknowledge a generation of new writers whose work was beginning to appear in the late 1950s and 1960s. It also sought to challenge the dominance throughout that period of Enid Blyton's fiction by insisting on alternative criteria and proclaiming that only the best was good enough for the country's children. Perhaps, too, there was also the implied idea that, if a genuine children's *literature* could be made to exist, it ought to take on the transitional role of leading young readers towards adult literature. Indeed many writers of the period deliberately and with serious commitment wrote *literary* novels for the young that did genuinely provide lessons in how to read adult fiction.

What constituted a *literary novel* would be hard to define: it had to do with language and style, and with new narrative modes; but a frequent characteristic was a wide allusiveness to other works of literature, so that children reading one such novel would have their attention directed to a variety of other literary (or musical, theatrical, artistic) works. Even without that allusiveness, a child reading Gillian Avery, Lucy Boston or Leon Garfield could move comfortably to Muriel Spark, Iris Murdoch or Charles Dickens.

Once established, the term 'children's literature' was then applied retrospectively to Carroll, Nesbit, Hodgson Burnett and the rest, with the slightly misleading implication that a concern to provide an exclusive *literature* for the young had been an abiding, continuous and self-conscious intention for more than a hundred years – a Little Tradition working modestly alongside the Great Tradition of English literature.

Few would subscribe to such a view today. Its implied absolutism can have little appeal to sceptical postmodernist thought. But the evangelical excitement associated with the enterprise in the 1960s was considerable, especially as there was a generation of new writers whose work required determined and attentive readers, and at the same time gave great pleasure to adults. Some of that fiction came to be seen as too difficult for young readers, and was founded on an aesthetic that was essentially exclusive. Alan Garner's later novels, for example, frustrated at a stroke the traditional expectation that an authorial voice should provide constant explanation and reassurance. The plots are driven often by anxiety or fear – often with long episodes of unattributed dialogue – and the only explanations the reader is given are those of the puzzled characters themselves. Nor do his endings provide the clear and comforting resolutions usually associated with children's fiction.

But for the determined and responsive reader, this new aesthetic offered a dynamic sense of private and communal experience, often muddled and only partly understood by the fictional characters themselves. It tried to do justice to fleeting, fragmentary and half-understood experience. Above all it was an aesthetic offering readers new challenges and left them gaps to fill and puzzles to work out. Any similarities between a Blytonesque *explanatory* aesthetic and the new *literary* aesthetic are superficial: each was in the most fundamental way opposite to the other, the one committed to an absolute and simplified surface clarity, the other to a permeable suggestion of infinite depths and shadowy insights. The shock of Mayne's *Choir School* quartet, or of Garner's *The Owl Service*, or of Antonia Forest's *Peter's Room*, to a reading culture based on *explanatory* fiction can hardly be exaggerated; and the excitement it generated in teachers, librarians, academics and many young readers was real and inspirational.

Then came a moment in the history of children's books at which – to the dismay of many – there was a conscious move to abandon the *literary novel* in favour of accessible and popular fiction generally. It was a debate between literature and teaching – a failure of precisely that relatedness with which *Where Texts and Children Meet* is concerned. And it set children's writers a fresh challenge – to write narratives that were richly evocative and multilayered in language and form, but which were at the same time straightforwardly accessible to inexperienced young learner readers; or, to put it more bluntly, to make fiction whose complexities and subtleties do not act as a deterrent. A few writers managed it, none more successfully than the incomparable Jan Mark;[1] others adapted, as can be seen by comparing the early novels of Philippa Pearce with her latest, *The Way to Sattin Shore*.

So the term 'children's literature' was not always a blunt weapon. For thirty years it helped to shape the way children's books were understood and valued. However, the *classic* has a less elevated history. The ways in which a work comes to be regarded as a classic are both fascinating and problematic. In the last five or six years, I have noticed a readiness to think of Enid Blyton as a great classic writer and to regard some of her works – *The Magic Faraway Tree* and its sequels, perhaps, or *The Famous Five* series – as great classics of their time. I draw attention to this phenomenon not to reawaken old controversies about Blyton's work but simply to remind readers that it was not always thus. There is an interesting anomaly here: when Blyton's books were being consumed by young readers in their millions, adult criticism was content to regard them as little better than *rubbish*. And now, in a nice irony, we seem to be willing to concede classic status at the precise moment in history when children themselves are beginning to turn away from what they see as dated and rather silly stories. So we got it wrong – twice.[2]

'Rubbish', too, is a problematic term. There are those who argue that bad writing is simply bad writing and that we should do everything in our power not to infect our children's minds with its dangerous influence. There are others who believe that it is mostly harmless, or that a healthy literary diet needs some roughage in it, or that you cannot appreciate good writing if you have no experience of bad. A rather different kind of defence might call it popular fiction and argue that it provides an important transitional reading, possibly leading later to a developing interest in more nourishing literature. Another argument is one concerning empowerment – that young readers are discriminating and know exactly what they are doing when they choose to read popular fiction; that if they choose to read escapist novels it is probably because they wish to escape; that the act of reading is itself a locus of complex personal and ideological pressures; and that in any case the reading strategies involved in reading a Point Romance are not unlike those involved in reading *Pride and Prejudice*. And, finally, there is the view that *rubbish* is just as culturally determined as *literature*, that a good deal of it is actually very well-written, and that yesterday's *rubbish* may be tomorrow's *classic*.

One deplorable consequence of the notion of the classic is that it encourages selective histories, omitting 95 per cent of what children actually read. Yet it hardly needs to be said that an account of children's reading is not the same as an account of the classics; a *social history* of children's reading is badly needed. The concept of the classic gets in the way of such an undertaking, so that the less well-known writers whose works lasted only for a generation – but who in their own time made possible thousands of forgotten readings – are not remembered. Although a few distinguished scholars have for many years contributed a substantial body of bibliographical research, the critical overview of the history of children's books remains incomplete and distorted. So much has been entirely omitted – for example, the massive contribution of magazines and annuals[3] as a central and abiding contribution to the reading of children for the last 150 years. And until recently information books suffered a similar neglect. The contribution of series fiction has yet to be appreciated. Finally, the ways in which the largely forgotten children's authors of the 1940s and 1950s have been obscured by the overwhelming output of Enid Blyton[4] exemplifies how history can become so preoccupied by the most successful writers that their success is magnified.

A book entitled *Where Texts and Children Meet* might reasonably prompt this question: *Where*, precisely, *do* texts and children meet?

The traditional value-laden muddle of journalistic criticism is inclined to the sentimental or nostalgic view, associating children's literature with bedtime reading under the blanket with a torch. This is not entirely wrong, and we should not lose sight of the fact that determined children have an infinite variety of ways of finding the reading they want. But we also need to accept the fact that all meetings between texts and children – whether they take place in quiet libraries, in crowded classrooms, in drama studios, or at screens of one kind or another – in a very real sense take place in a marketplace, within the apparently implacable realities of publishing and marketing economics. In the end, considerations of value and quality point to the suppliers and providers. To whom are publishers and booksellers accountable?

The realities of the marketplace are acknowledged in every chapter in this volume – except one. Elizabeth Grugeon, in her chapter on playground lore and language, describes perhaps the only arena left where market economics have no power over the mercurial inventiveness of children. Playground lore is a literacy for which no participant has to have *bought* anything – not even a skipping rope. To take part, all you must have is a body, a voice and a willingness to join in. (And it helps to be a girl.) Although these children's games and rhymes are in all manner of ways enmeshed with their cultural lives, the market has no impact at all on the freewheeling, improvising, mischievous literacies that develop there.

That is deeply comforting. However, the provision of all other kinds of children's texts is largely dependent on producers and vendors in a marketplace that is in many ways profoundly unsatisfactory. And yet I do not believe there is any need to be defeatist about it. If those of us who are concerned with the provision of children's texts can be clear where power lies, and where decisions are made, it is possible that we might come to understand what needs to be done if this marketplace is to work in the interests of children.

And a great deal needs to be done. Changes must be made in both publishing and bookselling. There must be higher production values and better marketing. Bookshops must show a greater commitment to employing and training specialists in their children's departments. There must be an end on the part of publishers to short, half-hearted print runs; and new titles must not be taken out of print before they have had time to become known.[5] There needs to be a constant revisiting of back lists in search of books that might be reissued – it is a peculiar irony that, at a time when *heritage* has become an educational slogan, a good deal of heritage lies buried and forgotten in publishers' back lists. And, most importantly, ways must be found to value and extend the influence of the tiny handful of gifted editors currently working in the field.[6] And, incidentally, why cannot these big international publishers provide a wide international literature? Why, for example, has children's literature in the United Kingdom been almost entirely untouched by the extraordinary renaissance currently taking place in South Africa?

Is it ridiculous to talk in such idealistic terms in a world of profit and loss? I think not. Publishers must look to their laurels: if the great classics of adult literature can be bought for one pound, and if Internet providers offer access free of charge, publishers might be asked some embarrassing questions about the service they provide. Why should books for children cost more than books for undergraduates? There is a role here for central government: provision for access must be wide and egalitarian. Free books for some schools, sponsored by major newspapers, are all very well, but affordable books for everyone would be better.

It is not enough, though, for teachers, librarians and academics to complain: we must find ways of helping those beleaguered children's editors who cannot get a book reissued unless they can guarantee a publishing committee that at least 2000 copies will be sold – at a time when library budgets are being cut. Let us make no mistake about this: many children's book editors are sympathetic, along with some dedicated and highly skilled booksellers. So what can be done to help them? I do not ask this as a rhetorical question – those of us with an educational interest in children's books should consider what formal or institutional structures might be established to support the editors and booksellers.

And let us not have too many awards. One for each genre ought to be enough. Where there are too many prizes, some publishers will be tempted to discontinue new titles unless they get shortlisted. That would serve no one's purpose and operate as an unofficial and arbitrary censorship.

On the other hand, there need to be more – and more widely and quickly available – reviews and criticism. In any marketplace, value for money is important and issues of quality will continue to matter. Critical opinions *of both adults and children* should be made widely available. I do not believe that young readers should be allowed to have the last word; but nor do I believe that adult reviewers should be allowed the *only* word. In literary criticism, there is no last word – only dynamic exchanges of provisional and avowedly subjective judgements. But I cannot see how there can be any development of critical literacy unless there is a flourishing literary criticism, and I cannot see any reason why young readers should not become young critics. Anyone who doubts their ability to engage in criticism should consult *In Brief*, an in-house review magazine distributed free at a major chain of bookshops, whose young critics have established new standards for intelligent and uncompromising directness, clarity and accessibility.

As *Where Texts and Children Meet* shows, what used to be called 'the world of children's books' is changing rapidly. With luck – and with the application of articulate and intelligent political pressure – the marketplace might change for the better. The providers might be persuaded to make direct eye contact with the children who come there to buy.

There is no need for those of us who are concerned about children's reading to feel dispirited about current developments. Marketplaces are often rather exciting.

Notes

1 There can be no better illustration of what I mean than her *Trouble Half-Way*, which is simultaneously both immensely complex and immensely simple.
2 It is worth remembering, perhaps, that more Enid Blyton books have fallen out of print than works by *any* other writer.
3 There are various lively works on the history and development of comics and annuals, but they are intended mostly for collectors and rarely engage analytically with the texts.
4 Blyton seems to me to be of special importance. Quite apart from debates about the value of her work, she hijacked children's literature and defined, for a generation of children, parents and publishers, what it was. In doing so, her massive and relentless output not only overwhelmed alternative critical views of her time, but has also determined how historians today see her period.
5 The success of J.K. Rowling's *Harry Potter and the Philosopher's Stone* would not have occurred at all if the publisher (Bloomsbury) had not kept it in print long enough for its quality to become known, largely by word of mouth.
6 There are one or two publishing editors interested in reissuing out-of-print works; but they are few and far between.

Reference

Hollindale, Peter (1997) *Signs of Childness in Children's Books*, Stroud, Glos. Signal Press.

Part I

The old meets the new

This book begins by looking at what happens when new readers meet old texts. Very often they are introduced to each other by well-meaning adults who, with proper social concern, want to make these encounters as pleasant as possible so that good and enduring relationships can be established. But the contributors to Part I question the whole idea of smoothing the way and making introductions easier, suggesting that it's a more complicated business than it might at first seem. Sometimes adults who want to simplify first meetings just get in the way, making it more difficult for children to have a genuine conversation with a text. Books can seem like older friends in the dialogues children have with them, but the apparent playfulness of a text can mask sombre thoughts. Sometimes adults might try to prevent close attachments forming, fearing that certain texts might offer danger to their young readers; at other times, young readers enjoy dialogues with texts written by young writers. All of these possible relationships between texts and children, the old and the new, are represented here.

Janet Bottoms criticises those who try to make Shakespeare too 'familiar', pointing out that 'space and time are needed for a true meeting with something as complex as a Shakespeare play'. She reviews the ways in which Shakespeare has been used for teaching over the centuries and how this has resulted in 'versions', 'tales' and explanatory notes, which tend to mask the subtleties rather than enhance them or make it easier for young people to enjoy the works. She feels that adult interventions can be intrusions: 'If we want children to meet Shakespeare we must stand out of the way as much as possible, let them *be there*, ask their own questions, even answer back in their own way.'

Many adults, in the UK at least, would remember their first meeting with Robert Louis Stevenson as one that seemed effortless; here was an adult who could speak with the voice of a child. But is this true? Certainly, Stevenson's poetry remains some of the best loved by adults and children alike, suggesting accessibility and easy conversation between the reader and the texts, but when adults probe the nostalgia surrounding *A Child's Garden of Verses*, for example, they may find an adult whose childlike tones seem both pretence and pretentious. Morag Styles considers some issues surrounding this collection of well-loved poetry, reminding us that Stevenson had a darker side and that he certainly did not feel 'proud or particular' about his 'rimes'. While he did not claim to 'go for eternity', there is nevertheless an enduring appeal in his work. Styles suggests that perhaps when children meet Stevenson they find someone who, as an adult, can 'gaze at the immensity of the world and wonder at it', while adults may be seeking the 'child of air' from their own lost childhoods.

Adults are properly concerned that any new encounter for children should not be dangerous. This has meant that over the years some stories – particularly, perhaps, fairy stories – have been heavily censored. Even today, the versions collected and published by the brothers Grimm can worry adults because of negative images of certain groups of people. Stepmothers have certainly suffered at the hands of fairy-tale makers and Nicholas Tucker takes a new look at these traditionally threatening but strangely alluring figures. He looks at modern views of family groups and parenting, reminding us that fathers and stepfathers may now be seen as more of a threat in some encounters with children and that 'images of wicked stepmothers are more easily accommodated than ideas about wicked stepfathers'. Tucker offers no palliatives. While reassuring today's step-mothers that they often do better in the eyes of their new charges than their fictional counterparts in Grimms' stories, he points out that it is easy to exaggerate the effects on young readers of meetings with such demonised characters.

Part I ends with the meeting of young readers with young writers. Victor Watson reviews what he calls the forgotten history of writing by young writers – Daisy Ashford, K.M. Peyton, Pamela Brown and others – who were writing early in the twentieth century. There have been fewer examples more recently, and Watson argues that there must be young writers still 'out there' but that perhaps modern publishing robs us of their texts. One of the greatest appeals of the books written by children in the 1930s and 1940s was a powerful sense of sharing with adults, even if the adults were kept in the background. The whole of Part I has a message for adults who want to mediate between older texts and new readers – the contributors show that children can tackle profound texts for themselves, can meet writers as equals in delight, can distinguish between literary texts and life, and can be writers of texts for children when they are still very close to childhood themselves. It adds up to honouring the child as a reader and writer, who is capable of more than adults might imagine.

Chapter 1

'Familiar Shakespeare'

Janet Bottoms

'Although in naming the best books of the world, Shakespeare is usually mentioned after the Bible, comparatively few of the great reading public are familiarly acquainted with Shakespeare's plays.' So wrote Lois Hufford in 1902, and many people would argue that little has changed since (Hufford 1902: vii). Yet it is undeniable that the majority of adults, and even of children, in the British Isles are familiar with *a* 'Shakespeare' of some kind – a name, an icon, revered or rejected – vaguely associated with 'quotations' and parodies of quotations; with history and tourism; above all with school, and the social and intellectual divide signalled by 'doing', or being judged incapable of 'doing', him. This Shakespeare – this 'familiar ghost' of the national psyche – is largely the product not of the theatre, or even of direct experience of reading the plays, but of all the *Family Shakespeares*, anthologies, *Tales* and annotated school texts which have poured from the presses in the last 200 years. A major industry has grown up to feed Shakespeare to the nursery and schoolroom, and it is on foundations acquired in childhood that the superstructure of much of our knowledge is built.

So accepted has the idea become that Shakespeare should be taught to children that we hardly query why or where it arose. Shakespeare is 'great', and therefore greatly good even for children, enriching 'the fancy' and strengthening virtue ·(Lamb and Lamb 1809: xi) or, in the terminology of today, conveying 'rich and subtle meanings' and 'universal values' (DES 1989: 7.16). The intention is admirable; the approach, reverent. Hufford described the aim of her *Shakespeare in Tale and Verse* as:

> to tell the stories from Shakespeare's point of view; to interpret sympathetically and truthfully the motives of the dramas and of the characters; to omit unessential details, and to select for quoting passages that are notable for strength and beauty.
>
> (Hufford 1902: viii)

More than half a century later Leon Garfield wrote of his *Shakespeare Stories* that his intention was 'to be true to the play, and always seek to bring my readers to Shakespeare, rather than Shakespeare to my readers' (Garfield 1990: 46). Indeed every *tale* teller and abridger has claimed only to act as a 'gateway', an 'introduction' to the plays themselves. Yet what does it mean to be 'true to the play'? Who is to say what Shakespeare would have considered 'unessential'? And what happens to Shakespeare when a child has been 'introduced' to him? It is, perhaps, salutary to recall Alice's introduction to the pudding in *Through the Looking Glass*: 'Pudding – Alice. Alice – Pudding. Remove the pudding!' Invited to a feast, Alice was left hungry.

It is not, of course, inevitable that children must or will meet Shakespeare's plays in such a way. Some have always had their first encounters with him through a – perhaps imperfectly understood but personally experienced – theatre performance, and such memories will often remain with them, and the adults they become, for years. 'Children's Shakespeare', however, was born at the beginning of the nineteenth century, when publishers for the new juvenile and educational markets discovered his commercial value. Since then – as a corpus of 'works' fronted by the vaguely monumental figure of the 'author', rather than any single text – he has been regarded as a resource to be drawn upon by moralists and writers for children, in much the same way as they have drawn upon classical and popular myth and story. The basis upon which such reworking commonly takes place, according to a study by Zohar Shavit, is a collection of 'assumptions held by the editors about childhood, especially about *the child's capacity to understand and the themes to which he should be exposed* [italics in the original]'. On this basis, traditional stories are filled out with minor details 'according to contemporary fashion or prejudice', while elements considered unsuitable are 'either omitted or revised' (Shavit 1986: 28–9). Shakespeare himself, of course, engaged in similar activity, drawing his stories from a common stock which was, and still is, equally free to others. In the plays, however, these stories have been consciously shaped into new and complex forms, and such 'authority' as is given them by his name must surely be bound up in the forms their 'author' gave them. In these forms they have already departed from any 'clear opposition between "bad" and "good"', and live by such 'ambiguous values and characterizations' as, according to Shavit, are inconceivable to writers within the 'children's system' (Shavit 1986: 29).

The history of 'children's Shakespeare' bears out Shavit's thesis. 'It was no easy matter to give the histories of men and women in terms familiar to the apprehension of a very young mind', said Mary Lamb, at times almost despairing of her task.[1] Despite claims that 'Shakespeare's plays suit all ages', the protection of mediator and censor has usually been thought necessary (Allman 1883: v). The assumption that children are too young to understand text written as dialogue, or its 'glorious' but 'rather difficult and old-fashioned language', justifies putting the stories 'back into simple modern language', disentangled from the competing plots and extra characters with which the dramatist complicated them and their moral (Miles 1976: 8). Sometimes, too, that moral has seemed inadequately drawn, the text failing in its 'obligations towards the child … that the child should gain something for their spiritual welfare' from it (Shavit 1986:17). 'Theatre', as David Hare says, 'is a moral form', and therefore 'it is almost impossible to stop the audience drawing moral implications', but in 'children's Shakespeare' they are seldom left to draw the conclusions for themselves: the narrator-intermediary must interpret 'the motives of the dramas' for them (Hare 1996: xv). How they have been interpreted has tended to vary from one version, and from one century to the next.

Shakespeare became our 'familiar Shakespeare' largely through three media – the anthologised passages from which the quotable quotes known to everyone are drawn; the prose narrative versions; and various selected and abridged texts, from the Bowdlers' *Family Shakspeare* to the recent *Animated Tales*. As Noel Perrin points out in *Dr. Bowdler's Legacy*, even most apparently unexpurgated school editions, down to the present day, have in fact been tacitly 'bowdlerized' both in the texts themselves and in the accompanying 'explanatory' notes. The process began even before the Bowdlers got to work, in Bell's 1774 edition of the texts used at the Theatre Royal, from which those 'glaring indecencies' which had survived on the stage were omitted in order to make Shakespeare 'more instructive and intelligible, especially to the ladies and to youth' (Perrin 1992: 93). The supposed needs of these two categories were the motive force that produced 'familiar Shakespeare', and the more detached from the theatre Shakespeare became the easier it was to make him both safe and instructive. Pleasure came a poor third.

Shakespeare the moral philosopher

Shakespeare's entry into the world of education can be traced first in the eighteenth-century anthologies for the use of schools, primarily grammar schools for boys of the middle classes. These books, modelled on the earlier Latin 'grammars', were designed for two purposes: as aids to learning the techniques of public speaking, and for moral teaching through the 'authority' attached to aphoristic or meditative passages committed to memory. Shakespeare was a relatively late entrant in this company. *The Virgin Muse* of 1717, for example, 'a collection of poems from our most celebrated English poets', did not include him, and neither did the *The Pleasing Instructor* of 1756. In 1774, however, William Enfield's *The Speaker* introduced a number of passages from Shakespeare's plays, drawn predominantly from the histories. From the comedies he took only those stoical or melancholy summaries of Life or The World which would continue to appear in similar collections for many years to come. Enfield's *Speaker* proved immensely popular, going through at least sixty editions and introducing large numbers of boys to what are even today the most familiar lines and speeches. In 1810, Charles Lamb complained about the number of times he had had to listen to the words of Henry V '*spouted*' by schoolboys, and confessed himself:

utterly unable to appreciate that celebrated soliloquy of Hamlet, 'To be or not to be', or to tell whether it be good, bad or indifferent, it has been so handled and pawed about by declamatory boys and men, and torn so inhumanly from its living place and principle of continuity in the play.

(Lamb 1811 [1924 edition]: I, 126–7)

Other collections followed the pattern of the even more popular *The Beauties of Shakespeare*, compiled by William Dodd, who arranged his chosen passages under indexed headings such as 'Conjugal Fidelity', 'Conscience', 'Consent of a Father' and 'Constancy'. The morally dubious was thus avoided: dramatic context was of no relevance.

The plays were available in increasing numbers in the homes of the educated classes, however, and were read within the family circle. This was the means by which girls were most likely to encounter Shakespeare, if they did so at all. Shakespeare had long appealed particularly to women as *their* classic, the philosopher whose understanding of the human heart came 'from *nature*', not the theories of 'the school-men', and who was concerned particularly with 'those moral duties which are the truest source of mortal bliss – domestic ties, offices, and obligations' (Griffin 1775: ix–xiii). His heroines, though lively and witty, were also devoted to their families and friends, and either were, or became, models of wifely duty, while the tragedies could 'furnish themes on which to ground much appropriate and instructive conversation'. As Hannah More argued, works which might appear to 'promise nothing better than mere entertainment' could, 'in the hands of a judicious preceptor' and 'when properly selected and judiciously animadverted on', not only 'delight the imagination, and gratify the feelings, but carry instruction to the heart' (More 1805: 176). Aphorisms and extracts alone would not do this: story, character, romance might all be justified, provided that the 'judicious preceptor' was at hand.

This presented no problem where there was a parent or teacher qualified to mediate between text and child. Dr Bowdler remembered his father reading with such 'good taste' and 'prompt discretion' in omitting anything 'dangerous' that his children 'listened with delight to Lear, Hamlet, and Othello, without knowing that those matchless tragedies contained words and expressions improper to be pronounced' (Bowdler 1825, cited in Perrin 1992: 65). Such discretion, however, was not always to be relied upon – especially as the volumes of Shakespeare became increasingly available to the growing, wider reading public. England was becoming a mercantile and rapidly industrialising society, with a rising middle class, desirous of acquiring a 'polite' education. This was the public that Coleridge hoped to attract to his lectures on Shakespeare, since, as he said:

it can rarely happen that a man of social disposition, altogether a stranger to subjects of taste (almost the only ones on which persons of both sexes can converse with a common interest), should pass through the world without at times feeling dissatisfied with himself.

(Morley 1932: 138–9)

Such men, according to Coleridge, were marked by their anxiety to secure for their children the accomplishments they did not have themselves. There was, therefore, a market for a Shakespeare guaranteed not to 'give pain to the most chaste or offence to the most religious of his readers' (Bowdler 1818: I, viii), a Shakespeare who would be, to his young readers, 'a withdrawing from all selfish and mercenary thoughts', teaching them 'courtesy, benignity, generosity, humanity' (Lamb 1809: viii).

It was into this cultural context that the two works which might be said to herald the arrival of 'Shakespeare for children' were published, coincidentally in the same year. It is probably not a coincidence, however, that both the Lambs' *Tales from Shakespeare: Designed for the use of young persons* and the first (1807) edition of *The Family Shakespear* were mainly the work of women, and written primarily with girls in mind. Though the larger, second edition of *The Family Shakspeare* appeared under the name of Thomas Bowdler, the first was published anonymously by his sister Henrietta, aiming perhaps to do for others' families what her father had implicitly done for her. In an unsigned preface, she claimed that, since 'everything that can raise a blush upon the cheek of modesty' had been removed from the text, it could even be 'placed in the hands of young persons of both sexes' – without intermediary (H. Bowdler 1807: preface). Similarly, though they were not at first attributed to her, fourteen of the twenty stories in the Lambs' *Tales* were written by Mary, to whom it is probable that the original commission was given. They were described as intended principally for 'very young children' and 'young ladies', but the advertisement for the second (1809) edition admitted that their style had been found to be 'not so precisely adapted for the amusement of mere children, as for an acceptable and improving present to young ladies advancing to the state of womanhood' (Lamb and Lamb 1809). For much of the nineteenth century, the main markets for the many selections, adaptations and narrative versions of Shakespeare that followed the lead of the Lambs and the Bowdlers were in the home, and in schools for girls. As the Rev J.R. Pitman said, in the preface to his *School Shakspeare*, 'The attention of young females, both in schools and in families, has, of late years, been carefully directed to the study of our English classics' (Pitman 1822: preface). Caroline Maxwell introduced her *Juvenile Edition of Shakspeare: adapted to the capacities of Youth* with the assertion that 'an early knowledge of this excellent author is a most desirable acquisition', since 'polite education cannot be complete without it' (Maxwell 1828: preface) and Thomas Bowdler's nephew concluded:

The readers of Shakspeare will henceforth probably be multiplied tenfold; the Family Shakspeare will be the edition which will lie upon the table of every drawing-room, and the name of the editor will be remembered, as of one who has perhaps contributed more than any other individual to promote the innocent and rational amusement of well-educated families.

(Bowdler 1825: 321–2)

Thus was 'familiar Shakespeare' born.

Shakespeare, the 'Girl's Friend'

Until the expansion of education in the second part of the nineteenth century, Shakespeare appears still to have been seen as peculiarly well suited to the needs of girls. The plays most often selected, as well as the method of treatment, reflect what were thought to be the interests of girls, focusing principally on romantic and family relationships, and omitting all lowlife antics. With the advent of the Victorian era the range of plays selected also tended increasingly to be limited. The romantic comedies were popular, along with *Hamlet*, *Lear* and *Macbeth*, but *Othello* caused difficulties most easily solved by omitting it, and even *Romeo and Juliet* could be problematic. So far as the histories were concerned, *King John*, with the pathetic Constance and Prince Arthur, was popular, as was the tragic Queen Katharine in *Henry VIII*, but even Bowdler had said of the *Henry* plays that 'to clear them of all indecent and indelicate expressions, without destroying the wit and spirit of Falstaff' was 'an arduous undertaking' (Bowdler 1818: V, 96). Falstaff might be highly regarded by the adult world, but he was not suited to children, especially girls.

The heroines, on the other hand, were everything that could be wished, 'models of courtesy, gentleness, grace, and every combination of moral beauty' (Slater 1836: xi) who combined 'delicacy and tenderness' with a 'devoted, self-denying and sustaining power', which enabled them to 'brave dangers and perils from which a sterner nature would shrink' (Anon 1848: vii). Shakespeare, it was believed, could speak to and on behalf of women with peculiar authority, for, as Mary Cowden Clarke, author of the immensely popular *The Girlhood of Shakespeare's Heroines*, put it, he was 'the Girl's Friend'.

For moral introspection and self-culture Shakespeare is a grand aid, as well as for mental discipline; ... since he, the most manly thinker and most virile writer that ever put pen to paper, had likewise something essentially feminine in his nature, which enabled him to discern and sympathize with the innermost core of woman's heart.

(Clarke 1887: VIII, 562)

Lively, witty, loyal, capable of devoted female friendship, and yet impeccably dutiful daughters and wives, Shakespeare's women fed the romantic dreams of middle-class Victorian girls, without leading them into dangerous paths. Even at the end of the century an experienced woman teacher was advising a young student that 'in this age of feminine eagerness and prominence', the 'would-be "new woman"' would do well first to learn to be a 'Shakespeare woman', since 'without the deep heart of Cordelia, the devotion of Imogen, the patience of Hermione, the generosity of Portia, the gentleness of Desdemona, the joyousness of Rosalind, and the grace of Perdita, all the enlightenment and freedom of the nineteenth century' would prove but a snare and a delusion (Knox 1895: 223).

At the younger end of the age group, the emphasis was placed less on Shakespeare's insight into character than on his 'beautiful stories'. Here we find A *Midsummer Night's Dream* coming into increasing prominence. E. Nesbit's account of the genesis of her *Children's Shakespeare* locates it in the aftermath of a visit to Shakespeare's house in Stratford, with the children 'poring over a big volume of the Master's plays, lent them by the landlord', while she 'with eyes fixed on the fire, was wandering happily in the immortal dreamland peopled by Rosalind and Imogen, Lear and Hamlet' (Nesbit 1897: 5–6). Out of this she is dragged by the children's complaint that they can't understand a word, in spite of having been promised that it was 'so beautiful' and 'a fairytale'. To justify Shakespeare's claims – or her claims on his behalf – she has to tell them the story, and to the complaint that it doesn't look like that in the book, replies with the classic apology that it is only 'put differently' and that they will understand when they grow up 'that the stories are the least part of Shakespeare'.

'But it's the stories *we* like,' said Rosamund.

'You see he did not write for children.'

'No, but you might,' cried Iris, flushed with a sudden idea.

'Why don't you write the stories for us so that we can understand them just as you told us that, and then, when we are grown up we shall understand the plays so much better.'

(Nesbit 1897: 5–6)

The result of nearly a century of 'introducing' Shakespeare is that the plots, previously criticised by scholars as Shakespeare's weakest point, have come to be seen as valuable in themselves because they are *his*: 'No one before he lived ever made up such beautiful stories', claims Adelaide Gordon Sim (1894) in *Phoebe's Shakespeare*. The *Dream* becomes simply a fairy-tale, and Shakespeare the creator of a 'dreamland' of 'pleasure' and 'truths' which wait to be discovered sometime in the future, but meanwhile have to be taken on trust.

Shakespeare, man and boy

Meanwhile, another aspect of our 'familiar Shakespeare' had begun to develop with the mid-century expansion of elementary and 'middle-class' schooling.

Though the public and old-established grammar schools might continue to focus almost exclusively on the classics, a growing number of educationists were arguing for the importance of the so-called 'English subjects' – English language, English history, geography, and finally English literature. 'I think', concluded Professor Henry Sidgwick, in 1867, 'that a course of instruction in our own language and literature ... ought to form recognised and substantive parts of our school system' (Sidgwick 1867: 140–1). In such a course, Shakespeare, the national poet, must obviously have pride of place, though for many years there was uncertainty as to just how he should be taught. An educational tradition based on the parsing and translating of Latin texts did not lend itself easily to study of the native literature, and 'doing Shakespeare' in school became, for many, little more than an exercise in linguistic analysis. However, a new impetus had been given to the 'children's Shakespeare' industry in general, and the last decades of the century saw the publication in increasing numbers of new narrative or abridged versions of the plays, as well as the Lambs' *Tales*, now with notes and glossary, in cheap formats designed for schools. 'More and more is a knowledge of Shakespeare coming to be regarded as a necessary part of an Englishman's education', Alfred Ainger wrote in his edition of 1879 (Ainger 1879: xiii).

This was not the 'Girl's Friend', however, but a new, more masculine Shakespeare, the patriotic hymner of British manhood and glory. What the people – the newly enfranchised, newly literate people – needed was 'political culture', instruction in their duties as citizens, and to be 'impressed sentimentally' by examples of heroic and patriotic action 'brought vividly and attractively before them' (Collins 1891: 148). Emphasis switched from the comedies and tragedies to the history and Roman plays. The text most frequently selected for study in the early years of the Cambridge Local Examinations was *Julius Caesar*, while, at the other end of the spectrum, the Requirements in Reading for Elementary Schools, in the Code of 1882, specified that Standard VI pupils should read a 'passage from one of Shakespeare's historical plays, or ... from a history of England'. Now the (discreetly softened) character of Falstaff came into his own again. F.J. Furnivall made up for the Lambs' deficiencies by adding the histories to a new edition of the *Tale*, and Sir Arthur Quiller-Couch brought out his own *Historical Tales from Shakespeare*, 'not to extract pleasant and profitable stories, as one might (and as the Lambs did) from the masterpieces of Shakespeare's invention', but to quicken an 'early patriotism' and interest in history (Quiller-Couch 1899: iii). No one, after all, could read Shakespeare 'and be deaf to the ringing, vibrating note of pride, of almost fierce joy to be an Englishman, to have inherited the liberties of so great a country and be a partaker of her glory' (Furnivall 1901: 13–14).

This accepted, it followed naturally that Shakespeare must also have a useful unifying and emollient influence in a time of social unrest and growing working-class solidarity. As the Spens Report was to argue in 1938 – and it is an argument which still, perhaps, informs some of the pronouncements of politicians and journalists – among the reasons for studying literature is 'the bond it can create between all who speak the same language'. It is 'part of the common inheritance which helps to build up a national consciousness and to forge invisible links of union between those who at first meeting may think they have little in common' (DOE 1938: 226).

Attempts were also made to break down the distance which had developed between the Master and his worshippers. Furnivall introduced his readers to 'young Will Shakspere', who, 'with his chestnut hair, blue eyes, and rosy cheeks', was always in the thick of whatever 'fun or mischief was going on':

> Only think what good company he must have been, and what jolly stories he told the boys he was with! Don't you wish you'd been one of them, even if you did have to put your meat in your mouth with your fingers instead of a fork? I do.
>
> (Furnivall 1901: 13–14)

It was odd, said Furnivall, that the Lambs, themselves 'such humourful folk … who so enjoyed Shakspere's fun', should have decided 'to keep all that fun (or almost all) out of their *Tales*' (Furnivall 1901: 13–14). This, however, was because they were afraid the humour would be lost in condensing them. He himself couldn't help thinking 'that most boys would like the fun put into the *Tales*, and the stories cut shorter', but they could easily 'get it all in the plays themselves', so, after all, there was 'no harm done'. Thus was the promise again held out and fulfilment deferred.

'Universal values'

Those who write for children, says John Stephens, usually aim 'to foster in the child reader a positive apperception' of the writer's own sociocultural values and the morality of the day (Stephens 1982: 3). Examination of the ways in which the plays have been reworked or abridged shows not only how strongly each of these representations relates to contemporary morality, but how they are tied to the age, gender, social class and race of the interpreter, and how much may not only be added to, but also lost from, the possible 'meanings' of the play.

Sometimes the differences of moral outlook are obvious. *Romeo and Juliet*, for example, was not at first seen in such a romantic light as it later acquired. Charles Lamb gave full weight to the Rosaline factor, describing Romeo as 'a sincere and passionate lover' *before* he was 'suddenly struck with the exceeding beauty' of Juliet, and laying stress on the 'hasty and inconsiderate passion' of both protagonists (Lamb and Lamb 1809). Later nineteenth-century versions treat the 'undying love' of the couple more romantically, so foreclosing any critical questioning of their secret marriage, but condemn the suicides as 'selfish'. If Romeo had only remembered that 'he had no right to kill himself just because he was unhappy … everything might have ended happily' (Sim 1894: 145).

More recently, much has been made of the relevance of feuding communities or gangs to the play's themes, but few interpreters have registered (or perhaps had the courage to handle) comparison with the issues of arranged marriages, and father–daughter relationships, causing tensions within the cultures of some ethnic minority groups in Britain today.

Changing ethical values are even more obvious in the treatments of *The Merchant of Venice*, one of the plays most consistently featured in narrative versions and recommended for schools. For Mary Lamb, the hero is Antonio, 'the kindest man that lived', and 'greatly beloved by all his fellow-citizens' apart from Shylock, who hated him 'because he used to lend money to people in distress, and would never take any interest for the money he lent' (Lamb and Lamb 1809). Shylock's race is not an issue so much as his hardheartedness, and the central moral emphasis is on the strength of the friendship between Antonio and Bassanio. When Bassanio declares that he would sacrifice every-thing, including his wife, to save his friend, she is 'not at all offended with her husband for expressing the love he owed to so true a friend as Antonio in these strong terms'. For much of the century the play continued to be interpreted as 'a picture of devoted, unalloyed, manly friendship, such as Shakespeare loved to paint' – though with no hint of homoeroticism, of course (Mathias 1867: 100). Bassanio's behaviour gives Portia 'the full proof of the depth of her husband's love', since 'a man who could act and speak as he had done could be no vulgar heiress and fortune-hunter' (Mathias 1867: 107). There are no tensions, no ambiguities in this triangular relationship. By the turn of the century the Jewish dimension began to come to the fore, however, in a way it had not done previously. 'Shunned, hated, despised, insulted', wrote Mary Macleod, 'the Jews in the Middle Ages led a cruel and embittered existence among their Christian brethren' (Macleod 1902: 68). A few years later Thomas Carter drew a Shylock conscious of 'whole centuries of insult and wrong ... inflicted upon his ancient race' (Carter 1910: 4), and concluded his account with Shylock's now famous lines, 'Hath not a Jew eyes ... ' – a passage to which no reference had been made in earlier versions (Carter 1910: 26–7). Carter saw the play as a confrontation between two people – Portia and Shylock – shaped by environ-ment:

> she from the palace where wealth and security had made her life all sunshine, he from the home of an outcast, where present darkness only faintly typified the sorrow and gloom of a persecuted alien. Circumstances had done much to mould their characters. The daughter of Day was facing the son of Night.
>
> (Carter 1910: 19)

Even when no overt moral is drawn – or added – the very act of reconstruction inevitably affects the meaning. Ainger, pointing out how Mary Lamb 'shortened and resolved into a harmony more intelligible to the child' Prospero's 'long and intricate narrative ... broken by grief and anger', noted approvingly that 'in this way, a kind of running annotation or commentary is provided for the reader – unsuspected by him or her' (Ainger 1879: ix). Thus the figure of paternal authority was saved from possible criticism, elevated to the role of all-wise philosopher of 'familiar Shakespeare'. Reduction of the dialogue in narrative versions is generally also accompanied by the addition of descriptive detail, or 'stage carpentry' as Leon Garfield has called it, and this can have an even greater effect. Macleod's Shylock, for example, influenced perhaps by Irving's performance, is a tragic figure, who leaves the court 'crushed and beaten ... followed by the yells and hooting of the crowds collected to hear the result of the trial' (Macleod 1902: 84). By contrast, Garfield makes his exit, under the 'gentle regard' of the merciful Portia and, as he goes, 'the thronged candles tugged after him, as if to lend him a little of the radiance of a court in which, not justice, not the law, but mercy had triumphed' (Garfield 1985: 98).

As it begins to be perceived that Shakespeare might himself be charged with religious, race, class or gender prejudice, an increasing uneasiness can be sensed in his interpreters and a good deal of special pleading surreptitiously incorporated into their work. He and the 'values' taught by his plays have been given such unique authority that those who interpret him for children feel both a need and obligation to make sure he is 'rightly' understood We may not, today, focus so overtly as earlier mediators did on the 'moral' of a play, but we still find it difficult to leave children to judge for themselves the characters, actions and relationships Shakespeare dramatises and, while maintaining 'the right of individuals, regardless of age, to think for themselves and form personal opinions', are still 'caught by the underlying belief that given enough knowledge' – or guided gently in the right direction – 'everyone should and would make the "right choice", the one we prefer' (Beehler 1992: 219–20).

Re-animating Shakespeare

The attempts of later narrators to put back the 'fun' might be said to vindicate the Lambs' point of view. Though twentieth-century writers have redressed the balance, giving children Falstaff, Sir Toby, a drunken Caliban, and Bottom and company, they have rarely found a way *in words* to convey the visual and physical comedy of their scenes. Even 'lily lips' and 'cherry nose' and 'yellow cowslip cheeks', though relished by children in performance (particularly when they are the performers), read coldly on the page, and an exaggerated effort to convey the 'fun' tends to sound merely patronising.

Turning the 'two hours traffic of the stage' into a short story is not an easy business. Something has to give. The later twentieth-century tale-tellers have, on the whole, been more respectfully conscientious than their predecessors in their attempts to follow the structure of Shakespeare's plays, and to include all the plot strands, but too often this has meant compressing so much into a narrow compass that only the bare bones of the play are left. As Mary Lamb discovered, and Leon Garfield has pointed out, the comedies are particularly intractable in this respect, since they are generally much more complex in structure than the tragedies, yet it is the comedies that tend to be considered more suitable for 'introducing Shakespeare' to children.

The same difficulties can be seen in the *Animated Tales*, an attempt at 'popularising' Shakespeare through the use of animated graphics rather than printed text (Edwards 1992). Though these are abridgements rather than narrative versions, the requirement to compress each play into less than thirty minutes necessitated savage cutting and the addition of extensive narrative links. Leon Garfield, who was responsible for the script, has admitted that as the lines selected had 'to carry the weight of narrative' this often meant 'using half a line and perhaps skipping twenty lines'.[2] As in the writing of his own *Shakespeare Stories*, he had to 'leave out the poetry and concentrate on the stage carpentry', yet in spite of this many children still find the video versions difficult to follow (Garfield 1990: 107–8). The *Animated Tales* therefore raise all the old questions posed by previous attempts to 'popularise' or 'introduce' Shakespeare to a wider audience. What is 'Shakespeare'? What are we trying to do when we offer him to children? What do we value in his plays that we believe may be of value, also, to them? Is it more than a historical, 'cultural' interest?

The arrival of the National Curriculum means that every child educated in Britain will be legally compelled to acquire *some* familiarity with Shakespeare's plays. The question must be: What kind of acquaintance will this be, and in what personal way will they be affected by it? It is debatable whether examinations and SATs (Standardised Assessment Tests) will enable them to discover 'rich and subtle meanings', or any values, universal or specific. 'Test leaves pupils bored by the Bard', as the *TES* headline put it (*Times Educational Supplement*, May 1997: 13). On the other hand, the knowledge of a couple of 'stories', with the names of a few characters, even backed by the ability to repeat some lines of verse from memory, is hardly likely to register with them as of significant value.

A more dynamic engagement with the play is needed if children are to experience for themselves anything like the mental and emotional excitement felt by those Shakespeare enthusiasts whose claims for his greatness were and are the foundation of 'Shakespeare for children'. Every intermediary has her or his own 'familiar' Shakespeare, and eager desire to share this with children, but, in the increasingly diverse society which is Britain today, Western Christian, white and middle-class values can no longer be automatically assumed to be 'universal', and neither can the 'ghost' Shakespeare formed in their image. Perhaps we need, instead, to begin to see him as the presenter of universal – or at least widespread – *dilemmas* . Family tensions; sexual rivalry; the duties and relationship of rulers and subjects; realpolitik; the feelings of outsiders, whether by reason of race or illegitimacy; the means by which crafty politicians, in the widest sense of the word, manipulate others – these are the stuff of which Shakespeare's plays are made. To weight the scales on one side or the other is to appropriate his 'authority' for our own ends, while robbing children of the right to ask their own questions and form their own judgements. We do not need to present Prospero as the all-wise father, or Caliban as either a comic grotesque or wronged and colonised 'native', if we let children encounter them both through their own words and actions. Nor should we forget Miranda, also, may have a point of view to be discovered in her words and her silences. Hannah More was not wrong when she said that Shakespeare's 'mixed' characters and their actions 'furnish themes on which to ground much appropriate and instructive conversation', but to arrogate to ourselves the role of instructor is to quench the conversation (More 1805: 182). We must help children to enter into and *wrestle* with the characters and their dilemmas, as actors do in the rehearsal process. They need to improvise on the text, speak the lines, discuss the dilemmas and speculate on what will happen next. Even 'watching the video' is not enough: the impenetrable screen, the crystallised images that abide no question – in fact hardly abide at all, in their race against the clock – are still a barrier to real engagement.

Space and time are needed for a true meeting with something as complex as a Shakespeare play. As a group of children, whose performance of *Macbeth* I had watched, told me:

> 'If you just went to the story, and tried to make a play, you wouldn't understand it or anything – you've got to do it bit by bit, you can't just go straight onto the play.'

> 'He says old words, Scotland words and you don't understand them, but then, but if you were back in that time you would – we're learning about Macbeth and history, you see, and you feel like you're there … '

> 'Actually, there – it makes you think about it.'
>
> (Bottoms 1996: 135)

The Cox report was right: Shakespeare's plays *are* 'so rich that in every age they can produce fresh meanings', but they do not produce them of themselves, and neither is an overdependence on the meanings discovered in them by tellers of *Tales*, writers of Prefaces, and devisers of explanatory notes likely to produce much freshness. It is possible for Shakespeare to become overfamiliar. If we want children to meet Shakespeare, we must stand out of the way as much as possible, let them *be there*, ask their own questions, even answer back in their own way, and 'think about it'.

Notes

1   Most of the Preface to *Tales from Shakespear* was written by Mary, as Charles made clear in a letter to Wordsworth. See Marrs, E. (1976) *Letters of Charles and Mary Lamb II*, Ithaca and London: Cornell University Press, pp. 256–7.
2   Leon Garfield speaking on *Animating Shakespeare*, BBC2 in 1992.

References

Ainger, A. (1879) *Tales from Shakespeare*, London: Macmillan & Co.

Allman's English Classics for Elementary Schools (1883) *Selections from Shakespeare, No 8, 'King John'*, London: Allman and Son.

Anonymous (1848) *Readings from the Plays of Shakespeare; in Illustrations of His Characters*, London: John W. Parker.

Beehler, S. (1992) 'Censorship and Teaching Shakespeare', in Merrix, R. and Ranson, N. (eds), *Ideological Approaches to Shakespeare*, Lewiston/Quanston/Lampeter: Edwin Mellen Press Ltd.

Bottoms, J. (1996) 'What's a Cultural Heritage When It's At Home?', in Styles, M., Bearne, E. and Watson, V. (eds), *Voices Off: Texts, Contexts and Readers*, London: Cassell.

Bowdler, H. (1807) *The Family Shakspeare*, London: Hatchard.

Bowdler, T. (1818) *The Family Shakspeare*, 10 vols, London: Longman, Hurst, Rees, Orme and Brown.

Bowdler, T. (younger) (1825) *Memoir of the late J. Bowdler Esq.; To which is added some account of the late Thomas Bowdler*, London: Longman.

Carter, T. (1910) *Stories from Shakespeare Retold*, London, George Harrap & Co.

Collins, J. C. (1891) *The Study of English Literature*, London: Macmillan & Co.

Clarke, M. (1887) 'Shakespeare as the Girl's Friend', *The Girls' Own Paper* VIII.

Department for Education and Science (1989) *English for Ages 5 to 16*, London: Her Majesty's Stationery Office.

Department of Education (1938) *Report of the Consultative Committee on Secondary Education with Special Reference to Grammar Schools and Technical High Schools*, London: His Majesty's Stationery Office.

Edwards, D. (series producer and director) (1992) *The Animated Tales*, Soyuzmiltfilm Studios, Moscow/SC4, Channel 4 Wales; distributed by Island World Communications.

Furnivall, F.J. (1901) *Tales from Shakespeare*, London: Raphael Tuck & Sons.

Garfield, L. (1985) *Shakespeare Stories*, London: Gollancz.

——(1990) 'The Penny Whistle: the problem of writing stories from Shakespeare', in *Essays by Divers Hands*, n.s. XLVI: 92–108, Woodbridge: Boydell Press.

Griffith, E. (1775) *The Morality of Shakespeare's Drama Illustrated*, London: T. Cadell.

Hare, D. (1996) *Plays I*, London: Faber and Faber.

Hufford, L. (1902) *Shakespeare in Tale and Verse*, London: Macmillan & Co.

Knox, K. (1895) 'On the Study of Shakespeare for Girls', *Journal of Education*, n.s. XVII: 309.

Lamb, C. (1811) 'On the Tragedies of Shakespeare', in Hutchinson, T. (ed.) (1924) *The Works of Charles and Mary Lamb*, London: Oxford University Press.

Lamb, C. and Lamb, M. (1809) *Tales from Shakespear: Designed for the use of young persons*, 2nd edition, 2 vols, London: M.J. Godwin.

Macleod, M. (1902) *The Shakespeare Story Book*, London: Wells, Gardner, Darton & Co.

Mathias, D. (1867) *The Prince's Shakspere; A Selection of the Plays of Shakspere Carefully Expurgated and Annotated for the Use of Families and Schools*, London: Richard Bentley.

Maxwell, C. (1828) *The Juvenile Edition of Shakspeare: Adapted to the Capacities of Youth*, London: Chapple Hailes, Wells.

Miles, B. (1976) *Favourite Tales*, Twickenham: Hamlyn Publishing.

More, H. (1805) *Hints Towards Forming the Character of a Young Princess*, vol. 2, London: T. Cadell & W. Davie.

Morley, E.J. (ed.) (1932) *Blake, Wordsworth, Coleridge, Lamb &c being Selections from the Remains of Henry Crabb Robinson*, Manchester: Manchester University Press.

Nesbit, E. (1897) 'How the Stories Were Written', in *The Children's Shakespeare*, London: Raphael Tuck & Son.

Perrin, N. (1992) *Dr. Bowdler's Legacy: A History of Expurgated Books in England and America*, Boston, MA: David Goodine Publishers Inc.

Pitman, Rev. J.R. (1822) *The School Shakspeare: Or Plays and Scenes from Shakspeare*, London: C. Rice.

Quiller- Couch, A. (1899) *Historical Tales from Shakespeare*, London: Edward Arnold.

Shavit, Z. (1986) *The Poetics of Children's Literature*, Athens, GA/London: University of Georgia Press.

Sidgwick, H. (1867) 'The Theory of Classical Education', in Farrar, F.W. (ed.), *Essays on a Liberal Education*, London: Macmillan & Co.

Sim, A. G. (1894) *Phoebe's Shakespeare*, London: Bickers & Son.

Slater, E. (1836) *Select Plays from Shakespeare; adapted chiefly for the Use of Schools and Young Persons*, London: J. Souter.

Stephens, J. (1982) *Language and Ideology in Children's Fiction*, London: Longman.

Chapter 2

'Play-business'

Issues raised by Robert Louis Stevenson's classic collection, *A Child's Garden of Verses*[1]

Morag Styles

Robert Louis Stevenson published *A Child's Garden of Verses* in 1885 and it has never been out of print.[2] He had been dabbling with children's poems since 1881 and sent out copies of a version called 'Penny Whistles' to his friends Sidney Colvin and William Henley in 1883. Rejecting 'New Songs of Innocence', which he described as blasphemy, he finally settled on *A Child's Garden of Verses* which was an immediate success when it was published on 6 March 1885, went into a second printing three months later and came out in America the same year. Charles Robinson was the first illustrator and his richly textured, art nouveau decorations complement the text beautifully (Stevenson 1885). Since then there have been countless editions, translations and illustrated versions.

Apparently, Stevenson had no great expectations for his slim volume of sixty-six children's poems, although it was close to his heart. As he wrote to Edmund Gosse in March 1885, ' there is something nice in the little ragged regiment for all; the blackguards seem to me to smile, to have a kind of childish treble note that sounds in my ear freshly; not song, if you will, but *a child's voice*' (Gosse 1913: 279). It is worth pointing out that most Victorian poetry written for children – indeed, most poetry for children – has a short lifespan. Only a handful of pre-twentieth-century poetry collections for children has any currency with the advent of a new millennium, and Stevenson's is one of them. In this chapter I will try to suggest some of the reasons for the collection's longevity, including the contentious issue of Stevenson's so-called 'child's voice'.

In seeking to analyse why these poems seem to resonate for so many children and adults half a dozen generations after they were first written, Cornelia Meigs wrote in 1969:

> if we ask why adults also get so much from it, we see that the power of this collection of simple verses lies in the fact that it offers, not a glimpse, but *the whole contour of the child's hidden world*. It shows the life that a child lives within himself and takes so completely for granted … Stevenson has recaptured … the whole of that hidden life, and has set these recollections forth

in just the terms that children would use, could they put them into words at all.

(Meigs 1969: 270)

A *Child's Garden* made the same sort of impression on E.V. Lucas, a contemporary of Stevenson, who wrote one of the earliest essays devoted to poetry for children in 1896: 'It stands alone. There is nothing like it, so intimate, so simply truthful, in our language, in any language ... he has recaptured in maturity the thoughts, ambitions, purposes, hopes, fears, philosophy of the child' (Lucas 1896: 393).

Both Lucas and Meigs could be criticised for taking an essentialist and Romantic view of childhood for granted and for neglecting the artistic recreation of childhood which Stevenson performs so skilfully. As Harvey Darton put it, 'There are few thoughts in that little 1885 volume ... that children have not felt ... *even though here and there the grown-up can be detected using his literary art to express them*' [my emphasis] (1932: 314). Quite so. Darton tells us what he thinks the special appeal of the collection is: ' ... the substance is in the fabric of a child's mind – the child who was always in Stevenson ... ' (1932: 314). He goes on to suggest that Stevenson was doing something that no other poet achieved before, capturing, as faithfully as it is possible for an adult to do, what it feels like to be a child.

> And does it not seem hard to you,
> When all the sky is clear and blue,
> And I should like so much to play,
> To have to go to bed by day?

This leads to contentious territory, including debates about constructions of childhood and issues of class, gender and culture, which I would prefer to largely sidestep in this essay. While recognising that there are many versions of childhood, and acknowledging that Stevenson's experience of childhood was privileged, middle-class, European and male, I would still dare to venture that he was better than most, before or since, at constructing childhood in a way that is convincing to many adults and children, and that the dual-audienced appeal is one of the reasons for the collection's success.

H.W. Garrod, Oxford Professor of Poetry in the 1920s, suggested that Stevenson created the genre of children's poetry (Garrod: 1929: 184), and in saying this apparently discounted the work of authors as diverse as Bunyan, Watts, Blake, Ann and Jane Taylor, Lear, Carroll and Christina Rossetti, among others! However, the point Garrod was making was a valid one, insofar as he asserted that *A Child's Garden* was a pivotal collection, radically redefining how children could be written for, and about, in poetry. Garrod also talked about the '*pretended* naturalness of the *Child's Garden* which has no greater element of pretence than accompanies any other attempt at communicating between grown-ups and children' (Garrod 1929: 184). He was right, I think, about the 'pretended naturalness' and in suggesting that Stevenson is gifted at addressing children in ways that strike a chord with many readers, while simultaneously speaking to adults about what they have lost by growing up. But there are dissenting views.

A pretty pretence?

In *The Natural History of Make-Believe*, one of the most controversial but interesting recent books on children's literature, John Goldthwaite states:

> No-one has ever lied up a stereotype so sweetly or at this artistic level before ... He [RLS] enshrined his age for his readers by detailing his own childhood as an habitual daydreamer creeping about behind the furniture, climbing a cherry tree, studying the passing scene through the window of a railway car. The lilting verses are all as beautifully laid out as toy soldiers parading across his sickbed covers in 'The pleasant land of counterpane'.
>
> (Goldthwaite 1996: 28)

Goldthwaite goes on to charge Stevenson with dishonesty: admittedly 'a pretty pretense ... but the seduction is sweet, and generations of parents took Stevenson's book to heart as the gospel truth of who they thought they had been and wanted to see in their own children' (Goldthwaite 1996: 31). So Goldthwaite suggests that Stevenson presented a view of childhood that (middle-class) parents wanted to hear and that is one key reason for its enduring appeal.

Many of Stevenson's friends and admirers believed he was gifted with a special intuition, which gave him acccess to the supposedly real essence of childhood. This presumes, of course, an essentialist view of childhood, in line with the thinking of the day, which many contemporary critics would question. Certainly Garrod and members of Stevenson's large circle of friends suggest that he *was* genuinely playful and childlike. Andrew Lang, for example, said:

> The peculiarity of Mr Stevenson is not only to have been a fantastic child, and to retain, in maturity, that fantasy ripened into imagination: he has also kept up the habit of dramatising everything, of playing, half consciously, many parts, of making the world 'an unsubstantial fairy place' ... Perhaps the first quality in Mr Stevenson's works ... which strikes the reader ... is the survival of the child in him ... It was the unextinguished childish passion for playing at things which remained with him.
>
> (Lang 1891: 25)

Edmund Gosse tells a similar tale:

> ... his gaiety ... a childlike mirth leaped and danced in him; he seemed to skip upon the hills of life. He was simply bubbling with quips or jests ... his laughter-loving mood was never wholly quenched by ill health, responsibility and the advance of years.
>
> (Gosse 1913: 279)

This playfulness is all the more remarkable when one discovers that Stevenson as a child, as well as an adult, was more often ill than well. In a letter to William Archer on 29 March 1885, he confides:

> ... you are right about my voluntary aversion from the painful sides of my life. My childhood was in reality a very mixed experience, full of fever, nightmare, insomnia, painful days and interminable nights; and I can speak with less authority of Gardens than of that other 'land of counterpane'. But to what end should we renew these sorrows? The sufferings of life may be handled by the very greatest in their hours of insight; *it is of its pleasures that our common poems should be formed*; these are the experiences that we should seek to recall or to provoke ...
>
> (Stevenson 1885: 218, my emphasis)

This seems a clear-sighted acknowledgement of the partially escapist nature of the collection. Here Stevenson goes some way to explaining why his poems have been loved by so many over the years: he sought to celebrate the pleasures of childhood, editing out the miseries most of us experience as well – rather like the selective memory that is so evident when speaking to old people about the past. The reference to 'common poems' may relate to his themes which are, indeed, common to many readers – playing alone or with friends, commenting on the people around him and the little ups and downs of everyday life. It could also mean poems for everyone, the 'common touch', which Stevenson had in abundance.

But Goldthwaite's charge is severe – the dishonesty of intention behind Stevenson's version of childhood. To some extent, I can understand Goldthwaite's position; for example, the yearning little voice that asks the reader to sympathise in 'Bed in Summer' is a kind of fake:

And does it not seem hard to you,
When all the sky is clear and blue,
And I should like so much to play,
To have to go to bed by day?

This is clever adult artifice, not a child's voice, though the point of view is convincingly childlike. But is it a 'pretty lie' or the lesser charge of 'pretended naturalness'? Stevenson's own adult perspective on his childhood, made available through his letters, journals, essays and poetry, leads to other conclusions.

He clearly thought he was selectively but authentically drawing on genuine memories which, because of the combination of frequent bouts of illness and a vivid imagination, were more developed in him than others. And in an article entitled 'Robert Louis Stevenson and Children's Play' Michael Rosen speculates as to whether 'it is not fanciful to see one aspect of the origins of the *Child's Garden* as an Arcadian relief from the pain of his illness' (Rosen 1995: 55). In his letters Stevenson goes some way towards acquitting himself of Goldthwaite's charge of dishonesty by admitting the suffering involved in childhood but also choosing to emphasise the positive in his poetry. And why not? In life as well as in the poetry, he is rarely sorry for himself, though he is sometimes a little wistful.

> When I was sick and lay a-bed,
> I had two pillows at my head,
> And all my toys beside me lay
> To keep me happy all the day.
>
> And sometimes for an hour or so
> I watched my leaden soldiers go,
> With different uniforms and drills,
> Among the bed-clothes, through the hills;

Readers will have to make up their own minds.

The voice of innocence?

Commentators often use Stevenson's life to interpret the poems. He was an only child of loving parents who were deeply involved in each other. Stevenson said wryly in later life that he often felt like an intruder on his parents' happy marriage. However, he did have a nurse, the famous Cummy (Alison Cunningham), who looked after him devotedly and gave him a taste for fantastic stories and to whom *A Child's Garden* is dedicated:

> The angel of my infant life
> From the sick child, now well and old,
> Take, nurse, this little book you hold!

In a letter telling her of the dedication, Stevenson wrote; 'I am not altogether unconscious of the great debt of gratitude I owe you. This little book which is all about my childhood should indeed go to no other person but you, who did so much to make my childhood happy' (Stevenson 1885, cited in Mehew 1997: 218). Cummy was also a religious bigot, who frightened the impressionable child half to death with tales of hellfire and damnation. The themes of sickness, isolation and night-time fears strongly pervade the poetry and we know from the letters and conversations of the adult Stevenson that Cummy was both a comfort to the invalid and a source of religious terror and guilt: 'I have three powerful impressions of my childhood: my sufferings when I was sick, my delights in convalescence at my grandfather's manse of Colinton, and the unnatural activity of my mind after I was in bed at night' (Stevenson 1880 :220). In the middle section of *North-West Passage*, he softens these painful memories, ignoring 'the sorrow and burden of the night' and the 'hideous night-mares', but retaining something of the fear and dread of his early memories. Of course, it is an adult understanding that Stevenson brings to bear on his childhood experiences.

> All round the house is the jet-black night:
> It stares through the window-pane;
> It crawls in the corners, hiding from the light,
> And it moves with the moving flame.

> Now my little heart goes a-beating like a drum,
> With the breath of a Bogie in my hair;
> And all round the candle the crooked shadows come
> And go marching along the stair.

> The shadows of the balusters, the shadow of the lamp,
> The shadow of the child that goes to bed-
> All the wicked shadows coming, tramp, tramp, tramp,
> With the black night overhead.

Certainly one of the most powerful impressions that comes out of A *Child's Garden* is the sense of a child's absorption in the world of play and how it is inti-mately bound up with the child's imagination. In the article mentioned earlier, Rosen (1995) shows how Stevenson was wrapped up in the twin themes of play and childhood around the time he was writing his poetry for children, publishing in succession 'Notes on the Movements of Young Children' (1874), 'Child's Play' (1878) and *Memoirs of Himself* (1880). Rosen suggests that the ideas he was developing in these prose pieces came to fruition in the poetry.

Ernest Mehew tells us in the *Selected Letters* that Stevenson's essay of 1874 was inspired by watching children playing with a skipping rope underneath his window in Hampstead, and by memories of a child called Nelitchka, whom he encountered while convalescing in Mentone in France the same year. His letters are peppered with lively observations of her: 'An organ came into the garden this afternoon and played for some time, Nelitchka dancing up and down in front of the hotel, with solemn delight' (Mehew 1997: 74), and

> Whenever she cries, and she never cries except from pain, all that one has to do is to start 'Malbrook s'en va-t-en guerre', she cannot resist the attrac-tion, she is drawn through her sobs into the air; and in a moment there is

Nellie singing, with the glad look that comes into her face when she sings, and all the tears and pain forgotten.

(Mehew 1997: 76)

Stevenson has documented how visits to his cousins in Colinton provided scope for play with friends of his own age. Here is a typical example:

When my cousin and I took our porridge of a morning, we had a desire to enliven the course of the meal. He ate his with sugar, and explained it to be a country continually buried under snow. I took mine with milk, and explained it to be a country suffering gradual inundation. You can imagine us exchanging bulletins; how here was an island still submerged, here a valley not yet covered with snow; what inventions were made; how his population lived in cabins on perches and travelled on stilts, and how mine was always in boats ...

(Stevenson 1878, quoted in Harman 1992: 59)

The poet here demonstrates his talent at recollecting and transforming what was probably a mixture of childhood memories, family stories of his childhood, and his own adult reflections on these events. We must be careful in going along with the so-called 'naturalness' of Stevenson's childlike imagination and give proper credit to the adult skill he employed to make it *seem* so realistic. As Goldthwaite put it more critically, 'A book about childhood can never really be a child's book. Stevenson gave innocence a voice' (Goldthwaite 1996: 28).

In a letter to Frances Sitwell in October 1874 the adult Stevenson describes a turbulent night, which appears to show the genesis of one of the poems:

Last night it blew a fearful gale; I was kept awake about a couple of hours, and could not go to sleep for the horror of the wind's noise; the whole house shook ... But the quaking was not what put me about; it was the horrible howl of the wind round the corner; the audible haunting of an incarnate anger about the house; the evil spirit that was abroad; and above all the shuddering silent pauses when the storm's heart stands dreadfully still for a moment. O how I hate a storm at night! They have been a great influence in my life I am sure; for I can remember them so far back – long before I was six at least ... And in those days, the storm had for me a perfect impersonation ... I always heard it, as a horseman riding past with his cloak about his head, and somehow always carried away, and riding past again, and being baffled yet once more, ad infinitum, all night long. I think I wanted him to get past, but I am not sure; I know ... I used to lie and hold my breath, not quite frightened but in a state of miserable exaltation.

(Stevenson 1874, quoted in Mehew 1997: 97)

Ten years later he wrote 'Windy Night':

Whenever the moon and stars are set,
　　Whenever the wind is high,
All night long in the dark and wet,
　　A man goes riding by.
Late in the night when the fires are out,
Why does he gallop and gallop about?

Whenever the trees are crying aloud,
　　And ships are tossed at sea,
By, on the highway, low and loud,
　　By at the gallop goes he.
By at the gallop he goes, and then
By he comes back at the gallop again.

Stevenson minimises the terror though he certainly creates unease and drama in the poem. The mystery at the heart of his childhood experience is retained along with the unforgettable personification of the wind as a horseman.

A good play

In 'Robert Louis Stevenson and Children's Play', Michael Rosen shows how Stevenson's ideas, though original and distinctive, were part of a growing interest in the empirical study of childhood, promoted by educationalists like Friedrich Froebel, philosophers like Rousseau and writers like Herbert Spencer, who popularised Schiller's famous observation that 'aesthetic sentiments originate from the play-impulse' (Rosen 1995: 58). So, Rosen tells us, 'Stevenson's essay and poems on childhood were produced at precisely the moment the issue of play was being formally discussed in Britain for the first time' (1995: 58). In his essay, 'Child's Play', Stevenson constitutes the essence of childhood as play:

> We grown people can tell ourselves a story ... all the while sitting quietly by the fire ... a child ... works all with lay figures and stage properties. When his story comes to the fighting, he must rise, get something by way of a sword and have a set-to with a piece of furniture, until he is out of breath. When he comes to ride with the king's pardon, he must bestride a chair ... lead soldiers, dolls, all toys, in short, are in the category and answer the same end. Nothing can stagger a child's faith; he accepts the clumsiest substitutes and can swallow the most staring incongruities ... this need for overt action and lay figures testifies to a defect in the child's imagination which prevents him from carrying out his novels in the privacy of his own heart. He does not yet know enough of the world and men. His experience is incomplete ... He is at the experimental stage; he is not sure how one would feel in certain circumstances; to make sure, he must come as near

trying it as his means permit … play is all. Making believe is the gist of his whole life.

(Stevenson 1874, quoted in Harman 1992: 56)

'A Good Play', an apparently simple poem, is written as if in the voice of a child, and is, perhaps, the key to A Child's Garden of Verses:

We built a ship upon the stairs
All made of the back-bedroom chairs,
And filled it full of sofa pillows
To go a-sailing on the billows.

We took a saw and several nails,
And water in the nursery pails;
And Tom said, 'Let us also take
An apple and a slice of cake;'
Which was enough for Tom and me
To go a-sailing on, till tea.

We sailed along for days and days,
And had the very best of plays;
But Tom fell out and hurt his knee,
So there was no one left but me.

Matter-of-factly, Stevenson states that the stairs and the back-bedroom chairs became the ship, pillows the sea; the fantasy is sustained until his playmate got hurt and the game abandoned. There is no extraneous detail; it is simply told and totally believable and therein lies its charm, immediacy and persuasiveness. This is one of the poems which probably draw on memories of playing with his cousins at his grandfather's manse in Colinton. But Stevenson was often a solitary child, as the section The Child Alone suggests. There is longing for companionship and a whiff of the hero worship children can feel for the most unlikely people in the ending of 'The Lamplighter':

And O! before you hurry by
    with lantern and with light,
O Leerie, see a little child
    and nod to him to-night!

'My Bed is a Boat' gives a near-perfect account of how children appear to recognise the boundaries of the fantasy world they create, yet how imagination allows them the escape route of adventure:

And sometimes things to bed I take,
As prudent sailors have to do:
Perhaps a slice of wedding-cake,

Perhaps a toy or two.

All night across the dark we steer:
But when the room returns at last,
Safe in my room, beside the pier,
I find my vesssel fast.

For a while the child appears to exist in a sort of halfway house, poised between fantasy and reality. At the same moment, he both knows that he is really in bed *and* imagines that his bed is a boat, 'Safe in my room, beside the pier'. To juxtapose such impossibilities is the prerogative of childhood and one with particular appeal to adults. However, one cannot ignore the adult knowingness of a phrase like 'As prudent sailors have to do' or the clever dualities in the final verse. In other poems, 'The Gardener' 'does not love to talk' and 'never seems to want to play'. In *The Land of Story Books* the child finds adults and their evening pursuits very dull, mostly because they don't 'play at anything'. Some of his memories of play were clearly idealised and, perhaps, half-recognised as such. He wrote to his cousin Henrietta Milne on 23rd October 1883:

> I shall never forget some of the days at Bridge of Allan; they were one golden dream … much of the sentiment of 'A Good Boy' which is taken from one evening at B. of A. when we had a great play with the little Glasgow girl … generally speaking whenever I think of play, it is pretty certain that you will come into my head.
>
> (Stevenson, quoted in Mehew 1997: 236)

Two of his close literary friends, Colvin and Henley, wanted him to dump 'A Good Boy' on the grounds that it was priggish, but he refused to do so.

I woke before the morning, I was happy all the day.
I never said an ugly word, but smiled and stuck to play.

And now at last the sun is going down behind the wood,
And I am very happy, for I know that I've been good.

I have tried to emphasise that Stevenson was exceptionally persuasive at writing as if in the authentic voice of a child bent on play, albeit one, as he would have been the first to admit, with all the advantages of late Victorian middle-class security and affluence. But there is one section of *A Child's Garden* where Stevenson's adult voice predominates – in the closing section *Envoys*. Here he writes elegiac poems for some of the people most important to him as a child: his mother ('You too, my mother, read my rhymes/For the love of unforgotten times'); his cousins, his name-child, and his Aunt Jane Whyte Balfour. He writes of the latter: 'The children of the family came home to her to be nursed, to be educated, to be mothered … all were born a second time from Aunt Jane's tenderness' (Stevenson 1885, quoted in Mehew 1997: 283).

Chief of our aunts – not only I,
But all your dozen nurslings cry –
What did the other children do?
And what were childhood, wanting you?

The wail of love, the awkwardness of 'and what were childhood' in 'To Auntie'
gives the poem emotional charge and is surely the grown-up Stevenson recognising and appreciating what a special person she had been for him and his
cousins in childhood, whereas 'Auntie's Skirts' is suggestive of a child's genuine
observation:

Whenever Auntie moves around,
Her dresses make a curious sound;
They trail behind her up the floor,
And trundle after through the door.

But the most poignant poem of them all is a lament, not for one human being
but for 'Any Reader', and it is about the loss of childhood itself.

But do not think you can at all,
By knocking on the window, call
That child to hear you. He intent
Is all on his play-business bent ...

... And it is but a child of air
That lingers in the garden there.

There are, however, other poems I have always been slightly perplexed by, as
the voice seems out of kilter with the rest of the collection. These are the
poems which appear to be moral or conformist, almost maxims. For example,
'A Thought' is too cosily self-satisfied for a radical and atheist like Stevenson:

It is very nice to think
The world is full of meat and drink,
With little children saying grace
In every Christian kind of place.

If he means to be ironic, most readers will miss it. The same is not true of
'Whole Duty of Children', where Stevenson's tongue is firmly in his cheek:

A child should always say what's true,
And speak when he is spoken to,
And behave mannerly at table:
At least as far as he is able.

It is hard to know what Stevenson is up to in a poem like 'System' – the point of view is too conventional and the cloying sweetness of the ending does no justice to Stevenson's outlook on poverty.

> The child that is not clean and neat,
> With lots of toys and things to eat,
> He is a naughty child, I'm sure –
> Or else his dear papa is poor.

But 'Looking Forward' is so obviously a contrived 'child's voice' that it is unconvincing to the young but perhaps amusing to adults:

> When I am grown to man's estate
> I shall be very proud and great,
> And tell the other girls and boys
> Not to meddle with my toys.

Where golden apples grow

Despite some small reservations and exceptions, I have tried to provide some explanation for the appeal of Stevenson's account of childhood and drawn attention to his facility for representing play in the poems. But there are other reasons for the enduring regard for *A Child's Garden*. One obvious factor in its favour is the strength of the poetry (though, as we know, not all good poetry books do well or stay in print). Stevenson is adept at using satisfying metre and phrasing. This melodious quality makes the verse especially appealing to very young children, though older readers respond to the same qualities in 'From a Railway Carriage'. Here the poet captures both the rhythmic speed of the train and the outlook of the young passenger trying in vain to keep pace with the myriad of impressions racing by the carriage window:

> Faster than fairies, faster than witches,
> Bridges and houses, hedges and ditches;
> And charging along like troops in a battle,
> All through the meadows the horses and cattle:
> All of the sights of the hill and the plain
> Fly as thick as driving rain;
> And ever again in the wink of an eye,
> Painted stations whistle by.

Stevenson avoids sentimentality in writing for children, though sometimes only just. He often uses diminutives: 'A *birdie* with a yellow bill', *Tiny* woods below whose boughs/Shady *fairies* weave a house', 'Where the *little people* play' (my emphasis). Commentators rarely mention his skill as a close observer of nature though, as Darton put it, 'the child is always, more or less, in an ordinary

English garden'. Stevenson describes birds' nests and wild flowers, autumn leaves and digging. Sometimes he roamed into wilder places, like the Highlands of Scotland:

> Down by a shining water well
> I found a very little dell,
> No higher than my head.
> The heather and the gorse about
> In summer bloom were coming out,
> Some yellow and some red.

Despite suffering from poor health, Stevenson craved adventure, found it in his life and wrote about it in his books. Goldthwaite likes that side of Stevenson:

> However much Stevenson veered from a child's true perception [sic] from verse to verse, at the centre of the book is a vision of the world and his voice as he tells us about this world he sees is the voice of a man who couldn't wait to be joined with it, and went.
>
> (Goldthwaite 1996: 31)

Several poems uncannily anticipate future adventures, such as his somewhat reckless wanderings at sea in the last decade or so of his life. Indeed, Stevenson did end up where 'Parrot islands anchored lie' – in Samoa, to be precise. A letter of June 1875 gives the first hint:

> Awfully nice man here tonight ... Telling us about the South Sea islands till I was sick with desire to go there; beautiful places, green forever; perfect climate ... nothing to do but ... sit in the sun, and pick the fruits as they fall ...
>
> (Stevenson, quoted in Mehew 1997: 109–10)

> I should like to rise and go
> Where the golden apples grow; –
> Where below another sky
> Parrot islands anchored lie,
> And, watched by cockatoos and goats,
> Lonely crusoes building boats; –
>
> (from 'Travels')

> Where shall we adventure today that we're afloat,
> Wary of the weather and steering by a star?
> Shall it be to Africa, a-steering of the boat,
> To Providence, or Babylon, or off to Malabar?
>
> (from 'Pirate Story')

When he reached the South Sea Islands, Stevenson had finally found a place where he could be relatively healthy and happy. He was interested in and appreciative of the different island peoples and their cultures, and many of them, in turn, grew to love him. He travelled widely, staying in Tahiti and Honolulu before settling in Samoa, appearing to thrive on dangerous sea voyages in untrustworthy vessels. 'I will never leave the sea I think,' he told Sidney Colvin (22 August 1889). Having left Britain in 1887, Stevenson never returned, despite many promises to do so. He died in Samoa in 1894 and his funeral was legendary. According to his wishes, Stevenson (or Tusitala, his native name) was buried on top of the mountain near his beloved house, Valima. Forty men worked night and day to clear a path through the jungle for the funeral cortege. Hordes of people came to pay their last respects. His tomb bore two bronze panels decorated by a hibiscus flower and a thistle with words from the book of Ruth: 'Thy people shall be my people … '

A child of air

One of Stevenson's greatest gifts was his ability to gaze at the immensity of the world and wonder at it, as children and poets are inclined to do, as if seeing it for the first time: ' … And I say with Thoreau, "What right have I to complain, who have not ceased to wonder?" ' (Stevenson, quoted in Mehew 1997: 283):

> The lights from the parlour and kitchen shone out
> Through the blinds and the windows and bars;
> And high overhead and all moving about,
> There were thousands of millions of stars.
> There ne'er were such thousands of leaves on a tree,
> Nor of people in church or the park,
> As the crowds of the stars that looked down upon me,
> And that glittered and winked in the dark.
>
> (from *Escape at Bedtime*)

It is extraordinary that in Frank McLynn's otherwise excellent biography, *A Child's Garden* merits a single paragraph and fails to appear in the index; nor does any reference to children or play, though McLynn does describe the poems as 'that prime source for his childhood'. He begins Stevenson's biography with these simple words: 'This book has been written in the firm conviction that Robert Louis Stevenson is Scotland's greatest writer of English prose' (McLynn 1993: 1). I would wish to add 'and poetry for children'.

In a reply to Sidney Colvin about the proofs of *A Child's Garden of Verses* in November 1883, Stevenson confided: 'I would just as soon call 'em "Rimes for Children" as anything else. I am not proud or particular … these are rhymes, jingles; I don't go for eternity … ' (Stevenson 1883, quoted in Mehew 1997: 285). He was wrong.

For long ago, the truth to say,
He has grown up and gone away,
And it is but a child of air
That lingers in the garden there.

Notes

1   This article was first given as a talk to the IBBYP (International Board Books for Young People) Conference at Roehampton Institute in October 1998. I developed some of the arguments and adapted material from 'The Best of Plays' (1998), in Styles, M., *From the Garden to the Street: 300 Years of Poetry for Children*, London: Cassell.
2   Stevenson, R.L. (1885) *A Child's Garden of Verses*, Longman and Green, London. All references to *A Child's Garden of Verses* relate to this edition, unless stated otherwise.

References

Garrod, W.H. (1929) *The Profession of Poetry*, Oxford: Oxford University Press.

Goldthwaite, J. (1996) *The Natural History of Make-Believe*, New York: Oxford University Press.

Gosse, E. (1913) *Critical Kit-Kats*, London: Heinemann.

Harman, C. (ed.) (1992) *Robert Louis Stevenson: Essays and Poems*, London: J.M. Dent.

Harvey Darton, F.J. (1932) *Children's Books in England*, Cambridge: Cambridge University Press

Lang, A. (1891) *Essays in Little*, London: Henry & Co.

Lucas, E.V. (1896) 'Some Notes on Poetry for Children', *Fortnightly Review*, ed. W. Courtney, vol. LX, London: Chapman & Hall.

McLynn, F. (1993) *Robert Louis Stevenson*, London: Hutchinson.

Mehew, E. (ed.) (1997) *Selected Letters of Robert Louis Stevenson*, New Haven: Yale University Press.

Meigs, C. (1969) *A Critical History of Children's Literature*, Canada: Macmillan.

Rosen, M. (1995) 'Robert Louis Stevenson and Children's Play', in *Children's Literature and Education* 26(1): 53–72.

Stevenson, R.L. (1874) 'Notes on the Movements of Young Children', *The Works of R.L. Stevenson, Essays and Poems*, vol. 22, London, 1912.

——(1878) 'Child's Play', *Cornhill Magazine*, September.

——(1880) *Memoirs of Himself*, Edinburgh, 1929.

——(1885) *A Child's Garden of Verses*, London: Longman and Green.

Chapter 3

The Grimms' wicked stepmothers

Nicholas Tucker

The standard nineteenth-century fairy-tale anthologies so familiar throughout Western Europe and America do not on the whole provide the female sex with a fair deal. Stories about genuinely sparky heroines have usually been left out, and editors have seen to it that male characters have often been rendered more sympathetic over the years, while some female characters have occasionally suffered from the reverse process.

This is particularly true of the stepmother characters in Grimm's fairy-tales, still the most popular and widely read collection. The starving peasants who mutually abandon their children in the earlier versions of *Hansel and Gretel* are recast in succeeding editions into the characters of a benign, if passive, father and a scheming, evil stepmother. Similarly, wicked stepmothers can be found in numbers of other Grimm stories, including well-known titles such as *Cinderella*, *Snow White* and *The Juniper Tree*. In contrast, there is only one story featuring an evil stepfather. Stepmothers today, faced by the already daunting task of contributing to the success of an already-existing family, must sometimes wonder what they have done to deserve this poor literary image. They can also hardly be expected to relish the *Oxford English Dictionary*'s definition of 'step-motherly' as 'harsh and neglectful'.

More harm than good?

There is something intrinsically disagreeable about always selecting villainous characters in children's literature from the same, limited cast of stereotypes that also often reflect and reinforce current popular prejudices. This could partially explain why some rehabilitation of the traditional wicked stepmother character is now found in numbers of modern children's books. Anne Fine has provided a far more sympathetic portrait of contemporary stepmothers in her novel *Step by Wicked Step*. Jenny Nimmo's *Griffin's Castle*, Gillian Cross's *Wolf* and Nina Bawden's *Granny the Pag*, all written during the last decade, have also started to redress the balance, this time, by creating deviant natural mother characters as the chief threat to their children. But these are stories written for older readers; younger ones are still more likely to come across those fairy stories first, collected and then published almost always by male editors, and within which evil stepmothers habitually emerge as some of the nastiest villains going. In the face of this bias, some might argue there is at least a case for restoring *Hansel and Gretel* in any future edition to its earlier version in the Grimms' collection, where both natural parents are seen as equally to blame for the abandonment of their children.

There are arguments for and against taking such a course, and not for the first time fairy-tales present something of a problem here. Parents are often eager for their children to enjoy these marvellous tales, but sometimes feel uncomfortable with particular characterisation or detail. Attempts to deal with the number of different concerns fairy-tales have given rise to both in the past and today have included suggestions to ban them altogether, rewrite them or reduce them to shadows of their former selves in picture books that contain hardly any text at all. An influential male critic like Bruno Bettelheim has continued to argue, meanwhile, that the Grimms' fairy-tales as they stand are essential to a child's psychological health (Bettelheim 1976). Female critics like Alison Lurie have been considerably less enthusiastic (Lurie 1980). Final agreement, as in other controversies involving fairy-tales, seems remote.

There certainly seem no sound reasons to continue celebrating and passing on to children every fairy-tale simply because it is there. A story from the Grimms' selection like *The Jew among Thorns* is both sadistic and anti-Semitic (the postwar Military Government Information Control in Nuremberg reissued it in 1947 as 'The Old Man in the Thornbush') (Bottigheimer 1987: 17). There are other tales in the Grimms' collection that are similarly anti-Semitic, two of which the brothers retained in the first smaller edition that they prepared especially for children. On another tack, Maria Tatar, in her excellent study of fairy-tales, *Off with Their Heads!*, makes a convincing case against *Bluebeard* as a suitable story for children (Tatar 1992: 110). The tale itself is crude and frightening, particularly when illustrators portray in gloating detail the hanging corpses of his previous wives. Its principal message, that women should never be over-curious, is boorishly sexist.

But sacrificing a classic story like *Hansel and Gretel* is unthinkable. Merely changing its wicked stepmother back to the earlier figure of a desperate, starving mother would indeed be fairer to stepmothers in general, but could create problems this time for young readers, a point I shall return to shortly. It is also possible that the wicked stepmother the Grimms helped create may not be so entirely a negative force as she initially appears. Getting rid of her could even end up doing more harm than good.

The ideal mother

The ostensible reason why the Grimms changed abandoning mothers into wicked stepmothers was the unacceptability, in their eyes, of stories where a natural mother is seen to turn against her offspring. This image did not fit with their own idealisation of all things Teutonic; they did not wish the common culture they believed the tales exemplified as part of the German nation's true identity to contain at the same time suggestions of formerly rejecting family practices. Yet the Grimms began collecting their tough, sometimes amoral folk stories at a time when such tales were less often being told to adult audiences as a way of making repetitive domestic chores or farm work pass more quickly. Instead, fairy-tales were beginning to be seen more particularly as the preserve of the young, and children themselves also tend not to relish the presence of uncaring, natural parents in their stories. For them, and particularly so as the nineteenth century developed and more mothers began taking a closer interest in bringing up their own young, parents and the home became even firmer symbols of ultimate security. In homes today that are genuinely unhappy or neglectful, infants still commonly turn, both in the imagination and in real life, towards the abusing parent whom they hope one day will prove more loving and nurturant.

Wicked stepmother characters, however, are far more acceptable to a young audience. While the image of the perpetually good, natural mother can be cherished as an ideal, whether she exists in reality or not, the wicked stepmother is there to be loathed without ever giving rise to feelings of infantile guilt or disloyalty. Child readers or listeners who identify with her victims can positively wallow in the self-pity that flows so naturally from tales of the cruel victimisation of the young within the family. It is no accident that the story of *Cinderella*, that monument to puerile self-pity, is easily the most popular fairy-tale in the world, found in many different versions and cultures.

In children's games among themselves, this witch/wicked stepmother figure also makes a splendid villain, chasing everyone in sight with threats of cannibalism or something almost as bad. When she eventually catches a victim, it is then their turn to act out this marauding termagant. Few object – indeed, teachers, dinner ladies and pupils themselves will attest that in playground games loosely based on *Hansel and Gretel* every child wants to be the witch first or Gretel second. Nobody wishes to play Hansel or the weedy father. If the wicked stepmother is a part every little girl desires, this character must possess something of definite worth to children. It is surely not too hard to work out what that might be.

One of the besetting inadequacies of so many of the Grimms' fairy-tale heroines is their passivity. They were not ever thus, particularly in the more bawdy folk tales that were rarely allowed into nineteenth-century anthologies. Female characters here could often be as lusty, scheming and devious as the best of them. But the Grimms, and other collectors of folk stories increasingly aiming at a young audience, preferred heroines who were chaste, domestically hard-working, modest and who always knew their place, which was largely to be obedient to both father and husband. If these heroines did not always behave like this when the stories were first published, their characters were often rewritten in this direction in succeeding versions. Tidy morals were also now attached to the end of their stories of a type that had no place in the rougher, tougher tales on which they were based, but which were no longer thought fit for the edification of younger readers.

But, as Freud suggested years ago, attempts at wholesale repression and denial cannot succeed indefinitely: important emotions denied one outlet are bound in the end to find expression elsewhere. Generations of girls as well as boys have either heard the fairy-tales or read them for themselves. Too often denied representations of their own spirit of assertiveness in the person of the new literary fairy-story heroines, could they instead have sometimes warmed to the sheer energy and general level of patriarchal defiance shown by the character of the wicked stepmother? The adult narrator, when this was a woman, as often seemed to be the case, may also have found other types of fulfilment when it came to giving life to evil stepmothers in fairy stories. In both French and English, for example, the words 'stepmother' and 'mother-in-law' were synonymous until the mid-nineteenth century. Marina Warner suggests that some older women narrators might therefore have derived grim satisfaction from recalling in the character of the wicked stepmother their own once oppressive mothers-in-law (Warner 1994: 218). Taking revenge in the imagination is a pleasure that can still be enjoyed at any stage of life.

It has been fairly said that this 'stepmother character was a handy one for the moralists who collected the fairy stories to use in presenting the antithesis to the desired feminine traits they wished to extol' (Smith 1998: 37). But there is always the danger of arousing an audience's unconscious approval for splendid, over-the-top, rule-breaking villains, especially female ones. In any performance of Humperdinck's operatic version of *Hansel and Gretel*, the stepmother-turned-witch (since they are usually sung by the same artist) always manages to light up the stage with her wild cackling and energetic dancing. This would be very untypical behaviour in the Grimms' fairy-tale heroines, so often reduced by their editors to what was thought of as a becoming modesty and silence (Bottigheimer 1987: 5–6).

Noisy, demanding and fearless wicked stepmothers also often have the effect of reducing their male consorts in fairy-tales to the status of wimps, as happens in the story of *Cinderella*, *Snow White* and various others. The brothers Grimm, setting out to improve the story of *Hansel and Gretel* by demonising the wife, also succeeded in emasculating the father who so weakly fails to oppose her. This character could have been rewritten to the extent that he was shown never knowing that his wife was intent on turning their children out. The situation whereby one trusting person is sadly deceived by another is found in other fairy stories, but not this one. So the paradox remains, that by creating bad stepmothers in some of their stories the Grimms also made it almost impossible for their fairy-tale husbands to look anything other than weak and pathetically deluded. Without realising what they were doing, the brothers ended up by themselves attacking concepts of patriarchy in the stories, at the same time as trying to bolster it by so often placing all the blame on the aberrant female.

Female listeners and readers will of course consciously side against these wicked stepmother characters: it is not just the small boys who cheer in Disney's film when Snow White's malignant enemy falls to her death. But unconsciously it might be a different matter – why else would little girls want to play the part of this frightening lady in their games? This occasional identification with the chief villain can sometimes cross over into consciousness. The little girl who once said of J.M. Barrie's menacing Captain Hook, 'I do love that man', the moment after Hook puts his head through the door to glare at Peter Pan innocently asleep, is by no means the only child to have sent fan mail to this particular villain and no doubt to many others too (Lancelyn Green 1954: 114). That Captain Hook is a male in this case is irrelevant: he is still the only real threat to uppity Peter Pan, whose own patriarchal values extend to reconstructing the family with Wendy firmly cast as the nurturant, hard-working mother-figure with little or no time for any exciting adventures outside the home.

Wicked fictional stepmothers also have undeniable style as well as power; another possibly source of unconscious admiration. If they are witches into the bargain, they avoid the hooked nose and shabby clothes that would never have attracted their gullible husbands in the first place. In Disney's film version of *Snow White*, the wicked queen, up to that moment a glamorous Duchess of Windsor lookalike, is shown changing into an old hag by magic. This particular transformation does not occur in the text itself; wicked stepmothers generally manage to stay looking coldly beautiful throughout their stories. If they were to appear genuinely unprepossessing, this would serve as another implied criticism of the taste of their feeble husbands.

Big spenders, ruthless manipulators, vain, amoral and unashamedly self-serving, these evil stepmothers hold out the delicious prospect of a female who breaks all the rules and, for a time at least, gets away with it. Often a would-be murderess into the bargain, she is not someone to tangle with. While children glory in her final fall, they must also recognise some of their own occasional destructive fantasies of jealousy and general mayhem in this wicked creature. Her ultimate defeat represents their own rejection of the idea of taking evil action against their own families. But this return to following the moral rules is rendered more bearable by the splendid, temporary outing of the various bad thoughts made possible either by reading about such wickedness or else by representing it in noisy games played with others.

Another argument for the retention of the wicked stepmother is the sad fact that, according to the evolutionary psychologists Martin Daly and Margo Wilson, having a step-parent in real life continues to be 'the most powerful risk factor for severe child maltreatment yet discovered' (Daly and Wilson 1998: 7). Could those fairy-tales featuring wicked step-parents also be expressing this point of view in the sense of warning children and the rest of society about the inherent dangers that can arise when a new parent is brought into the family? Did the brothers Grimm, in their rewriting of some of their traditional tales in order to convey a better picture of the natural German mother, also touch upon these deeper fears? As it is, their stories carry ample warnings about the possibility of other excesses; there are plenty of indications in them about the type of cruelty later responsible for the Holocaust. Banning or bowdlerising fairy stories will not get rid of evil in the human condition, but could merely disguise its possibilities even further.

But the dangers facing stepchildren today come overwhelmingly from evil stepfathers, not stepmothers, whose actual numbers in comparison with stepfathers are fairly small, especially where the very youngest children are concerned (currently there are around seven times more resident stepfathers in the United Kingdom than there are resident stepmothers). Child abuse, sexual and otherwise, is a threat posed predominantly by males, and is particularly represented among stepfathers. Continuing to pick on wicked fairy-tale stepmothers as the sole source of danger to the child could therefore be seen as a monstrous act of injustice, and particularly so in the case of the brothers Grimm. Writing about their collection, Maria Tatar states, 'For the one story ... that openly depicts a father's persecution of his daughter, there are twelve that recount a girl's misery at the hands of her stepmother' (Tatar 1987: 155).

Fathers and stepfathers

The argument that fairy-tales still carry valid warnings for children would therefore work better if it were stepfathers rather than stepmothers who were mainly featured. But, although this would be fairer, the results in fiction at least for infants would surely be much too terrifying. Perhaps this is why there are far fewer folk tales featuring wicked stepfathers. In those evil fairy-tale stepfathers that do exist, the two overriding motifs the American expert on folklore, Stith Thompson, has picked out are 'cruel' and 'lustful'. It seems better for children to imagine these terrifying figures well outside the home in the shape of those ogres and bogeymen who roam abroad in fairy-tales. These are frightening enough in their own right; incorporating them into a domestic story as the scourge of their own stepchildren could well be too much, at least to a young audience.

Early infantile fear of the male is not confined to ogres and bogeymen. Even ordinary fathers have, at least until very recently, usually been more feared by their children than is generally the case with mothers. Psychoanalytic explanations for this phenomenon state that the father is always unconsciously resented by infants of both sexes for his claims on the beloved mother. Evolutionary psychologists prefer explanations harking back to a distant time when fathers, like other mature mammals, might occasionally have been dangerous rivals to their growing children. Even today, when both parents go to work, fathers are still more likely to represent the world outside, authority, and a certain distance to children, while mothers usually stand for the home and the domestic. Fewer modern mothers now utter threats like 'Wait till your father comes home!' over matters of family discipline. Yet, so long as the father represents strength rather than intimacy to the small child, some residual fear, of course usually mixed with more positive feelings, is always more likely in infants living in families where the father is still less known and less visibly present than is the case with the mother.

Modern picture books and fiction for children follow contemporary reality by showing fathers as active, involved members of the family rather than as authoritarian figures chiefly responsible for discipline. At the same time, the cruel, murderous and incestuous fathers or stepfathers familiar in some older versions of folk tales have long been omitted from standard fairy-tale anthologies, not least by the Grimm brothers themselves. They retained only one, altering the other older versions they came across towards what they felt were more acceptable plots. They were surely right to take this step; were such characters to continue to exist in popular anthologies, they could conceivably exacerbate lingering feelings of distance still felt by some children about some fathers. In a few tragic cases, tales of cruel fathers or stepfathers could be too much like the real thing anyhow. Although this possibility also exists in tales about wicked mothers and stepmothers, the threat to children in terms of physical or sexual abuse remains on the whole a male phenomenon.

The widespread existence of wicked stepmothers in fairy stories could therefore be seen as a tribute to all mothers, step- or otherwise, rather than merely as a sad example of victimisation. It is far more acceptable to children to play or read about evil creatures who do not normally offer them a threat in real life. Good-humoured games and stories about witches, for example, could only exist for pure enjoyment at a time when most children and adults had given up actual belief in witchcraft itself. When the idea of witches still provided a potent threat, stories about them were horrific rather than any sort of fun, and rituals of protection would have been more likely than light-hearted games involving these characters. By the same token, few children would want to join in games today involving pretend sexual abusers. The fact that they still like to play at or read about wicked stepmothers suggests that they do not feel that too many of these evil creatures exist in reality. Violent and dangerously unpredictable fathers or stepfather characters, in contrast, have little part in the way children entertain themselves now or for some time in the past. Such characters, I would suggest, have always been too menacing to provide any suggestion of pleasurable fear when encountered in game or story.

I would not therefore countenance revising the Grimms' tales to lessen what has often been an act of literary injustice against stepmothers. Children need shared objects of fear in their imagination, and I believe that images of wicked stepmothers are more easily accommodated than ideas about wicked stepfathers. In his autobiography, Jean-Paul Sartre remembers that being read to as a small child was as if his mother 'leant over, lowered her eyelids and went to sleep. From this mask-like face issued a plaster voice. I grew bewildered: who was talking? About what? And to whom? My mother had disappeared' (Sartre 1964:

31). In this sense, even loving mothers turn, at least for the duration of a story, into the dreadful, cruel stepmothers they are doing their best to bring to life from the book they are reading. No child could bear this experience unless they knew that their ordinary, affectionate parent was going to reappear at the end of the story. The nastier the wicked fictional stepmother, the closer most infants should feel to their real mother afterwards.

As Bruno Bettelheim puts it,

> The fantasy of the wicked stepmother not only preserves the good mother intact, it also prevents having to feel guilty about one's angry thoughts and wishes about her – a guilt which would seriously interfere with the good relations to Mother.
>
> (Bettelheim 1976: 69)

Wicked stepmothers therefore have the effect of making everyone feel better about themselves. Real mothers, by comparison, can only look reassuringly so much nicer, and children, identifying with the put-upon young victims in the text, can enjoy the sensation of feeling, at least by proxy, very much more sinned against than sinning. Opportunities to feel morally superior to parents, even only in fiction, are not to be missed by small children normally expected to follow rather than avoid adult example. Fantasies of gruesome revenge can also be very sweet, especially when safely directed at a fictional character.

A child, meanwhile, who already possesses a second mother and hears her read aloud one of these tales that vilify stepmothers should also soon note the difference between fiction and reality, since it is unlikely that an unloving step-mother would go to the trouble of reading them anything at all. If a child is unfortunate enough to possess a genuinely neglectful, cruel stepmother, then these stories serve as warnings from the past that still sometimes have meaning for the present. If such warnings stay in public consciousness partly as a result of fairy-tales, this is not necessarily a bad thing. Good step-parents will have nothing to fear; bad ones should at least feel that others may always feel more suspicious about them if and when the children in their care seem to be suffering. It is sometimes stated that the uncomfortable topic of child abuse, sexual or otherwise, is too often avoided in children's literature. This could never be said of fairy-tales: in the Grimms' collection alone, there are no less than twenty-five stories 'in which the main focus is on children who experience some form of abuse' (Zipes 1988: 120). Ridding the stories of abusing adult characters, stepmothers included, would be at the same time to cease warning about a particular threat to children that shows no real sign of disappearing.

But to return to the question posed earlier, is it fair to besmirch the names of all step-parents as part of the same process? In answer to this question, there is some evidence that stepmothers did indeed sometimes act against their new children in the past. There was a time, for example, when widowers could often be expected to remarry quite quickly. Marina Warner writes that 'in Tuscany in the fifteenth century almost all men widowed under the age of sixty took another wife and started another family. In France, 80 per cent of widowers remarried within the year in the seventeenth and eighteenth centuries' (Warner 1994: 213). A final share of the father's money and property for whoever's children were going to be lucky could mean the difference between riches and poverty. Fairy-tales featuring jealous, scheming stepmothers may therefore often have been quite near the mark, with magic in the imagination the only solution to a displaced child who in real life might sometimes have been suffering from a raw family deal

The burdens of virtue

Today in Britain, quarrels about inheritance rarely have quite such important economic significance. Maternal cruelty and abandonment are also much less of a feature than was once the case, although the comparatively tiny number of abandoned babies has actually tripled over the last ten years. Daly and Wilson claim that stepmothers remain greatly overrepresented in recent cases of child maltreatment (Warner 1994: 213). But they concede that the numbers involved remain very small, with the overwhelming dangers facing stepchildren still coming from males rather than females. Continuing, therefore, to demonise stepmothers in fairy-tales is at best – although always with some exceptions – an irrelevance with little real-life meaning for most modern children or for society as a whole.

Such characters can therefore lead to pleasurable excitement rather than sheer terror in stories or during games. It is also easy to exaggerate the effect on young readers and listeners of this demonising process, given that common experience dictates that any new parent in the family is going to be at least initially resented by already existing children whether these have come across fairy-tales or not. The tales themselves, therefore, are more likely to act as safety valves than slow-burning time bombs. Despite recent criticisms of the Grimms for some of the ways in which they altered the tales they originally wrote down, it should surely be conceded that in the matter of exculpating natural-parent characters from blame for cruelty to their own children the brothers got it right. They were, after all, catering for an increasingly new form of family life, with a greater emphasis on chldhood as a period of intimacy and education, more distanced than before from the adult world of work. The enormous subsequent popularity of their collection which, from a slow start, eventually became the second most popular book in Germany after the Bible, suggests that these were the type of stories both parents and children were looking for. A contemporary fairy-tale anthology put together by Ludwig Bechstein, more popular to begin with than the Grimms' work, has since faded away. In Bechstein's book it is natural fathers and mothers rather than wicked step-parents who are seen to be equally responsible in those stories where children suffer within their own families. Could this be one reason young readers soon came to prefer the versions that the brothers Grimm were offering to them?

As for the vast majority of good-enough stepmothers today who still resent such an appalling literary image, they should also bear in mind that in most cases they can only eventually do so much better than this in the eyes of their new charges. Imagine the problems for them if literary stepmothers always came over as paragons of sweetness and light? It is not too hard to appear nicer than Cinderella's stepmother; being expected instead to emulate her fairy godmother every day of the year could be a sorry burden indeed.

References

Bettelheim, B. (1976) *The Uses of Enchantment: The Meaning and Importance of Fairy Tales*, London: Thames and Hudson.

Bottigheimer, R.B. (1987) *Grimms' Bad Girls and Bold Boys: The Moral and Social Vision of the Tales*, New Haven: Yale University Press.

Daly, M. and Wilson, M. (1998) *The Truth about Cinderella: A Darwinian View of Parental Love* London: Weidenfeld & Nicolson.

Lancelyn Green, R. (1954) *Fifty Years of Peter Pan*, London: Peter Davies.

Lurie, A. (comp. and ed.) (1980) *Clever Gretchen and Other Forgotten Folktales*, New York: Thomas Crowell.

Sartre, J.-P. (1964) *Words*, London: Hamish Hamilton.

Smith, D. (1998) *Stepmothering*, New York: Harvester Wheatsheaf.

Tatar, M. (1987) *The Hard Facts of the Grimms' Fairy Tales*, Princeton: Princeton University Press.

——(1992) *Off With Their Heads! Fairy Tales and the Culture of Childhood*, Princeton: Princeton University Press.

Warner, M. (1994) *From the Beast to the Blonde: On Fairy-Tales and their Tellers*, London: Chatto & Windus.

Zipes, J. (1988) *The Brothers Grimm: From Enchanted Forests to the Modern World*, London: Routledge.

Chapter 4

By children, about children, for children

Victor Watson

In 1937, two child authors, Katharine Hull and Pamela Whitlock, aged 15 and 16, sent a thick bundle of manuscript to Arthur Ransome claiming with an ironic disingenuousness that if he was too busy to bother with it he might like to 'ask Titty or Roger, as they might like it'. The work, *The Far-Distant Oxus*, was published the same year and two sequels followed it. In his Introduction, Ransome explained that the children's 'slogan was "By children, about children, for children" … In fact, "Do without the grown-up author altogether"' (Hull and Whitlock 1937: 12).

The young writers' slogan was an implied challenge to the traditional assumption that literature for children must invariably be written by adults, though this challenge was compromised a little by the fact that they needed Ransome's support with the publishers, and the novel they had written was in any case imitative of Ransome's own *Swallows and Amazons* stories. More about that later. However, the success of their novel invites us to consider the dynamics of *children* writing *children's books* and to ask such questions as: Can they actually do it? If so, are their works in any way different from children's books written by adults? Have they something to say to young readers that only they can say effectively?

Although poetry by children is quite frequently published, little attention has been given to novels written by young authors. There have been more of these than is generally realised. This chapter will begin by considering the most famous, Daisy Ashford's *The Young Visiters* (1919), and go on to consider a number of other works, more interesting in that they really were written *for* and *about* children. The chapter will then go on to argue that it is impossible to understand this phenomenon without at least some consideration of the largely unwritten history of children's books between 1930 and 1960, in particular pony stories, and the 'camping and tramping' fiction which formed such a large part of published children's books during that period.

Children's literature is inherently strange. It is unlike any other literature. Though there are many kinds of fiction written for specific groups of readers (gay literature, for example), such literatures invariably involve a reader/writer negotiation between equals. But children's literature is unique in this respect:

that its writers and intended readers are biologically and socially different from one another. Even when writers genuinely believe they are writing from ' the child within', or are adept at capturing a child's authorial voice, I do not believe that children ever lose sight of the fact that the books they are reading are produced by adults; nor do I believe that any author would really seek to deny the careful adult 'crafting' that is put into the production of a children's book, even the most apparently zany and childlike.

When a child reads a children's book there is an encounter between two minds imaginatively facing in opposite directions; the adult writer to some extent at least looking back towards childhood, and young readers always, at whatever deep level, aware of themselves as moving ahead into a future adult life. One of the reasons I find Philippa Pearce's *Tom's Midnight Garden* (1958) so especially interesting is that it enacts this imaginative meeting with great precision. It concerns an older person with her own needs and memories, and a young person with his own needs and interests, who share briefly an imaginative experience that is both his and hers and becomes the narrative. Philippa Pearce makes it clear, however, that they are different people, of different times, and when their brief meeting is over they will go their separate ways, having encountered one another in a space, which Peter Hollindale might call 'childness' (Hollindale 1997).

But is there some fundamental difference when children write for children, and when the generational difference clearly does not exist and the reader–author 'meeting' is one between biological and social equals? Does some new transforming alchemy come into play? Or is the strange and elusive magic of children's literature lost when the magician is not a grown-up?

I think I had better say at this point that I do not intend to consider Anne Frank. Although she is in my view one of the greatest writers of the century, she falls outside this study because she was not writing for publication, and she certainly was not writing fiction for children. And, since I will be limiting myself to British writers, neither will I be looking at *The Outsiders*, that extraordinarily powerful representation of a violent and exclusively male world, written by S.E. Hinton when she was 17 years old.

Here is a list of works written by child authors. I will later look in some detail at four of them, and then try to put these young writers into a historical context. First, the list almost certainly incomplete:

1919   The most famous is probably Daisy Ashford's *The Young Visiters* written when she was 9.

1930   *Tally Ho, The Story of an Irish Hunter* by Moyra Charlton, who started just after her 11th birthday and finished it thirteen months later.

1934   Primrose Cumming was a teenager when she wrote her first book, *Doney*, which was admired by Rudyard Kipling.

1936   15-year-old Shirley Faulkner-Horne wrote a book of instruction, *Riding for Children*.

1937   *The Far-Distant Oxus*, by Katharine Hull and Pamela Whitlock, aged
        15 and 16.
1938   *Plain Jane*, written by Mary Colville, aged 13.
1939   *Fortune's Foal*, by Garland Bullivant, written when she was a teenager.
1941   *The Swish of the Curtain*, by Pamela Brown, written when she was 14,
        and later to grow into an extended series.
1945   *Flame* by Daphne Winstone, written when she was taken ill at the age
        of 12, and illustrated by Lionel Edwards, the celebrated draughtsman of
        the hunting field.
1946   *It Began with Picotee*, by the three Pullein-Thompson sisters, Josephine
        and the twins Diana and Christine, when they were teenagers.
1948   *Sabre the Horse from the Sea*, written in 1948 by Kathleen Herald at the
        age of 15.
1948   *Satin and Silk*, written by April Jaffe when she was 14.
1953   *Black Marigolds* (*not* a pony story) by Gillian Bell, aged 16, was
        published in 1953 with illustrations by John Verney.
1954   Catherine Harris was in her teens when she wrote *We Started a Riding
        Club*.
1957   *Horse of Air*, written by Lindsay Campbell, aged15.
1963   *Runaway Riders*, written by Bernagh Brims, aged 15.

The extent of this list may surprise you. And it will not have escaped your
attention that a good number of these books were pony stories. At this point I
must acknowledge my debt to a colleague with a specialist's knowledge of pony
stories, Alison Haymonds, who provided me with a good number of these
details. I have only recently begun to appreciate that, in what is sometimes
referred to as 'the world of children's books', pony stories constitute their own
entire continent.

Innocence and ironies: Daisy Ashford

Daisy Ashford's *The Young Visiters* constitutes a special case. Here, a complex
game was being played *between adults*, a game that had very little to do with
children's literature and a great deal to do with adults and concepts of childhood. It is almost always the first text most people think of when child authors
are mentioned. It was written when the writer was only nine, published by
Chatto and Windus in 1919, became an immediate best seller, and was
reprinted sixteen times in its first six months. It had a preface by J.M. Barrie,
and the original child's spelling and grammar were retained: clearly part of the
book's appeal.[1] It begins:

> Mr Salteena was an elderly man of 42 and was fond of asking people to stay
> with him. He had quite a young girl staying with him of 17 named Ethel
> Monticue. Mr Salteena had dark short hair and mustache and wiskers

which were very black and twisty. He was middle sized and he had very pale blue eyes. He had a pale brown suit but on Sundays he had a black one and he had a topper every day as he thorght it more becoming. Ethel Monticue had fair hair done on the top and blue eyes. She had a blue velvit frock which had grown rarther short in the sleeves. She had a black straw hat and kid gloves.

One morning Mr Salteena came down to brekfast and found Ethel had come down first which was strange. Is the tea made Ethel he said rubbing his hands. Yes said Ethel and such a quear shaped parcel has come for you. Yes indeed it was a quear shape parcel it was a hat box tied down very tight and a letter stuffed between the string. Well well said Mr Salteena parcels do turn quear I will read the letter first ...

(Ashford 1919: 19–20)

The letter turns out to be an invitation for Ethel and Mr Salteena to stay with Mr Bernard Clark. The reader is clearly hearing an authentic child's voice here and, as she describes her two characters' arrival at Bernard's mansion, it soon becomes apparent that she is a reader of popular romances.

When they had unpacked Mr Salteena and Ethel went downstairs to dinner. Mr Salteena had put on a compleat evening suit as he thought it was the correct idear and some ruby studs he had got at a sale. Ethel had on a dress of yellow silk covered with tulle which was quite in the fashion and she had on a necklace which Mr Salteena gave her for a birthday present. She looked very becomeing and pretty and Bernard heaved a sigh as he gave her his arm to go into dinner ...

Well said Mr Salteena lapping up his turtle soup you have a very sump-shous house Bernard.

His friend gave a weary smile and swollowed a few drops of sherry wine. It is fairly decent he replied with a bashful glance at Ethel after our repast I will show you over the premisis.

Many thanks said Mr Salteena getting rarther flustered with his forks.

(Ashford 1919: 29–30)

This is impressive writing! The 9-year-old author is handling with great skill a number of different narrative interests and themes: romantic comedy, snobbery, poverty and the embarrassments of etiquette. She cleverly removes Mr Salteena from Bernard's mansion, despatching him to meet the Earl of Clincham and 'by mixing with him ... probably grow more seemly'. Left to themselves, the two youngsters decide to go 'up to London for a weeks Gaierty' and their departure and subsequent arrival in town is one of the book's highlights.

Well goodbye Minnit [Bernard] cried to the somber butler take care of your gout and the silver and I will pay your wages when I come back.

Thankyou kindly sir murmered Minnit when may I expect your return.

Oh well I will wire he said and dashed down the steps.

Ethel followed with small lady like steps having bowed perlitely to Minnit who closed his eyes in acknowlegment of her kindness.

… Arrived in the gay city Bernard hailed a cab to the manner born and got in followed by Ethel. Kindly drive us to the Giaerty Hotel he cried in a firm tone. The cabman waved his whip and off they dashed.

We shall be highly comfortable and select at the Gaierty said Bernard and he thourght to himself how lovly it would be if he was married to Ethel. He blushed a deep shade at his own thourghts and gave a side long glance at Ethel who was gazing out of the window. Well one never knows her murmerd to himself and as one of the poets says great events from trivil causes springs.

Just then they stopped at the gay hotel and Ethel was spellbound at the size of the big hall…Bernard poked his head into the window of the pay desk. Have you a coupple of bedrooms for self and young lady he enquired in a lordly way.

A very handsome lady with golden hair and a lace apron glanced at a book and hastily replied Oh yes sir two beauties on the 1st floor number 9 and 10.

…They went upstairs and entered number 9 a very fine compartment with a large douny bed and white doors with glass handles leading into number 10 an equally dainty room but a trifle smaller.

Which will you have Ethel asked Bernard.

Oh well I would rarther you settled it said Ethel. I am willing to abide by your choice.

The best shall be yours then said Bernard bowing gallantly and pointing to the biggest room.

Ethel blushed at his speaking look. I shall be quite lost in that huge bed she added to hide her embarassment.

Yes I expect you will said Bernard …

(Ashford 1919: 62–4)

The enormous popularity of *The Young Visiters* suggests that the public at large loved it and responded with eagerness to its many varieties of irony and ambiguity. There is the (probable) irony Daisy Ashford enjoyed at the expense of the romantic fiction she read; indeed, her pastiche so very nearly becomes parody that it is impossible to know where, or whether, the young author's insouciance ever shades into a self-conscious archness. This complicates matters; for the additional irony the adult reader enjoys at Daisy's expense is a shade uncertain, since we cannot be totally sure that she does not fully understand all those risqué comments about beds and blushing.

Yet it is even more complicated than that, for Daisy may have been 9 when her story was written but she was 38 when it was published, and presumably fully aware of those ironies in her childhood manuscript. And a further complication is the Preface written by J.M. Barrie, the arch-ironist himself and master of ambiguity, well aware of all the ironies and rejoicing in the childishness which in some ways was similar to the fictional childhood created by him.

But is this a children's book? Was it for children? Did children read it? Or was it in fact *the other way round* – a child writing for the entertainment of adults? (Children do a good deal of that, in fact.) Through a series of circumstances, this child's writing became public property, was championed by a famous writer and acclaimed by thousands of adult readers; it tells us a good deal about the complex myth of childhood that existed in the years immediately after World War I, the years that took us from Peter Pan to Christopher Robin. But it does not tell us much about my central question because it was not written by a child for other children to read.

'Different from any grown-up book': *The Far-Distant Oxus*

The Far-Distant Oxus is an altogether different matter. The story of how it came to be written and published is a remarkable one. According to Ransome, Katharine Hull and Pamela Whitlock met while sheltering from a thunderstorm while they were at boarding school. They fell into conversation and conceived the idea of writing a book about children, ponies and moors, one which would be 'by children, about children, for children'. Their systematic and level-headed approach to planning the operation was impressive: they did not write a word until they had plotted the entire novel chapter by chapter, and got to know the characters. They then began to write alternate chapters, swapped them and revised each other's work. Their biggest difficulty in a girls' boarding school was the supply of paper. They ruthlessly removed parts that were misleading, 'unnecessary and drivelling descriptions', repetition, and words they particularly disliked such as 'graceful', 'poised' and 'children'.

What impressed Arthur Ransome was the girls' extraordinarily well-organised approach to composition and the businesslike way in which they dealt with correcting their copy, providing illustrations, and so on. 'Its readers will not find themselves', he remarked in a sideswipe at *The Young Visiters*, 'laughing at quaint spellings, or making any kind of allowances on account of its authors' age. Instead, they will find with delight that they are reading something different from any grown-up book' (Hull and Whitlock 1937: 15).

But was *The Far-Distant Oxus* in fact 'different from any grown-up book'? The publishers seemed anxious to emphasise its similarity, or at least relatedness, to their other children's books: it was produced by Cape in exactly the same format as the *Swallows and Amazons* series, though in a different colour, with maps on the endpapers and illustrations by the children. With its two sequels, the three novels were marketed to suggest that they were related to, but independent of, the longer series by Ransome himself .

It could be argued that really Hull and Whitlock were writing for adults, for they knew they had to impress Arthur Ransome as well as an adult publisher. However, I am not persuaded by that, for they were undoubtedly writing what they thought of as a children's book, acknowledging their debt to Arthur Ransome's great series. I believe *The Far-Distant Oxus* is a book genuinely for child readers by two child authors.

What will a reader find here? These two child authors effectively employed many of the narrative habits of the *Swallows and Amazons* series to produce a story of camping and exploring in the countryside, but – outsmarting Ransome – with the additional interest of ponies. Like Titty and Susan and the rest, the fictional children in *The Far-Distant Oxus* map their patch of Devonshire countryside and imaginatively rename it and repossess it in the language of Matthew Arnold's *Sohrab and Rustum*. The novel is as absorbing as Ransome at his best, with humour, liveliness, a fast plot, frequent touches of lyrical descriptive prose, and some arresting similes.

> It was very warm. A mist had crawled up from the valley like the attack of a crumpled army ...
>
> ... Bridget and Peter sat on the five-barred gate swinging their legs. Before them stretched the great golden sea of corn rippling like water in the breeze. Here and there it was scattered with clumps of flaming poppies and looked, as Jennifer said, 'as though a giant had run through it with a bleeding knee.'
>
> (Hull and Whitlock 1937: 31–2, 157)

They are especially good at a kind of descriptive diminuendo effect:

> ... The hill-side was gloriously covered with bracken that was slowly bronzing ... The three ponies had to break a path for themselves through the stalks, which crackled under them like new straw that is dropped from the first wagon and run over by another.
>
> The children were so intent on steering the best course that they did not see the top until unexpectedly they climbed the last lap and were on the ridge of the moor. A hundred rabbits listened, started, and were gone.
>
> (Hull and Whitlock 1937: 39)

Surprisingly, there is a hint of sexual interest in the form of a mysterious and good-looking boy 'of about fourteen, tall and dark and lithe'. All through the book and its two sequels nobody knows where this mysterious boy comes from, where he lives, or where he goes to school.

Far away in another valley a boy lay on a rock, basking in the warmth of the setting sun. He was tall and dark, his long limbs bronzed to the colour of polished walnut, and by his side a black Labrador sat, snapping at flies and waiting expectantly.

(Hull and Whitlock 1937: 26)

These two young girl-authors have no misgivings about describing this romantic male hero swimming up to a waterfall and letting 'the water shower down upon his naked body' (Hull and Whitlock 1937:131).

One of the most revealing features of *The Far-Distant Oxus* is the fact that practical problems are always smoothed over, as if the authors felt that there was no need to slow down a good story with realistic accounts of practical difficulties. So a camp – with a wooden hut and a tree house! – gets built and furnished in a single afternoon, with hardly a hint of any of the difficulties we know would really have been involved. And this is so throughout: every undertaking is a success; frustrations are rare and short-lived, and there are no disasters. This is a determining characteristic: the narrative becomes a wish-fulfilling narrative and the reading excludes suspense and uncertainty of outcome; you are *imaginatively experiencing and savouring the satisfactions* that almost each chapter offers. To call this escapism would be wide of the mark; it calls for an unhurried, disciplined and almost ritualistic attentiveness to detail. It has the seriousness of pretending.

Hull and Whitlock do this brilliantly! They give the sympathetic reader an almost paradisiacal impression of intense shared pleasure. You get a sense of it here when, after several chapters in which the children have been journeying downstream, they triumphantly arrive at the sea.

… The marshy valley seemed forlorn. Twilight made everything seem unreal. There was one bright star in the grey mist of the sky. The golden ocean flowed nearer and nearer. They could hear the noise of the waves. The raft suddenly became difficult to manage because of the tide … The water grew wider, but there was still shadowy banks hemming them in. All at once there was a strange light feeling beneath the raft, and a salt wind stirred their hair. The two steersmen looked up. The bright evening star shone down on the ocean and they were floating on its gilded waves.

'The sea! The sea!' Bridget cried ecstatically.

'The Aral Sea, and it belongs to us because we've discovered it,' Jennifer said. 'The sea!'

(Hull and Whitlock 1937: 254–5)

Katharine Hull and Pamela Whitlock were gifted young writers with a genuine narrative aesthetic. There is in their writing a glorious narrative commitment to intense and serious pleasure. The converse is that there is little of Ransome's greater psychological depth,[2] and no concern at all for moral or emotional growth. Maturation is not a theme though the acquisition of new skills certainly is. 'They are not old enough to be afraid of their youth', Ransome said. 'We elders look back to a world that once was young. For them the dew is still on the grass' (Hull and Whitlock 1937: 17). These two young authors repeatedly in this novel represent what it is like to appreciate the dew on the grass, passionately and joyously. The larger view – time, maturation, growing up – is missing; in its place you get intense youthfulness written from inside.

Ransome's words are a reminder that no child's writing makes its appearance in a cultural vacuum. That reference to the dew on the grass places him firmly in a long Wordsworthian tradition; his view of the young authors' writing is coloured by his Romantic understanding of childhood. The reception by adults of books written by children is a complex process: there was probably considerable cultural reciprocity, since Hull and Whitlock's writing was avowedly influenced by Ransome's representation of childhood, which he then joyously recognised and celebrated. This could hardly be more different from Barrie's view of the young Daisy Ashford, with what he describes as her 'unholy rapture as she drew near her love chapter'. Barrie had ironically dismissed any Chattertonian view of her burning the midnight oil, playfully pointing out that 'there is documentary evidence that she was hauled off to bed every evening at six' (Ashford 1919: 7). Despite the jokes, it was the young Daisy's professionalism that seems genuinely to have impressed Barrie: 'It seems to me to be a remarkable work for a child, remarkable even in its length and completeness, for when children turn author they usually stop in the middle, like the kitten when it jumps.' Barrie was impressed that his young author had behaved like a grown-up; Ransome was impressed by his young writers because they had a uniquely different young persons' perception of life.

The support child authors receive from adults is probably crucial. How, for example, did 12-year-old Daphne Winstone get her book, *Flame*, illustrated by Lionel Edwards, one of the country's most revered and distinguished 'draughtsmen of the hunting field'? And *Black Marigolds* was illustrated by the distinguished author/illustrator John Verney, though its young author, Gillian Bell, had to endure a patronising introduction by Noel Streatfeild who commented that the young 16-year-old would one day 'grow up to be a real writer'.[3]

Amateur theatricals

In many respects Pamela Brown's *The Swish of the Curtain* (1941) is similar. It was begun when the author was 14, and it too ran into many editions and was later developed into a series. It concerns a group of children who decide to form a stage company, and tells of their success in converting a disused chapel into a small theatre. The children mount various productions – extracts from Shakespeare, a Christmas play, entertainments composed by themselves – and they finally enter and win a contest, which convinces their parents that they should be allowed to take up acting as a career.

But it is not an unrelieved or idealised success story. The setbacks and the numerous practicalities of stagecraft are all documented with a vivid faithfulness and the young writer is particularly good at capturing the children's moods, emotional flash points and sudden reconciliations.

> ... Lyn [the young producer] was the only one to take it seriously that night; all the others were exchanging jokes and quips during the scenes. When Bulldog appeared as a shepherd with his grey trousers beneath his short tunic she stifled a laugh, then looked as if she were about to cry; finally she picked up her coat and walked out of the door. Outside it was cold and sharp, and little snowflakes were fluttering to the ground. She found that she was not really cross, only tired, and she remembered the old stage superstition held that the worse the dress rehearsal the better the first night. Perhaps it would be all right on the night, and really it was too near Christmas to concentrate on anything.
>
> Back in the hall the rest looked at each other.
>
> 'We *are* brutes,' remarked Nigel penitently, 'to goad her like that.'
>
> 'She's so darn short-tempered,' said her brother.
>
> 'Well, so should I be in her place,' confessed Sandra. 'You know how I get when you won't stand still to be fitted.'
>
> 'Come on,' cried Nigel, darting into the dressing-room for his clothes, 'we'll catch her up and apologise.'
>
> Lyn was surprised as she walked through the gaily lit town to hear running feet behind her and Nigel's voice, 'Hi, Lyn!' He was first to catch up with her, and pressed into her hands a bag of roast chestnuts bought from a roadside vendor as a peace-offering. No one actually apologised, but as they munched the steaming nuts, leaving a trail of shells behind them, the atmosphere was very 'peace-on-earth-goodwill-unto-men-ish,' as Maddy described it. The next morning they went early to the theatre, through the snow, and performed the play perfectly.
>
> (Brown 1941: 162)

Here too there is a commitment to an aesthetic of pleasure, though here the pleasures are those of acting, composing and music. There are, as there were in *The Far-Distant Oxus*, rules within this aesthetic, implied, never spelt out: the only pleasure worth anything is one which has to be *planned and worked for*; group activity and friendship are to be celebrated; and for every difficulty there is a solution. Again, there is no concern for inner maturation, though there is a strong sense of growing older, with school certificate approaching, and the uncertainties of a future career. The young author's own sense of an imagined future and a shared past is apparent in the neatly theatrical way she concludes the novel:

'I shan't be sorry to come back to Fenchester,' said Sandra. 'I mean, we owe it something, don't we? It gave us the theatre and nice audiences.'

'And each other,' added Vicky.

'Of course, "each other" is the most important.' They smiled round affectionately.

'I feel friendly towards the world in general,' announced Jeremy. 'To-day is a perfect day.'

'It's the kind of day that sticks in your memory.'

'It seems to be sort of between the past and the future.'

The past was clear and colourful as a tapestry as they gazed out across the sea that was shrouded and misty as the future.

THE CURTAIN FALLS

(Brown 1941: 345)

The girl and the pony – a love story

The Far-Distant Oxus and *The Swish of the Curtain* both employ an already existing form – *Swallows and Amazons* for the former, and for the latter the career novel established by Streatfeild in 1936 with *Ballet Shoes*. And, because they have so much in common, it is tempting to use them as a basis for generalisations about the work of child authors. But alas, there are no universalities or absolutes here, for *Sabre the Horse from the Sea* (1948) by Kathleen Herald is significantly different.

Kathleen Herald was 15 when she wrote it and later became known as the distinguished author, K.M. Peyton.

Unlike the previous two works I have considered, *Sabre the Horse from the Sea* is not about a group; on the contrary, its young protagonist, Liza, is obsessively private. And, unlike them, this narrative does not bypass difficulties; it emphasises them. Pleasures do occur, but they are intense, utterly private, and short-lived. Loneliness and longing are the main themes. The writing is passionate, rather than lyrical. The only thing it has in common with the two novels I have already considered is that it is derivative, influenced to some extent by the already established formula of the girl-and-pony story which, in Alison Haymonds' (1994) words, represents the relationship between girl and horse as a rehearsal for future sexual and maternal emotions.

Its opening is impressively direct and seductive, recounting a moment of passionate recognition.

The horse was a great big-boned creature, dark grey in colour, with large gentle eyes staring out from beneath its forelock. It stood on the beach with its hooves planted apart in the wet sand, its tail half-raised, as if in doubt whether to fly or whether to remain. Its nostrils quivering with curiosity, its ears pricked, it was to Liza a creature of infinite beauty, a horse out of the sea.

She did not know anything about horses. But she was not afraid of them. She stood with bare feet in a pool of water left by the receding tide and looked at the grey. It did not seem strange to her to find a horse standing half in and half out of the sea, no stranger than it felt to be standing there herself. She only thought that she had never seen anything so beautiful as this animal, with the sea-water running down his legs and with a piece of seaweed caught up in his tail.

She stretched out her fingers to him. His ears came up and forward, and one hoof took a step towards her. She murmured:

'Come on, you beautiful fellow,' and he walked straight up to her and rubbed his nose against her dress. Liza took off her belt and buckled it round his neck, standing on tip-toe, and holding her breath. But the grey horse only knuckered deep in his throat, and pushed his muzzle against her hips, searching for her pockets.

'Oh, you lovely creature,' she whispered. 'What are you doing here?'

She looked round. There was no one in sight; the beach was flat and clear; only her footsteps running in a trail from the cliffs to the water's edge, and the horse's hoofprints coming up out of the sea to meet them, scarred the wet sand. The horse might have been wild, but for his gentleness, and the fact that horses such as he were not found wild in England, as Liza, even in her ignorance, knew. The child's eyes gleamed: in London, finding had been keeping.

(Herald 1948: 1)

This is complex writing of a quite different kind. With its physicality, its emphasis on the mutuality of their discovery of each other, the girl's rapture, its background of World War II and the loneliness of evacuees, it simultaneously evokes other classical arrivals out of the sea: Aphrodite, perhaps, and Robinson Crusoe stunned by a footprint in the sand.

Sabre the Horse from the Sea is a love story, passionately told. Sabre is as much in love with Liza as she with him. Two creatures meant to be together have found and recognised each other. And what follows is a powerful and totally convincing account of an obsession.

Liza is an evacuee, with no father. She has brothers away at war, and is unhappy, living with rich and unsympathetic relatives. She is curt, rude, deceitful and disobedient; her obsession is not *analysed* by this young writer, but it is brilliantly conveyed in the way the other characters are represented. They are sketchy, fragmented, half-real, set against a background of Spitfires and a 19-year-old pilot who is reported missing and simply disappears from the story. Other people – and all the realities of World War II – are shadowy and distant, making little impact on Liza's secret passion for the great stallion. She lies under him in his stall, studying 'his lean, almost black legs, and the chipped hooves' and discovering 'a strange line of white spots running under his belly like a string of beads, [wondering] how anything could be more beautiful' (Herald: 1948: 9).

> She followed the line of white spots up from under his belly, up over the dappled sides, the withers, out along the crest of his neck to his head, to the dark eyes shining out of the gloom like lazy fires, flickering and smouldering as the breeze came in through the door to blow the shadows back and forth.
> 'Oh, I love you, I love you,' she thought.
>
> (Herald: 1948: 24–5)

The story itself is not particularly unusual. There is the very disaster the reader has predicted: the stolen horse's owner appears and he is taken away. Liza, in disgrace and wretched, is sent away to relatives where, to her delight, her cousin runs a stable. Gradually she is brought back into touch with other people again. And eventually she gets Sabre back.

What distinguishes this book is its language, its insistently convincing representation of passionate feeling and of doomed and ecstatic obsession.

The historical context

When I started this study, I wondered if it might be possible to identify features that would prove to be distinguishing characteristics of the work of young authors. And I think it can be said that it displays an absence of that interest in the larger perspective of time, change and character growth which we have come to expect as a feature of so many of the greatest novels for children. In its stead, there is directness, linguistic and narrative passion, and an ability to communicate the excitement and intensity of adolescence. It is not, in these novels, a heady, uncontrolled or anarchic excitement; whatever the ecstasies, intensities and joys the young writers are dealing with, they are in all three cases represented as *having to be worked for and planned for*, with every contingency anticipated. Perhaps the very activity of writing such extended narratives (like looking after horses, perhaps) imposes on young writers its own sense of the necessary disciplines of pleasure.

In all other respects, though, they differ from one another as much as novels by adults differ from one another.

But why were so many young writers able to succeed as published authors in this particular period between the 1930s and the 1960s? There are, I think, three reasons worth considering.

The first is socioeconomic. It is no coincidence that so many young authors began with pony stories. There were thousands of boys and girls playing football in the back yards and backstreets of the country, but none of them, as far as I know, wrote a novel about it or got one published. They came from different social and cultural backgrounds. To quote Alison Haymonds again:

All that was needed was the expertise, and since girls who could afford to ride ponies were likely to be middle class and literate, they were also more likely to write a book. The novelty value of a teenage writer and the great demand for pony stories also made it easier for the young writers to get published in the 1930s, 40s and 50s than it would be now.

Another possible reason, I have heard it suggested, is that there was not much competition. But I am not persuaded by any argument that assumes that books written for children in this earlier period were inferior to books written today. It is simply untrue: it seems that way because only a handful of works from the period have survived to become canonical texts. But we need to remind ourselves repeatedly that there is only a very small correlation between what children actually read and what gets established as children's literature. The history of children's books is not a history of the classics.

Throughout the 1930s, 1940s and 1950s there was a huge and flourishing provision of good fiction for children. If you go into any good secondhand bookshop, you will find shelves of discarded and forgotten children's books. If you buy and read any one of them, you will find it is not dross; it will probably be a well-written story with action, humour and a love of its subject. The values implicit in much of the children's fiction of that period would probably be unacceptable today; and the action in a good number of them proceeds at a very leisurely rate. But they are *not* badly written. And it is simply not true to suggest that our young authors succeeded because there was not much good writing around.

A good deal has been heard recently about the role of children's literature to introduce and welcome children into their culture and to confirm and celebrate their place within it. This seems to be a more promising idea. The 1930s and 1940s (I write as much from memory as from what I have read) were characterised by a willingness of children and adults to *share* in dozens of activities. Groups of Boy Scouts and Girl Guides were the most institutionalised and successful manifestations of this communal spirit but there were many others, often associated with local church groups and other benevolent organisations. The countryside was full of groups of adults and children sharing their favourite activities – walking and hiking, cycling, fishing, exploring, boating, birdwatching, riding – and there was a literature to express and respond to these interests: the camping and tramping stories, to which the pony story was closely allied.

If we are to begin to understand this period in the history of children's books, we must understand the peculiar nature of this fiction and its appeal. Camping and tramping narratives were mostly devoted to the excitements of hiking, exploring, boating, map reading and the practicalities of camping, and there were *hundreds* of them! Their fictional children had ready access to camping equipment and free entry to friendly farmhouses. Fairly typical was the *Fell Farm* series by Marjorie Lloyd, in which a family of children spend their school holidays on a farm in the Lake District. The series exhibits both the worst and the best features of camping and tramping fiction – not much action, characters who are of little interest, a stereotypical farmer's wife fussily providing huge meals, and a generally cheerful and trusting world. But before we deride these books, we should bear in mind that the camping and exploring adventures of the children are represented with a detailed and affectionate authenticity that appealed to thousands of young readers.

Another popular series, beginning with *Out with Romany* (1937), by 'Romany of the BBC' (G. Bramwell Evens) and running through several titles and many reprints until 1949, was committed to the observation and understanding of British wildlife. In David Severn's *Crusoe* series, the fictional world represented was fundamentally conservative, the narrative posture reclusive, and the tone elegiac, but with some rapturous lyrical descriptions and outstanding illustrations by J. Kiddell-Monroe. Another series was the *Explorers* series by Garry Hogg – *Awheel*, *Afloat* and *On the Wall* (i.e Hadrian's Wall). A girl-centred series was produced by M.E. Atkinson between 1936 and 1961: her novels were about the Lockett family and were set mostly in the south of England. Finally, there was a wide range of camping and tramping novels produced specifically in association with the Boy Scout and Girl Guide organisations, so many and wide-ranging as almost to constitute a genre in their own right.

It is easy to ridicule this kind of fiction, but the formula was extraordinarily popular with young readers for three decades. Only Arthur Ransome, M.E. Atkinson and Malcolm Saville rose above the limitations of the subject matter. Nothing more powerfully demonstrates cultural change than the popularity of these books – and their subsequent disappearance. They were eclipsed by the 'new wave' of young writers in the 1960s, by rapid changes in reading habits, and eventually by the overwhelming popularity of Enid Blyton's series.

Camping and tramping fiction also assumed that the countryside was safe. The background to that assumption was the great agricultural depression that afflicted the British countryside until the end of the 1950s. World War II did not, I think, change this culture; it simply interrupted it for a few years. Since World War I, the young had left the countryside in their thousands, leaving a beautiful rather run-down rural landscape. Depressed rural Britain – appealing, mysterious, peopled by subservient farm workers and full of dilapidated and half-ruined buildings – was infinitely appealing to the middle classes, who could see it as a lovely playground full of history and mystery, and suitable for hiking, boating and all manner of adventures for children. The background to all those friendly and welcoming fictional farmers was, in reality, one of economic and social stagnation, in which farmers had to supplement their incomes in any way they could. When farmers began to prosper and agriculture became intensive, an entire genre of children's fiction was effectively wiped out by Common Market farming subsidies. And, at about the same time, the Beeching cuts closed down the railway branch lines that had taken so many fictional children by steam to their favourite holiday destinations.

The literature reflects that powerful sense of sharing within a depressed but lovely countryside. Adults are kept at a distance and children are given a free hand to organise themselves; but at the same time they are surrounded and sustained at a distance by a world of trusting and welcoming adults who *understand and share* the children's pleasures. In such a culture, children's books enjoy two enormous advantages: they have a variety of subjects of equal interest to both children and adults (riding, for example); and they can have a genuine role in drawing children into the shared culture, simply because there *is* a shared culture.

Children's books between 1930 and 1960 represented and held together a continuity of shared cultural and social interest between adults and children. It was, I suspect, a largely middle-class phenomenon. In such a culture, a young author who had the appropriate social and educational advantages could count on the sympathetic support of adults and, in some cases, practical help as well.

But what happens when the continuity is fractured – when there is (or is perceived to be) a *different* culture of the young, with its pop icons, rave parties and drug culture, and which many adults find alien and frightening? Childhood has changed; teenagehood has changed; its relationship with the rest of the cultures of our country has changed. And children's books have to change too. Perhaps they might benefit from a contribution from 'in-the-know' young writers?

In any case, perhaps everything is about to change dramatically and out of all recognition, for new young writers are publishing themselves freely now on the Internet, using the latest technology to publish works of all kinds 'by children, about children, for children', and without the assistance of adults.

If this trend develops significantly, we might have to consider seriously what exactly we mean by '*children's* literature'.

Notes

1   The sceptical view – that Barrie had as much to do with the composition of this work as with the publication – seems not to be supported by any of the known facts.
2   I know Ransome has been criticised for *lack* of psychological depth – a claim I find astonishing. One of his great gifts is the ability to suggest, rather than make explicit, the complexity and depth of his characterisation.
3   I am indebted to Jan Mark for drawing my attention to this novel and Streatfeild's somewhat ungenerous introduction to it.

References

Ashford, Daisy (1919) *The Young Visiters*, London: Chatto & Windus.
Brown, Pamela (1941) *The Swish of the Curtain*, London: Nelson.
Haymonds, Alison (1994) 'Rides of Passage', unpublished dissertation, Reading University.
Herald, Kathleen (1948) *Sabre the Horse from the Sea*, London: A. & C. Black.
Hollindale, Peter (1997) *Signs of Childness in Children's Books*, Stroud, Glos: Signal Press.

Hull, Katharine and Whitlock, Pamela (1937) *The Far-Distant Oxus*, London: Jonathan Cape.
Pearce, Philippa (1958) *Tom's Midnight Garden*, Oxford: Oxford University Press.

Part II

Crossing boundaries: where cultures meet

Part II highlights some of the transformations that happen when readers meet texts and act on them. At such interactions things change: there may be boundaries to cross and new routes into the hinterlands of understanding. Action-upon-texts is all the more important when the texts represent culturally significant experience. The conversations that take place forge new meanings, exploring culturally different ways of saying. The texts encountered in Part II have particularly complex – and sometimes shifting – structures. They represent the 'many voices' described by Bakhtin as *heteroglossia*: the different genres, dialects and styles within texts that reverberate with previously acquired knowledge and experience – cultural, social, linguistic, literary, visual and connotative (Bakhtin 1981). For Bakhtin, this concept helped to describe the dynamic relationship between reader and text as meaning is constructed. In order to enter new cultural territory, the reader may have to ask questions and be prepared to hear messages in unfamiliar languages 'to discover how we may be connected, woven together', as Gabrielle Cliff Hodges puts it. As she explains, enactment of the dialogues within one text led the silent speakers on the page out into a different cultural space, linking voices of the past from a different continent with the voices of student teachers in England.

However, it isn't always the reader who asks the questions and prompts the interactions. CD-ROM texts are specifically designed to invite active dialogues with texts, taking the readings in differently chosen directions. Texts are designed to include a variety of voices, inviting further exploration into the labyrinths offered by hypertext. There are also, as Lisa Sainsbury points out, some halting conversations or meetings where there is very little genuine exchange: despite their description as interactive, some CD-ROM texts aren't geared to dialogue. Those that are, however, 'provide children with exciting, challenging and alternative textual encounters'. Even familiar texts, encountered earlier as books, can ring (literally) with new resonances through the transforming medium of technology, and second meetings can take acquaintanceship towards familiarity.

Elizabeth Grugeon concentrates solely on oral texts whose voices echo down the years in the subversive forms of playground rhymes. Her interest is particularly in the meeting place between old, folkloric forms, the new popular texts of television, contemporary events, pop music and girls growing in assurance as powerful members of their own cultures. She identifies the universally recognisable rhymes and games as ideal vehicles for subversive and powerful appropriations. The texts are patterned and rule-governed; the experiences described in them threaten explosions of energetic rebellion. Grugeon points out that the playground, with its physical enclosures, provides a safe environment in which to push at the boundaries of taboo topics, 'present and future roles and relationships'.

Drama offers a particularly dynamic site for the many voices within texts and the possibilities of new dialogues with those who read, watch or enact them. Helen Nicholson uses the shape-shifting nature of drama to go beyond verbal encounters and to recognise that 'drama makes meanings through the languages of movement, visual images, sound and music as well as through the spoken word'. In the practice of drama, learners encounter not only a diversity of modes but the possibility of difference. Crossing boundaries into the unknown can mean confrontations with the challenges of working in a community. The different textual elements of drama hold 'multiple viewpoints, multiple forms of representation' and raise 'multiple questions'. Helen Nicholson reminds us that when we cross frontiers, meeting the heteroglossia of different cultural texts, such encounters allow us to value difference.

Reference

Bakhtin, M. (1981)*The Dialogic Imagination*, trans. C. Emerson and M. Holquist, Texas: University of Texas Press.

Chapter 5

One morning's reading of 'An Afternoon in Bright Sunlight'

Gabrielle Cliff Hodges

Cambridge, England. A cool, clear morning in May. A group of Postgraduate Certificate in Education (PGCE) students, training to teach English and Drama in secondary schools, are meeting for their final English seminar. They will then go into a range of schools, rural and urban, throughout East Anglia for a further five weeks' teaching before qualifying as teachers.

The seminar theme is 'Reading Texts from Different Cultures and Traditions'. The story I have chosen for close study has journeyed a long distance to reach these student teachers on this particular day. It is 'An Afternoon in Bright Sunlight' by Shirley Bruised Head (1987), a member of the Blackfoot Nation whose people once lived freely on the Great Plains of what is now Alberta in Canada. I have chosen the story from a collection called *Writing from Canada*, edited by Jim Rice and Mike Hayhoe. The anthology is one of a series, published by Cambridge University Press under the series title 'Figures in a Landscape'. From Shirley Bruised Head writing in Canada to the student teachers who will read it this morning, the tale has had to pass many gate-keepers. These include: the teachers who helped to find and select the stories, reading and discussing them with their students in Nova Scotia and Norfolk; Jim Rice and Mike Hayhoe, the anthology's editors from Canada and England respectively; the Cambridge University Press series editor; the CUP 'syndics', academics from the university who guard closely the reputation of the world's oldest printing and publishing house; and me, whose choice it is that we should study the text this morning.

The study of texts from different cultures and traditions within the English curriculum is problematic. The National Curriculum for English privileges the reading of 'major works of literature from the English literary heritage in previous centuries ... literature by major writers from earlier in the twentieth century and works of high quality by contemporary writers' (Department for Education 1995: 20). The requirement for students to read 'texts from other [sic] cultures and traditions' (Department for Education 1995: 19) is represented as an afterthought.

An informal group discussion about student teachers' encounters with texts in the classrooms where they have been training during the year reveals how these requirements are interpreted in practice. A majority of the texts read by students in English schools are by British or American writers, past and present, who represent the cultural mainstreams of their respective nations. The student teachers' own experience of reading in school and at university also reflects, for the most part, these mainstreams with only a few exceptions.

Even if individuals are widely read across a range of literary traditions, their reading of literature from Canada is often limited to a few well-known authors: Margaret Atwood and Michael Ondaatje, to name but two. We therefore embark on the reading of 'An Afternoon in Bright Sunlight' from a disadvantaged position – apart, of course, from the Canadian student teacher who is a member of the English and Drama group this year.

The dimensions of the story

The group have been issued with copies of the story prior to the session and have been asked to read it through beforehand. This they have done, but it does not initially elicit any particularly excited responses. Some people feel it is unexceptional. On a first quick read it does not appear to have very much to it, nor much of a point to make. The language is, for the most part, Standard English with very little even to mark it as Canadian English apart from a few words, mostly French in origin, such as 'coulee' (a deep ravine caused by heavy spring floods, but which dries out in summer). Others are aware that there may be more to the story than meets the eye, but have not yet had the time or inclination to reread it and consider where that sense stems from. So, what kind of story is it?

We are informed by the editors that it is an unsettling and enigmatic story, in which the author

> uses all her poetic skill to create an encounter between two ways of life, one immensely old and one relatively new. She also follows the great tradition of First Nations' storytelling, introducing her tale, setting up a predicament – and leaving you, the reader, to create its ending.
>
> (Rice and Hayhoe 1994: 55)

Who and what are we introduced to?

First there is a group of children – Hank and his younger sisters, Anne and Girlie (the first-person narrator), their admired 14-year-old companion, Les, who trains horses – and their mum (Mom) and dad. The children set off on a ride one hot prairie afternoon to hunt for arrowheads. Mom anxiously warns them not to go too far into the coulee and to watch out for rattlesnakes and the bear that Jerry (who is known to lie a lot) says he saw there last week. Looking back from a distance, they think they spot old Sam (whom everybody treats with respect) with their dad. Dad calls them back, but they decide to ignore him, even though they know he'll worry and be angry with them for disobeying him.

Soon they reach the coulee and, with the afternoon heat intensifying, they wander in, picking and eating cactus berries. They bicker over whether or not to worry about rattlesnakes and bears. Talk turns to the subject of old Sam again. No one seems to know much about him except that he's old, he's treated with respect (you don't walk in front of him) and then Les volunteers further information, unsmilingly: Sam guards the coulees. Why? Because 'there's things out here'. What kind of things? Animals? Other things? The heat builds up.

The children wander further into the coulee, picking chokecherries and raspberries, arguing about who should stand and hold the horses while they do so. There is a strange smell, the smell of sage or possibly dried mint. Anne has a headache. Girlie feels sleepy. The horses begin to get restless, flicking their ears and rolling their eyes. The strange, sage-like smell returns. Someone sees a shadow and Les stands in his stirrups to get a better view. He reports an old woman, at which point one of the horses bolts, only halting when Dad and Sam ride up. Dad yells at the children for riding the horses too hard. When they tell him about the old woman, he falls silent. He is disbelieving, but knows his children would not dare lie to him. He orders them home. Then he stands holding the two horses while Sam walks into the coulee.

That is where the story finishes. Although the language of the story is for the most part simple, it is not an easy story to précis and several things are lost in the summarising. Using the third person has a distancing effect compared with first-person narration. Much of the story is written as dialogue, which loses its immediacy when turned into reported speech. There are several characters, such as Emma, Jerry and Sam, who are named but who never speak and who, in Emma and Jerry's case, do not even make an appearance. Most importantly, every now and then throughout the story, there are very short italicised sections which punctuate the tale, and which seem to defy summarising altogether. Here is the first such section:

> *Ayissomaawaawa … I must be careful, I waited long. Need to grow. Strong. Strong. Strong as when I was young. It was good. Our power was strong. Must be careful. Haste betrays. I must wait. Come, boy. Come alone. Do not fear. There is nothing to fear.*

> (Bruised Head 1987: 59)

The counterpoint these sections provide is crucial. Without them the story is one-dimensional but, as we are reminded by the Introduction, the author represents here at least two dimensions: the old and the new (perhaps also the actual and the spiritual).

As the seminar begins, the student teachers are debating what the children might have encountered in the coulee and whether there is or is not any real point to the story. If so, what is it? Some are reluctant to accord the story more time and attention. I realise that some kind of intervention on my part may help to move the discussion on and help them to engage more closely with the story. At the moment it feels as if it is being viewed through the wrong end of a telescope, far off and inconsequential. How much more so might it then seem to students in classrooms with whom these student teachers might subsequently read it?

The problem, I think, stems from a difficulty, not with decoding the text but with knowing how to interpret it. Some people are having difficulty engaging with it because it is from an unfamiliar culture and they do not have enough cultural information readily available to begin to complete the text in, as Robert Scholes puts it, 'a fashion commensurate with the words [and] images' (Scholes 1989: 131). Because it is from a different narrative tradition there are some further barriers to understanding. We are more used to tales that tell, rather than this kind of story, which only hints. Because it is written to be read, not spoken (although it may, of course, have its origins in the oral tradition), the words lie flat on the page, their nuances difficult to distinguish without the prosodic features of the spoken word. Some of the student teachers, normally fluent readers, seem to find themselves uncharacteristically ill-equipped to read interpretatively, needing to discover different skills, or awaken others which may have lain dormant for a while.

Interacting with the text

David Wood, drawing on research from the United States, observes that children who can decode text but who still have problems reading are helped by having reading processes made explicit: 'Children who find difficulty in learning how to "interact" with text can learn how to do so if these normally unobservable processes are made an *explicit* part of what is taught' (Wood 1988: 177).

The student teachers do not normally have problems reading, but this story seems to require them to interact with it differently from others they have read. A task which may help them to achieve this shift, and which they can themselves use with students in classrooms, is to prepare a dramatised rereading of the story as if for broadcasting. At the end of the session the reading will be tape recorded, but there will only be time for one attempt at it, without a full rehearsal.

Before that, though, a picture. The front covers of all the anthologies in the 'Figures in a Landscape' series include a colour illustration. It is not easy to select one image to convey the idea of a nation, all its people, cultures and histories, especially if you want to avoid being stereotypical. *Writing from Australia* (Morgan 1994) has perhaps the most intriguing picture in the series. It is a reproduction of a detail from *The National Picture*, a collage created by Geoff Parr in 1985. A group of contemporary white Australians are arranged in a tableau, equipped with surveying instruments, cool box and ghetto blaster. Some link hands, others point to one another. But no two people meet each other's eyes. The most important-looking man in the group wears a black suit and a tie. He shakes the hand of a black person, dressed in white, with a scarf in

Aboriginal colours. This person's face is covered with a black-and-white photograph of an Aboriginal man. In the foreground stands a kangaroo hound. Lying on the ground are a wallaby skin and a couple of large emu eggs. In the background, again in black and white only, represented by photographs, not real models, are the half-obscured faces and bodies of more Aborigines.

The cover of *Writing from Australia*, with its multiple layers and meanings, conveys something of the complexity of the nation it represents. I suggest to the group the idea of making a tableau to explore some of the equivalent dimensions in 'An Afternoon in Bright Sunshine'. It could be construed as an illustration to advertise the radio broadcast of the reading in the radio listings pages. It is worth saying at this point that none of the characters in the story is described physically. We are left to build up our ideas about each of them from the way they speak, act and interact. From that starting point, one by one, members of the group take up a position in the tableau, discussing where each of them should go, what stance they should adopt and why. For example, it is decided that Hank should stand at the front looking ahead towards the coulee: 'Hank is boss. At least he thinks he is' (Bruised Head 1987: 55).

The statement 'Hank is boss' is immediately undercut by 'At least he thinks he is.' The justification for having him at the front is that it simultaneously suggests assertiveness *and* vulnerability. Leading from the front leaves a person in the most exposed position. Next, where should Girlie (the first-person narrator) stand? She is not important in terms of the story's events, but almost everything is mediated through her. The group decides she should stand to one side, towards the front, from where she can survey all the other characters so far. We, the viewers, look at her looking at them. Our Canadian student teacher has told us about 'the talking stick' and the tradition among First Nations people of handing the talking stick to whoever is speaking in a Council debate or discussion. Only the person with the stick may speak and they may keep it for as long as they want. It is agreed that our narrator should hold a talking stick. We pass her a rain stick, borrowed for the morning from the Music department, to serve the purpose.

Slowly the tableau grows as Les, Dad and Mom are fitted in. Then comes Sam. Where should he go? What do we know about him? Only that, for some reason, he commands respect and that you are not allowed to walk in front of him. So he comes to the front. But since he does not speak in the story he is a much more shadowy figure than Hank, who is constantly there. So Sam moves to the side, representative of older people, other people in other times – ancestors, perhaps.

At this point one of the student teachers suddenly admits with surprise that up until now she has subconsciously been imagining the characters as white Canadians, not First Nations people. Ironically (and interestingly), this new awareness seems to have been prompted by the physical presence of another member of the group in role, despite their being white as well. It reinforces the notion that interacting physically with a text can extend readers' understandings of it in quite startling ways.

To return to the construction of the tableau – can the whole story be represented in this way? Probably not. Decisions need to be made about the sections in italics. Whose voice is speaking? Whose thoughts are we hearing? The group is not sure, but decides that the sections will be read by several voices simultaneously, to enhance their strangeness. Several additional figures are therefore brought in to surround the rest of the group (like the ancestors?) in a semicircular shape. But can the narrator, Girlie, see them? Should she still be the one to hold the talking stick?

Eventually the tableau is complete. There has been considerable discussion about characters and their relative clarity or obscurity. People seem to understand the characters slightly better because a range of learning modalities (Fielding 1996) – auditory, visual *and* kinaesthetic – have been brought into play. For this task the student teachers are being asked to interpret certain elements of the story, not just verbally but visually and physically as well. Guided by Howard Gardner's work on multiple intelligences (Gardner 1983), we can see how the task requires more than one type of intelligence to work on the problem of interpreting the story; not just linguistic intelligence but spatial and bodily intelligences as well. This is probably why the student teachers' attitudes towards the story slowly begin to shift.

It is now time to start work on the reading. One section of the group adjourns to work out how to read the main narrative and to solve various problems that immediately present themselves. For example, will they leave in or take out the various verbs of saying. They decide to leave them out, since the different pitch and timbre of individual readers' voices as well as the content of the dialogue will help to identify characters. The group annotate their texts accordingly and decide to try a preliminary reading to see what it sounds like.

Meanwhile a second group have begun work on the italicised sections. They, too, have problems to solve, challenges that in silent reading are implicit rather than explicit. Take, for example, the first word of the section quoted on page 73: 'Ayissomaawawa'. It is the word which, standing alone, begins the whole story. But what class of word is it? What is its function? Is it a ritual story opening? Probably not, since it appears at various other points in the tale. Is it some kind of spell or incantation? Is it a chant or a cry of anguish? How do you speak it?

This group is also trying to decide to whom the words they are saying should be attributed. Are they the thoughts of an old woman? If so, who is she? How should the words be spoken? The grammar of these sections is marked. Some sentences are single words: sometimes adjectives, sometimes verbs, sometimes adverbs. Other sentences employ archaic syntax, have a subject but not a predicate, or vice versa. It is almost as close as it is possible to get to how one might represent the language of thought: Vygotsky's egocentric speech or speech for oneself (Vygotsky 1986: 86), stronger on predicate than subject, as distinct from more fully articulated 'communicative' speech, evenly balanced between subject and predicate. Is this, then, person or spirit? Voice or inner thoughts? The group let the text lead them and play around with voices and dynamics, beginning to create a slightly ethereal but somewhat menacing result.

In a third group, the students are working purely on sound and music to support the reading. They have been offered the rain stick, a CD player and a CD of Native American chants and dances, *Sacred Spirit*. They set to work. Before long they are reading the story very closely again, looking for moments when sound effects or music will contribute to the process of making the implicit explicit but without destroying the very delicate poise in which the different dimensions of the story are balanced. They like the atmosphere evoked by the first track of *Sacred Spirit*, which generates a sense of distance in both time and space and has a somewhat hypnotic effect suited to the strangeness felt by the characters in 'An Afternoon in Bright Sunlight'.

The session proceeds and it becomes clear that all three groups are now reading the text very closely, much more so than they did at first. Furthermore, they are impelled by the requirements of the task to talk about interpretation and to begin to take up a critical stance. Because the two speaking groups are occasionally recasting the text – the narrator-and-characters group reshaping it to suit the dramatised reading, the old-woman's-thoughts group repeating, doubling, chanting their lines – they need to communicate with each other to negotiate how to join it all together in the final reading. As they articulate their ideas about ways of reading the text, illustrating it with sound, they are forced to interpret the words on the page. As they argue between themselves for a particular way of reading, they adopt different critical positions to justify their views.

The most telling moment is yet to come, though. Some way into the story, just before the first italicised section, a change in the atmosphere is signalled in the narrative. The children's chattering and bickering stops. The narrator continues: 'It is hot. Horse tails switch lazily at slow-moving flies. Saddle leather squeaks. Hooves thud dully on dry grass. An occasional sharp crack echoes down the coulee' (Bruised Head 1987: 58). We can begin to feel the heat and hear only the switch, squeak, thud and crack break the silence. And then we read:

> She stands listening to the children's voices. An outcropping of rock hides her den. Inside it is cool and dry.
>
> *Ayissomaawaawa* …
>
> (Bruised Head 1987: 58)

On a first, silent reading we may gloss over these few short lines. It is the pressure to dramatise the reading that pushes us further towards interpretation. Who is the narrator here? To whom does that pronoun *she* refer? It does not appear to refer to Girlie, since Girlie is one of the children *she* is listening to. If it is not Girlie, who or what is it? (We don't know until the end of the story about the existence of an old woman.) *She* has a den. Is *she* some sort of wild animal? Is *she* the thinker or speaker of the italicised words? Or is *she*, in retrospect, Girlie, caught in a some kind of narrative time-shift by means of which she can be both young and old simultaneously? Can a mere pronoun achieve that effect?

The silent reader can remain in a state of uncertainty, but a decision has to be made for the dramatised reading. The narrator-and-characters group must confer with the old-woman's-thoughts group. They find an exciting solution, a way of representing aurally the complicated process that sophisticated readers enact subconsciously in their heads. However, there is no time to try it out and see if it really works until the final reading.

Crossing the frontier

Time presses. The morning moves on. It almost time to record the reading. Tables and chairs are moved, the tape recorder is switched on. The story will take about ten or fifteen minutes to read. There will be no chance to stop and start again. There is suddenly a sense of urgency, a will to do it well. People are feeling some affinity with their characters and the story. They do not know more than the bare bones of what the other groups have been working on. Now will be the first time they will hear properly how the various elements of the dramatised reading sound together.

'Play' is pressed on the CD player. *Sacred Spirit* begins. The rain stick is turned upside down, its dried beans trickling like shingle down inside. The reading starts:

> Ayissomaawaawa …
>   The Porcupine Hills look soft and brown as we stand gazing out over the sunburnt prairie grass.
>   'Come on, guys. Let's go for a ride,' says Hank.
>   Hank is boss. At least he thinks he is …
>
>   (Bruised Head 1987: 58)

The readers settle into the story and the atmosphere in the room becomes more highly charged. Everyone is both reading and listening to the story more carefully than ever before. Soon the narrative shift approaches. To add to the unease, the sound group have started to hum sustained, discordant notes. Against this background, how will the next lines work? The voice of the narrator, Girlie, begins 'She stands listening to the children's voices … ', but gradually her voice ceases to be alone. A whisper at first, but growing louder, she is joined by the multiple voices of the old woman until they have taken over and left the narrator's voice behind. It is and it is not Girlie speaking. It is and it is not the woman thinking. This is one of those stories which, as Jim Rice describes them, '*suggest* much more than they state' (Rice and Hayhoe 1994).

Listening and observing, I feel that the group here is on what Seamus Heaney calls 'the frontier of writing':

> the line that divides the actual conditions of our daily lives from the imaginative representation of those conditions in literature, and divides also the world of social speech from the world of poetic language.
>
> (Heaney 1995: xvi)

They are absorbed and concentrating, and, although the landscape of Canada and figures in that landscape, past and present, may still seem far distant, the process of engaging with them has begun.

In *How Children Think and Learn*, David Wood reminds us of the differences between spoken and written language and how, compared with the many subtleties of spoken language, the tools available for communicating in written text, for example punctuation, are relatively blunt instruments (Wood 1988: 166).

> Becoming literate must involve more than learning how to 'translate' written symbols into spoken ones. Reading demands *interpretation* ... Even when we listen to verbal accounts of what other people have said in conversation and narrative, the speaker can convey *how* something was spoken by imitating the tone of voice used. In text, however, we must use special *words* (like 'whispered') to get such messages across. The reader must make inferences about how a written text should be analysed to reveal its structure and has to decide where stress and emphasis should be laid. Expert readers usually perform these functions 'automatically' and without conscious awareness of how they do so. But children have to learn *how* to 'interact' with text in order to interpret its writer's intended meaning.
>
> (Wood 1988: 166)

Faced with a text like 'An Afternoon in Bright Sunlight', there are reasons why even ordinarily fluent readers have some new learning to do.

First, if (as here) the text draws heavily on characteristics more usually associated with oral storytelling, the absence of prosodic features can lead to difficulty in interpretation. Reinstating some of those prosodic features, through interactive tasks such as the one described in this chapter, may help to reanimate the telling and prompt interpretation, hitherto elusive. Such an activity also differentiates the reading and offers the chance for a range of learning modalities to come into play. If this results in greater engagement and understanding on the reader's part, then it has value.

Second, if the text is from a different tradition, then people's customary reading expectations may, temporarily at least, be unsettled. Lack of certainty may interfere with the otherwise smooth processes of reading and interpretation. In this particular case, the uncertainty derives from lack of explicitness in the telling as well as absence of obvious closure. Readers accustomed to closure may find it difficult to be left at the end of a story with questions rather than answers. Making a dramatised reading shifts the focus of attention away from the story's ending and on to the manner of its telling. If the process is pleasurable, then it may prove to be another way of learning to appreciate texts rather than simply reading to find out what happens in the end.

Finally, if the text is from and about an unfamiliar culture, there may be yet further difficulties facing even the most experienced of readers. The issue of knowing about the contexts in which texts are produced or written has been much discussed in recent years. It has been pointed out, however, by teachers such as Suzanne Scafe, that in educational institutions there is a tendency for texts from 'other' cultures to be studied predominantly for social, political, historical reasons, rather than for literary ones (Scafe 1989). As I have already said, this tendency is underpinned by the way texts other than those from the English literary heritage are represented in the the National Curriculum (Department for Education 1995: 19). Whatever the text or its origins, therefore, a balance needs to be maintained.

It remains the case, however, that if we are in the presence of a text from a culture with which we are not familiar, and if that text (like 'An Afternoon in Bright Sunlight') closely guards the detail of its people and cultural practices, then the reading process, temporarily at least, may be impeded. At that point we can choose to go on or to turn back. Which we choose to do may well depend on what we already know about textuality, its characteristics and rewards: 'The notion of textuality reminds us that we do nothing in isolation from others. We are always connected, woven together, textualized' (Scholes 1989: 154).

If that is the case, then we are bound to go on. Figures in a landscape, such as those in 'An Afternoon in Bright Sunlight', may seem very distant and different but they are recognisable 'because they are portraits of people living in a real world – recognisable but not familiar' (Rice and Hayhoe 1994: xi). What we have to do, of course, is find ways to familiarise ourselves with them further – as literary constructs and as representative of real peoples – to discover how we may be connected, woven together and textualised.

The idea of weaving and connections leads us to the Internet, which, ironically, appears to be one of the best ways to connect from the United Kingdom with First Nations cultures and traditions. A search using 'Blackfoot+Nation', for example, leads to many Web sites celebrating its history, its people, its spirituality, its schools, its art and craft, and a great deal more. But that is a different kind of connection, crossing different boundaries, to the frontier of writing. Writing is a frontier that connects and acts as a barrier simultaneously. But the reader, engaging with words and interpreting the ideas, connects with and oversteps the barrier. Our task therefore, as teachers and student teachers, is to learn how to be able to do that with all manner of texts and to teach others to be able to do it as well.

References

Bruised Head, S. (1987) 'An Afternoon in Bright Sunlight', in Rice, J. and Hayhoe, M. (eds), *Writing from Canada*, Cambridge: Cambridge University Press.

Department for Education (1995) *English in the National Curriculum*, London: HMSO.

The Fearsome Brave (1994) *Sacred Spirit: Chants and Dances of the Native Americans*, Virgin Records.

Fielding, M. (1996) 'How and Why Learning Styles Matter: Valuing Difference in Teachers and Learners', in Hart, S., *Differentiation and Equal Opportunities*, London: Routledge.

Gardner, H. (1983) *Frames of Mind*, London: Heinemann.

Heaney, S. (1995) *The Redress of Poetry*, London: Faber and Faber.

Morgan, W. (ed.) (1994) *Writing from Australia*, Cambridge: Cambridge University Press.

Rice, J. and Hayhoe, M. (eds) (1994) *Writing from Canada*, Cambridge: Cambridge University Press.

Scafe, S. (1989) *Teaching Black Literature*, London: Virago.

Scholes, R. (1989) *Protocols of Reading*, New Haven/London: Yale University Press.

Vygotsky, L. (1986) *Thought and Language*, Cambridge, MA: MIT Press.

Wood, D. (1988) *How Children Think and Learn*, Oxford: Blackwell.

Chapter 6

Tales from The Mouse House

Playing with reading on CD-ROM[1]

Lisa Sainsbury

Vibrant animations, oscillating words and bursts of tremulous music all perform to the click of a mouse as children interact with the multimedia surfaces of electronic fiction. The inheritors of a vast range of diverse media through which to investigate narrative – such as picture books, songs, films, plays, audio-cassettes, novels or comic strips – children are well equipped to explore the narrative environments presented to them through advances in computer technology. While the entire range of this inheritance should be valued, many media are overlooked by official hierarchies that tend to value the printed book over all other forms of narrative. In a recent newspaper article, James Naughtie refutes the notion that contemporary children read less because they are provided with more attractive options:

> ... sometimes it feels as if there is a conspiracy of pessimism. Computer skills? They surely mean that the machine will supplant the book. Television? It's the enemy of literacy. None of this need be true. Anyone who looks at the volume of good writing for children and teenagers ... will realise that the urge to read is still there, and it's being fed.
>
> (Naughtie 1998: A1)

Naughtie observes that this urge to read is being fed by engaging books, but I would suggest that it is also being fed by the very forms of narrative that are said to threaten it. In this chapter I focus on some of the nascent modes of electronic fiction published on CD-ROM, seeking to show that they have the potential to expand and complement the child's experience of reading printed books. I employ 'electronic fiction' as an expansive term, which includes the prolific game culture of the computer industry. While complementing more traditional modes of storytelling, computer games are increasingly reliant on progressive narrative structures that implicate children as readers as much as players. Adventure games are therefore treated as a form of electronic fiction and will be discussed alongside electronic books.

Theoretical foundations

I have already suggested that contemporary children are particularly well prepared for the multimedia environments of electronic fiction. However, as Lydia Plowman observes in an informative article on the use of narrative in pedagogic multimedia, although CD-ROMs 'superficially appear to combine media with which we are already familiar, such as film, television and books, the "reading" or interpreting skills we have acquired from exposure to these conventional media are not directly transferable' (Plowman 1996b: 92). Plowman is perhaps too ready to conflate the reading experiences allowed by films and books, which contrast and correlate to varying degrees, but she is right to suggest that learnt skills of negotiating narrative are not, or indeed should not be directly transferable to the reading of multimedia software.

Plowman introduces the Aristotelian notion of narrative coherence (which demands that no episode should be redundant and that it should take its place in a fixed sequence), in order to suggest that interactive multimedia challenges such 'traditional definitions of narrative because it can be suspended or altered at various decision points – the foci of interactivity' (Plowman 1996b: 92). She goes on to suggest that interactive multimedia thwarts the expectations of readers who are conversant with the linear narratives typical of many printed books or films and, in a related article, proposes that multimedia should be perceived as a multilinear form that invites its readers/users to make choices at various 'foci of interactivity' (Plowman 1996a: 48). Interactive multimedia are clearly multilinear, but this terminology is related to the formalist notions of story (*sjuzet*) and plot (*fabula*) – that invest in causality and linearity – which Plowman herself suggests are inadequate for describing the narrative dynamics of multimedia. As she says: 'these ways of slicing the narrative are too fixed for the medium and we need to find a way of describing narrative which takes account of its multidimensionality and includes its interaction with audiences' (Plowman 1996a: 48). Plowman's notion of multilinearity does start to evoke the multidimensional nature of CD-ROMs as narratives begin to branch off in accordance with reader/user selection. However, multilinearity cannot account for the *explicit* invitations to reader/user activity required at the numerous points of narrative suspension (or interactivity) which have come to define multimedia. This explicit demand for interactivity is not exclusive to multimedia, but multimedia is perhaps the medium best disposed to develop the potential of what I term 'elective' narratives. 'Compulsive' narrative and 'elective' narrative are associated terms, relating to my notion that narrative can be classified by the extent to which it expects reader participation.

A compulsive narrative, such as Roald Dahl's *James and the Giant Peach* (1961), is simply one that compels the reader to move from one sentence, image or page to the next; the reader is *not required* to make a choice as to the order in which the plot is presented. Elective narratives, like the *Fighting Fantasy Gamebooks* by Livingstone and Jackson, for example, *require* the reader to make directive decisions that can affect both plot and story. However, I must stress that this classification of texts merely serves to highlight the emphatic tendencies within individual narrative modes. As reader-response theorists such as Wolfgang Iser (1974) confirm, all texts leave silent spaces to be interpreted by the reader's imagination and, irrespective of medium, there is no doubt that individual standards of literacy, temperament or cultural experience all contribute to the idiosyncratic nature of the reading process. None the less, there is a difference between the nature of the gaps left in compulsive and elective narratives. While both modes direct the reader to action through the *spaces* left in the textual rendering of plot and story, the elective narrative also motivates the reader through a *textual withdrawal* from the rendering of plot and story; the reader of an elective narrative is overtly asked to make choices affecting narrative construction.

This tentative foray into terminology provides a useful starting point for my exploration of electronic texts. Texts which are both multilinear and elective can be described as interactive because they expect readers to select the direction of narrative development, but although most multimedia packages claim to be interactive, such claims are not always justified. The ways in which CD-ROMs make use of multilinear and elective structures indicate the level of their divergence from other media, and signal their capacity to provide children with progressive textual encounters. Rob Stannard believes that 'new technologies create or offer opportunities for new ways of seeing and making sense of the world, for shaping and creating meaning' (Stannard 1996: 13) and, certainly, electronic fiction is capable of providing children with fresh perspectives of, and interactive engagement with, their texts. However, new technologies do not *necessarily* lead to innovative design and development. Therefore, while allowing that electronic fiction invariably effects a meeting between child and text, I want to propose that such meetings are only of consequence if they enable a stimulating reading experience that is different – to some extent at least – from that of reading other modes of narrative.

Electronic books

Electronic books constitute a large section of the children's multimedia market and, although they are often lively, colourful and enjoyable, they are rarely original. Multimedia has the potential to take narrative in new directions, but it frequently replicates the form and structure of printed books. Profit margins surely contribute to this trend, for many programs are based on successful children's books and publishers attempt to harness this success with derivative CD-ROMs. Another possible explanation lies in the prejudice towards computer technology, signalled by James Naughtie, which locates multimedia as an enemy of book literacy. In their desire to woo anxious parents, software houses are seemingly tempted to 'play safe' with programs that look and behave like the texts of a conventional children's library. This is not to suggest that electronic books are inherently regressive, but since they typically model themselves on extant texts they must work particularly hard to reinvent the stories they tell.

Robert Louis Stevenson would be rolling furiously in his grave over the multimedia treatment of *Treasure Island*, one of the titles in an unimaginative series called Living Classics (Europress 1995). The worst aspect of these discs is the diminished quality of the narrative, for Europress have effectively bowdlerised the original texts. The direct transposition of novels to CD-ROM is problematic, as electronic books cannot easily cope with a large number of words. Trawling through verbal text via a computer screen can be a frustrating and wearing process, since the reader only has access to limited portions of text at any one time. Europress are clearly hampered by the need to limit the verbal content of their products, but this is brought about by their apparent reluctance to deviate from recognised narrative models; they have forced CD-ROMs to behave like printed books, denying their readers a transformation of narrative experience.

A much more fertile source for electronic books is the picture book, since its inherent ability to balance word and picture (without employing large amounts of prose) means that it can easily be adapted to multimedia. Living Books is a prolific series which bases its CD-ROMs on published picture books – I will be discussing *The Berenstain Bears Get in a Fight* (Brøderbund 1995) by Stan and Jan Berenstain. Each Living Book conforms to a format whereby the home screen (equivalent to a title page) offers the options 'Read To Me' or 'Let Me Play', and visually duplicates an open book with screens (pages) to be turned at the click of the mouse (see Figure 6.1).

As Judith Graham suggests in a review of Living Books, most children will choose to play the story (Graham 1994: 15), but an examination of the read-through enables an interesting comparison with live storytelling. The linear narrative about argumentative siblings is narrated, screen by screen, supported by a combination of written text and animated illustrations. Each spoken word is highlighted, supposedly allowing children to read along, although the eye is constantly distracted by talking bears, prancing wildlife and numerous changes in visual perspective. Although the story is pleasant to watch and listen to, the Read-To-Me experience lacks the dynamism of 'real-life' story time. There is no opportunity for the child to interrupt this automated telling of the tale ('But *why* did Brother Bear do that, Mummy?'), or for 'Mummy' to improvise, as all the best storytellers do. The act of reading books with children can be an extremely interactive process and frequently departs from the linear narrative as questions are posed and answered. The Read-To-Me option of Living Books allows for no such collaboration and, though the child might discuss narrative events after they have taken place, the storyteller's ability to surround the child with story is lost. Admittedly, this process might usefully act as a surrogate storyteller for busy parents, but television has long filled this gap through a history of inventive programming. So, if story time can do it better and television already does it, what is the point of Living Books?

Figure 6.1   The Berenstain Bears Get in a Fight. Living Books are clearly modelled on printed books and, although they offer several narrative pathways, their structures are not necessarily multilinear.

Source: The Berenstain Bears Get in a Fight, copyright © 1995 Living Books. All rights reserved.

Their validity lies in the Let-Me-Play element of the disk, where the player can either read and play with each screen in sequence, or can choose to go straight into a favourite screen. Play is suspended until the text has been narrated, dialogue spoken and animations performed in exactly the same manner as during the read-through (revealing that the Read-To-Me option does not constitute an alternative reading and that these dual pathways do not establish multilinearity). When the mouse finally becomes live, a floating cursor invites children to explore the on-screen illustration in search of hidden animations (hot spots) which frequently develop the narrative. On page 4, Brother and Sister Bear wake to grey skies, signalling the impending argument of the title. This central theme is then echoed and confirmed by the actions of the player who, for example, might click on a biplane suspended above Brother Bear's bed – it immediately flies away, causing the grumpy young bear to complain, 'Great, that was my best plane!'.

These moments of interactive play are not elective in the fullest sense, since selection of hot spots is random (and does not constitute an informed choice), but the designers have withdrawn from the automatic telling of these story fragments, leaving the player to supplement the Berenstains' narrative. Admittedly, it could be argued that the play is so focused (and amusing in itself) that its link to the narrative might be overshadowed by the immediacy of the impulse to seek and expose animations. However, as Vygotsky's discussion of play and development suggests in *Mind In Society* (1978), the use to which such interaction might be put, and the degree to which it allows the evolution of narrative, is likely to vary, as children will be driven by different motives, inclinations, incentives and cognitive abilities (Vygotsky 1978: 92). Brøderbund recommend an age range of 3 to 8, which covers a large amount of developmental ground, suggesting that narrative might be transformed in various ways at different stages of development.

In terms of early childhood, there are at least two crucial factors surrounding the interactive play of *The Berenstain Bears*. First, the activation of animations involves physical participation, as visible objects on the screen are selected by the child; and second, the area of narrative play is restricted to a single screen at a time. Vygotsky suggests that the play of preschool children entails the construction of abstract concepts, but that movement within the field of abstraction involves methods that are situational and concrete (Vygotsky 1978: 101). Children physically act upon objects that have a pivotal role in the making of abstract meaning. As Vygotsky explains, the 'child at play operates with meanings detached from their usual objects and actions' and thus a stick becomes a horse in the child's playful transference of meaning (Vygotsky 1978: 98). Some narrative environments resist this impulse to physical interaction, potentially resulting in confusion or anxiety. In *Becoming a Reader* (1991), Appleyard cites the example of a child (age 2.11) who, with the aid of toy props, is told the story of a fat elephant who cannot climb a hill. Reaching into the story environment, she insists that 'He can go up' and literally pushes the toy elephant over the hill. She then becomes bewildered and agitated when the researcher asks her to imagine that the elephant cannot climb the hill (Appleyard 1994: 50). The adult in this situation consciously refuses to comply with the child's desire for interaction with the story – as her entry into its abstract conditions relies upon affective interaction – but there are also texts denying this complicity to some extent.

The printed version of *The Berenstain Bears*, for example, is not structurally open to the participatory play of early childhood. The child may well act out various story elements through conversation or play, but such a response is not overtly invited by the text. Conversely, the multimedia narrative explicitly encourages physical interaction through its elective structure, thus endorsing the young child's own methods of engaging with narrative. This is not to suggest that printed texts cannot accommodate children's active involvement; movable picture books, like the Ahlbergs' *The Jolly Postman* (1986), provide an obvious example of texts that invite readers physically to manipulate and extend the boundaries of narrative invention. However, the hidden programming of electronic books means that such operational play can equally be directed towards more abstract associations. The CD-ROM invites the child to play, but controls its outcome through pre-written code, thus encouraging children to make connections between related hot spots (narrative events).

Although a complete reading of *The Berenstain Bears* constitutes a linear narrative, it is unlikely that young readers/players experience it in this way. Cognitive limitations suggest that the random formation of narrative is likely to evolve in clusters as play centres around hot spots on a single screen. Depending on the child's associative abilities, these clusters may go on to form the strands of a highly flexible multilinear narrative, but children are not forced to read the compulsive, linear story in order to engage in meaningful play. Indeed, this haphazard selection of animated narrative episodes is consistent with the kind of structures – common in stories told by young children – described by Applebee in *The Child's Concept of Story* (1978). Children frequently make use of Applebee's 'sequence', which is a story containing a number of disparate events, 'linked together on the basis of an attribute shared with a common *center*' (Applebee 1978: 60). In the case of *The Berenstain Bears*, this centre might be Brother Bear or perhaps the siblings' argument. The program thus accommodates the story structures of early childhood, providing the security and encouragement necessary for children to make sense of more complex struc-tures and to perceive *The Berenstain Bears* as a unified, linear narrative. Of course, Living Books are not the only electronic books to stimulate this level of cognitive activity in young readers. *The Adventures of Peter Rabbit & Benjamin Bunny* (Mindscape 1996), for example, also encourages operative play through centred hot spots, setting this play within a scrolling landscape that is shared by the narration of both stories, thus encouraging players to make connections between Beatrix Potter's related texts.

Where young players might be excited by new-found connections between play and story, older readers are likely to overlook the narrative potential of *The Berenstain Bears* as it fails to encourage or challenge literate children. As an electronic picture book, *The Berenstain Bears* supposedly employs a balanced integration of word and image, but this balance is called into question by its emphasis on illustrative play, an issue that 'niggles' at Judith Graham, who observes that the written word is marginalised by picture-play, encouraging chil-dren to ignore the printed element of Living Books (Graham 1994: 16). Such a response is confirmed by Caroline Ford, a primary-school teacher, who says that the electronic books are 'enormous fun, but I've noticed the children twiddling their thumbs rather than following the narrated text on screen' (Ford, quoted in Richards 1995: 23). The written portion of the text is sidelined as dull and is ultimately dismissed, potentially damaging the ongoing development of print literacy. There is no stipulation that multimedia should encourage print literacy, but it could make much better use of *combined* media; if pictures can spring to life, so too can words. Instead, the narrative potential of such texts is reduced for older readers by the negation of words.

An electronic book which might be expected to stimulate print-literate chil-dren is an ambitious electronic book called *Lulu's Enchanted Book* (Organa 1997), written and designed for CD-ROM by Romain Victor-Pujebet. This metafictive package looks more like a printed storybook than most electronic books, for each screen conveys sepia-tinted pages of verbal text, accompanied by illustrations styled on the woodcuts and engravings of early printing methods. This is no derivative use of bookish style, though, for a central theme of this text is the relationship between the pre-technological world of Lulu's book and the digital technology which subsumes this fictive world as its story is written to CD-ROM. The tale tells of a bored princess whose world is suddenly enlivened by the crash-landing of a robot in a flying saucer. Her relationship with this robot draws attention to her status as fictionalised character, as it soon transpires that he has travelled from a place in space and time beyond the pages of the book that tells her story.

This type of postmodern play is not new to children's literature, of course; Aidan Chambers, Pauline Fisk, the Ahlbergs, and Scieszka and Smith[2] have all produced book texts which constantly challenge the narratee's perspective of narrative through metafictive sleight of hand. However, *Lulu's Enchanted Book* makes use of hyper-text, a multimedia tool automatically transporting the reader/user to different parts of the program, so that when characters lose each other mid-story, the reader is literally thrown around the pages/screens of this program. The abstractions of metafictive narrative are thus made tangible to older readers through tools specific to multimedia, so *Lulu's Enchanted Book* provides a cognitive challenge similar to that offered to younger players of *The Berenstain Bears*.

Like Living Books, however (and despite the fact that it theorises the book's status), *Lulu's Enchanted Book* still marginalises the written portion of its narrative. The verbal text is often dry and wooden, while elaborate animations or hyper-text links lead away from words into animated sequences that are often surprising and always beautifully presented. There are moments of elective choice in this package, which seemingly allow the player to take its multilinear narrative in different directions. No matter which direction is taken, though, the reader is lured towards the philosophical conundrum around which this tale is centred. The playful regions of this disc have a solemn purpose, which effectively stifles the imaginative impulses of the reader; the reader is rarely allowed to make connections for her/himself and has no creative impact on the outcome of the story. This CD-ROM understands its narrative so clearly, is so self-reflexive, that there is little space for the inquiries of imaginative players. *Lulu's Enchanted Book* may be admired and enjoyed, but it effectively closes down the playful possibilities of narrative invention that it seems to open up.

Returning briefly to Living Books, there is one package that begins to depart from other titles in the series. *Green Eggs and Ham* (Brøderbund 1996b) begins like any other Living Book, but as soon as the words have been narrated some differences start to emerge. The written text subtly changes as the screen awaits its player, replacing several words with 'Seuss-esque' icons which invite the player to click on them, thus revealing the hidden words which are spoken aloud. As Seuss's rhymes build and expand, so the designers have found ways of incorporating them into the visual play of each screen, sometimes secreting words in scrolling boxes. Most exciting, though, is the discovery of new rhymes, revealed as hot spots are uncovered. Exploration of each illustration results not only in delightful animations, but in the presentation of numerous rhymes that adhere carefully to Seuss's own style. This linguistic play draws attention back to the original words, adding depth to the pre-text in a way other Living Books seem unable to manage. The printed version of *Green Eggs and Ham* takes the form of a traditional accumulative rhyme, building to a heady climax of rhythmic repetition and, while the electronic text is true to the comic tone of the book, the CD-ROM is able to reach beyond the accumulative rhyme, branching off into playful digressions of rhyme and animation. *Green Eggs and Ham* really does take the player beyond the original text, without repeating or reducing it, into a multilinear playground that immerses the child in the zany world of Dr Seuss.

Green Eggs and Ham is also elective to a greater extent than other Living Books, for there are three games (completely taking me by surprise) hidden beneath hot spots on different screens. 'To play, or not to play' is the option presented at these foci of interactivity (to borrow from Plowman) and entry into these digressive sections of the disk reveals a game of Pelmanism, a word game and a rhyming game, each of which is thematically and rhythmically connected to *Green Eggs and Ham*. In a similar fashion, *Winnie the Witch* (Inner Workings 1996), an inventive adaptation of the picture book by Korky Paul and Valerie Thomas, involves children in thematic colouring and spell-making games. This sort of elective detail is typical of multimedia edutainment,[3] which combines stories or games with pedagogic puzzles, so encouraging children to engage with the text on different levels. The reading of fiction requires a different cognitive process from that of solving problems, for these activities involve two different 'modes of thought', as identified by Jerome Bruner in *Actual Minds, Possible Worlds* (1986). The narrative mode (manifest in stories or drama) and the paradigmatic mode (manifest in logical arguments, descriptions or explanations) are modes of thinking that are employed in both the production and reception of stories or arguments. Of course, it is not always possible to separate these two modes as clinically as Bruner suggests, and many multimedia packages (from works of reference to electronic books) involve both ways of thinking.[4]

There are several reasons for the successful transformation of narrative in *Green Eggs and Ham*: it allows the child interactive access to both word *and* image; it moves smoothly between the different modes of storybook, playground and puzzle, encouraging cognitive dexterity; it builds on the original text through the creation of new rhymes and illustrations; and it uses the 'secret paths' of multimedia (Plowman 1996a: 46) to surprise the reader continuously as the narrative alters course at various foci of interactivity. *Green Eggs and Ham* works hard to integrate and develop its narrative with puzzles and games, a process common to many different forms of children's literature – metafictive picture books, pop-ups and adventure gamebooks all integrate their literary structures with toys or puzzles in an invitation to the interactive construction of narrative. None the less, multimedia has the ability to combine text and game in new ways. Puzzles are, of course, a very particular type of game, which are not necessarily playful; the most complex of scientific theories might be classified as puzzles. However, the type of puzzles in *Green Eggs and Ham* and many other multimedia packages, exist in a kind of limbo, moving fluidly from paradigmatic to narrative modes of thinking as children are encouraged to make meaning from a number of perspectives.

Clearly, some electronic books do allow readers a degree of playful participation in (occasionally) elective and multilinear narratives, presenting children with new ways of seeing and meeting with familiar stories. However, as long as electronic books use printed books as formative templates, narrative experience is unlikely to be radically transformed. Much more promising, then, are the multimedia packages that depart from printed books and make explicit use of the gaming principles so successful throughout the field of multimedia.

Interactive adventures

Possibly the most exciting examples of electronic fiction are those that structure their narratives around interactive adventure games, for, as I have suggested, the most engaging CD-ROMs enable elective participation through the synthesis of game and story. Although the range of adventures for younger children is still rather sparse, such titles as *Darby the Dragon* (Brøderbund 1996a) allow children to participate in challenging virtual environments (see Figure 6.2). Part of *Darby*'s success is perhaps explained by its use of an original story, so avoiding the temptation to accommodate pre-textual structure.

An animated cartoon sequence introduces Darby, which, though not interactive, is necessary for the purpose of contextualisation. Prince Darby, a young dragon living in Dragondale, finds a wand with which he inadvertently shrinks Sparkle, his older sister. The quest now set up, Darby must discover a way of returning Sparkle to her original size. At this point the player takes control of the sibling dragons and starts to explore the immediate environment of their castle. The early stages of *Darby* are relatively compulsive and, apart from the random exploration of various 'hot spots' on each screen, there is little scope for directive choice. However, an extra dimension is added to the narrative structure of the game through a selection of storybooks located in the castle library. While these books do resemble printed texts, their function is expansive, for they provide the quest, taking place in the reader/player's present, with an historical context. Each book tells a fairy-tale, involving various characters appearing in the adventure, thus allowing for a kind of intertextual recognition as readers locate them on their journey. Moreover, the compulsive structure of these tales emphasises the elective nature of the primary narrative itself. The experience of reading these books is noticeably passive, when compared to the active involvement required of the adventurer in the wider environment of Dragondale.

Figure 6.2 The signposts in this screen from *Darby the Dragon* indicate the multiplicity of directional choices open to the young reader/player. The scroll (bottom right) 'contains' objects, which have been collected by the player, to be used at various points in the adventure.

Source: Software © copyright 1996 Capitol Multimedia, Inc. All rights reserved.

On leaving the castle, the player is increasingly required to make directional choices, resulting in a narrative that refuses linearity (although each section of the game must be visited at some point if the quest is to be finished) and relies on the child's active participation; the child is gradually introduced to the game's elective potential, ensuring that the experience is not overly bewildering. Eventually, solutions must be found to problems that simultaneously entail the ability to anticipate the outcome of various narrative threads and the application of the operative principles governing such games as hide-and-seek. Response therefore involves recourse to knowledge of both narrative and gaming structure, which need to be integrated if the adventure is to be successfully completed. *Darby the Dragon* is a multimedia venture in the broadest sense, making use of cartoon sequences, songs, inter-linked stories and various 'drag and click' games which develop letter recognition, hand–eye coordination and artistic creativity. Furthermore, each of these elements is thematically linked to the central adventure, thus extending the reader's experience of narrative in numerous ways.

Although it implicates an adolescent readership, *Terry Pratchett's Discworld* (Psygnosis 1995) allows a more useful comparison to electronic books like *The Berenstain Bears* as it does have an identifiable pre-text. While the CD-ROM does not allow straightforward comparison to any of the books in Pratchett's Discworld series, principal characters and plot elements of *Guards Guards* (1989) are worked into the narrative evolution of the game. In *Discworld*, the player takes on the persona of Rincewind, Pratchett's infamous wizard and, once the introductory sequence is over, the game begins in Rincewind's room. At least, it must be assumed that this is where it begins, since the mouse becomes live at this point; otherwise there is nothing to indicate what must be done, where 'you'/Rincewind should go, or to show why 'you' should be motivated to do anything in the first place.

In *Darby the Dragon* it is clear that Sparkle must be returned to her original size, providing immediate motivation for action and conversation. *Discworld*, however, provides no initial motivation for Rincewind's movements, so the obvious reaction from the player is to explore, to feel her/his way around the environs of what turns out to be Unseen University, the home of a fraternity of wizards. To the uninitiated, the experience of *Discworld* is disconcerting, since 'you' are forced to act within the game without knowing why; as Sherry Turkle observes in *Life on the Screen* (1996), 'In video games, you soon realize that to learn to play you have to play to learn. You do not first read a rulebook, or get your terms straight' (Turkle 1996: 70). Turkle suggests that such games demand 'emergent' thinking, effectively a process of bricolage, calling upon early responses to narrative, in which the reader/player takes physical hold of story elements, but this is not to imply that such responses are simplistic.

Discworld collapses the linear and compulsive sequence of Pratchett's texts, requiring the reader/player to engage with narrative on a different level. The emergent construction of narrative involves the elective selection of objects which must be placed in a hypothetical relationship with other objects/events as problems are solved and the narrative moves forward. Of some consequence to adolescent players, this process correlates with their new-found ability to 'reason in terms of the formal or logical relationships that exist among propositions about objects' (Appleyard 1994: 97). Furthermore, the emergent demands of *Discworld*, which render Pratchett's narrative unfamiliar, confirm the adolescent's sense that familiar environments are no longer associated with unproblematic notions of comfort, stability or self-confirmation, as the adolescent landscape accommodates the wraith-like contours of hypothetical possibility. Thus, while the bewildering demands of *Discworld* may deter younger players, enthusiastic interaction will probably be elicited from adolescents, who can relate to this disorienting environment.

Discworld also draws players into an uncannily literary dimension through the use of farce, irony and pure nonsense and, due to Terry Pratchett's participation in its design, his particular brand of humour has been maintained. However, its function is a little more than scenic, for an understanding of Pratchett's 'non-sense' signals the correct approach to many of the games' conundrums. In Act II, for example, Rincewind's quest involves the search for six golden objects. Conversation with a fishmonger reveals that his belt has a gold buckle, but there is no obvious way of obtaining it. Experience of the game suggests that a wider exploration of the fishmonger's environment might help – emergent thinking is *constantly* required – and so Rincewind turns the corner. Around the corner is an empty toilet. This is where an appreciation of Pratchett's humour is beneficial, for there is no overt connection between the toilet and the fishmonger. However, recourse to *Discworld* toilet humour (of course, taken literally!) suggests that the toilet will be central to solving this problem. When I arrived at this point, I was certain that claiming the buckle would involve a farcical scene in which the fishmonger sat on the toilet and took down his trousers, thus releasing the belt-buckle. I was also sure that in order to make this happen I would have to proceed in accordance with the nonsensical dynamics of the game (and all Discworld novels): *the player* would have to do something ridiculous, in order that *the fishmonger* might do something farcical. My assumptions proved correct, confirming that an understanding of the generic construction of Pratchett's books, as comic fantasy, facilitates the solution of the game itself, but that response to this comedy is transformed from passive enjoyment to participatory re-*action*.

Integral to the structure of the *Discworld* games are numerous 'set-pieces' of animated action, which are activated when a problem is solved, or a hidden hot spot is located. These fragments of animation tend to focus on specific traits of a known character, or on the workings of a particular place; small details of the books are magnified as these cinematic sections come into play. While these scenes do alter the reader's perception of the original texts, they also allow new ways of doing or participating. The set-pieces are only motivated by an action performed by the player, perhaps as a result of a piece of cognitive (un)reasoning; thus the player seems to bring the books to life, appears to animate a fictional realm. These elements are actually preprogrammed, but adventure games determine to disguise their workings, allowing players to activate the complex surfaces of the screen. Although the verbal/pictorial landscape of *Discworld* is actually two-dimensional, the propensity for reader interactivity brings it very close to a world of three-dimensional reality. In the context of such computer games, the words of the original text are also transposed into three-dimensional space, as words become pictures and pictures become a simulation of a fantasised reality.

Although they structure themselves around the theatrical acts of a play, the *Discworld* games are more than texts *in* performance: they are texts which *allow* performance as players push back the limits of narrative experience in the act of play. It is my contention that they present the way forward for electronic fiction, enabling readers not only to see what they are reading, but also to act upon it with autonomous self-conviction. *Discworld* is by no means perfect: many of its problems are notoriously difficult to solve, it is overly reliant on lengthy dialogue and, ultimately, there is only one conclusion to its many narrative threads. However, this is the mode of electronic fiction that comes closest to breaking the boundaries of compulsive literature, while simultaneously internalising the pre-texts it challenges.

Conclusions

Discworld certainly transforms narrative in a radical manner, but it also expands and complements the experience of reading Pratchett's original books (whether this takes place prior to, or after, playing the CD-ROM). Its reinvention of Pratchett's world is likely to elicit the kind of narrative desire described by Mary Hilton:

> ... through new forms of story *and* through understanding the workings of traditional narrative desire, we get children hooked on books. Through books *and* media texts, through the new and the popular *and* the ancient and the traditional, their worlds of cultural possibility are enlarged and enriched.
>
> (Hilton 1996: 91)

Discworld invites the child to participate in a new form of story, and takes its place in a 'formative chain' of novels, graphic novels and animated films (all Discworld narratives), each of which encourages readers to move from one medium to another as the desire to extend an enjoyable narrative, to recognise it in a new configuration, is conceived. Narrative desire is thus defined as a hook, propelling child readers from one narrative form to another. Though *Green Eggs and Ham* is one of several encouraging exceptions, electronic books are less likely to stimulate the narrative desire engendered by such programs as *Discworld,* since they frequently borrow too much from original texts to tempt the reader into rereadings of their printed form.

The computer industry is responsible for the most rapidly evolving encounters between children and their texts, but of course the digital revolution does not stop at CD-ROMs. *The Jolly Post Office* (Dorling Kindersley 1997), based on the Ahlbergs' *Jolly Postman* books, is not the most inventive of 'edutaining' CD-ROMs (and is certainly less interactive than its printed counterparts), but it does connect players with the expansive realms of the Internet. Children are encouraged to design stamps and then send them to an interactive site on the Internet, where stamps can be collected and swapped with visitors from all over the world. Figuratively speaking, then, *The Jolly Post Office* acts as Alice's rabbit hole, though which children can access the wonders of the World Wide Web. Where the child's creativity is necessarily bound by the invisible design of CD-ROMs, the Internet can provide children with an unusual degree of autonomy as they create, contribute to, visit and interact with different sites. Where children's software is written, produced and disseminated by adults, the Internet offers children the opportunity to participate in on-line adventure games or conversations; to write and publish stories, magazines or cartoons; to download picture books and novels ... the list is endless ... almost.

This creative expression is not quite as boundless as it might appear – phone bills are likely to grow at the same rate as an average child; impatience is liable to build as video, sound and graphics take an eternity to download; and supervision of some sort will be required to protect children from unsuitable material. CD-ROM is currently a much more efficient and viable mode of electronic narrative – especially for children who rarely have the means to pay the bills they create – as it can hold vast amounts of digitised information and, if the promise of *Green Eggs and Ham, Discworld* or *Darby the Dragon* is any indication, will continue to provide children with exciting, challenging and alternative textual encounters.

Notes

1   Inspiration for my title must be attributed to Jill Thomas, an MA student at Roehampton Institute London, who runs a CD-ROM business called The Mouse House.
2   The texts I have in mind here are: *Breaktime* (Chambers; 1978); *Midnight Blue* (Fisk; 1990); *The Stinky Cheeseman and Other Fairly Stupid Tales* (Scieszka and Smith; 1993); and *The Jolly Pocket Postman* (Allan and Janet Ahlberg; 1995).
3   'Edutainment' is a term used by the computer industry to describe children's software which is both educational and entertaining. Matthew Richards, editor of *PC Guide*, states that Brøderbund coined 'edutainment' to describe their innovative software package, *Where in the World is Carmen Sandiego?* (Richards 1998: 30), which teaches geography through a narrative framework.
4   My discussion of Bruner's modes of thought in relation to multimedia has previously been published by Ashgate Publishing Ltd. (Sainsbury 1998: 147–8).

References

Multimedia texts

Brøderbund (1995) *The Berenstain Bears Get in a Fight*, Novato, CA: Random House/Brøderbund.
——(1996a) *Darby the Dragon*, Hartlepool: Random House/Brøderbund.
——(1996b) *Green Eggs and Ham*, Hartlepool: Random House/Brøderbund.
Dorling Kindersley (1997) *The Jolly Post Office*, London: Dorling Kindersley Multimedia.
Europress (1995) *Treasure Island*, Macclesfield, Europress Software.
Inner Workings Ltd (1996) *Winnie the Witch*, Oxford: Oxford CD-ROM.
Mindscape (1996) *The Adventures of Peter Rabbit & Benjamin Bunny*, Macclesfield: Europress Software.
Organa (1997) *Lulu's Enchanted Book*, Hove: Wayland Multimedia (first published in 1995).
Psygnosis Ltd (1995) *Terry Pratchett's Discworld*, Liverpool: Sony Psygnosis.

Other texts

Applebee, A. (1978) *The Child's Concept of Story*, Chicago: Chicago University Press.

Appleyard, J.A. (1994) *Becoming A Reader*, Cambridge: Cambridge University Press (first published in 1991).

Bruner, J. (1986) *Actual Minds, Possible Worlds*, Cambridge, MA: Harvard University Press.

Graham, J. (1994) 'Trouble for Arthur's Teacher? A Closer Look at Reading CD ROMs', *The English & Media Magazine* 31 (Autumn): 15–17.

Hilton, M. (ed.) (1996) *Potent Fictions*, London: Routledge.

Iser, W. (1974) *The Implied Reader*, Baltimore: Johns Hopkins University Press.

Naughtie, J. (1998) 'Teenage Passions', *Daily Telegraph*, 18 July 1998: A1.

Plowman, L. (1996a) 'Narrative, Interactivity and the Secret World of Multimedia', *English and Media Magazine* 35 (Autumn): 44–8.

——(1996b) 'Narrative, Linearity and Interactivity: Making Sense of Interactive Multimedia', *British Journal of Educational Technology* 27(2): 92–105.

Richards, M. (1995) 'Class Action', *CD-ROM Today* 20 (December).

——(1998) 'Back to School', *PC Guide* 4(6) (September): 30–4.

Sainsbury, L. (1998) 'Information Playgrounds: Children's Reference & Multimedia', in Hancock, S. (ed), *A Guide to Children's Reference Books and Multimedia Material*, Aldershot: Ashgate.

Stannard, R. (1996) 'Texts, Language, Literacy & Digital Technologies', *English & Media Magazine* 34 (Summer): 11–13.

Turkle, S. (1996) *Life On The Screen*, London: Weidenfeld & Nicolson.

Vygotsky, L.S. (1978) *Mind in Society: The Development of Higher Psychological Processes*, Cambridge, MA/London: Harvard University Press.

Chapter 7

Girls' playground language and lore

What sort of texts are these?

Elizabeth Grugeon

At first glance, playgrounds seem rather unruly and formless: children seem to be constantly on the move, the noise level is daunting and seemingly impenetrable. Closer observation reveals recognisable patterns of behaviour; closer listening reveals texts that accompany unexpectedly complex play routines.

My first encounter with these texts was inspired by the publication of the Opies' *Children's Games in Street and Playground* in 1969. The 11-year-olds in my class compiled a dictionary of the games that they played – on the playground, but also in large groups in the streets of 1960s Lambeth. The games they mentioned often required as many as twelve to fifteen players and seem to have involved quite violent and provocative behaviour; games such as Knock Down Ginger, British Bulldog and Stuck in the Mud. All the games they described can be found in the Opie collection (1969) and all of them are still being played on the playgrounds that I have since visited in the 1980s and 1990s.

There was one, however, that I could not find and it was the only game that had a substantial text – a skipping rhyme, with the refrain

> Up and down, up and down
> All the way to London town.
> Swish, swosh, swish, swosh,
> All the way to Charing Cross.
> Legs swing, legs swing,
> All the way to Camberwell Green.

The school was in Camberwell and the girls had adapted the rhyme to make it their own. I have recently found a version (Opie 1997: 228) with the line 'All the way to Berlin'. It seems to have been widespread and has been played since the 1920s.

In the late 1970s I recorded more complex texts that accompanied singing and clapping games. The publication of *The Singing Game* (Opie and Opie 1985) encouraged me to observe and record a rich oral culture on a local playground. It seems as traditional as the culture itself to assume that children's oral culture is dying out – the influence of television, parental fears for children's safety and computer games are currently given as reasons for this assumption. However, as before, the culture thrives. In the 1980s and 1990s, playgrounds continue to provide a rich source of evidence of children's informal language development in a dynamic oral culture.

The texts of the playground are various and slippery: they do not exist, they are not in print or, if they are, the printing has been mediated by people who have not been involved in the production of these texts. They belong only to the moment of their performance, they are unstable texts varying from day to day. To a certain extent, they defy explanation: Why are they there? Who are they for? Where have they come from? They are a bit like mushrooms or dandelions springing up unexpectedly, blown on the wind. The texts I want to discuss are even more extraordinary – they belong only to girls and largely to girls under the age of 11 or 12.

The rules of the games

In the summer of 1997 I recorded the traditional games that were being played on two local school playgrounds during the fifteen-minute mid-morning break; groups of girls could be observed playing over twenty different games. All these games involved complex texts, which often accompanied highly structured clapping, skipping or dancing routines. Observing and recording them, I was forced to ask what kind of texts these are and why they are being played. Isolating only three or four examples, it is possible to ask many questions about their origins, transmission and endurance. Attempts to classify these often complex texts seem to require an approach which draws on such disciplines as folklore, sociology, psychology, linguistics, anthropology and musicology. Attempts to explain them might also involve looking at issues of gender, subversion and elements of carnival.

The texts I shall explore and discuss in this chapter are unique and paradoxical – they belong to children exclusively. The children who use them are entirely familiar with them, yet they have never seen them written down – nor can they, since they are liable to stay the same and yet be changed every time they occur. They are essentially existential and ephemeral and yet have a historical permanence and identity. Folklorists and other interested adults may capture them in writing, but their attempts to transcribe such idiosyncratic and dynamic texts can only provide a one-dimensional account of events that depend on music, action and ritualistic routines. For the children who play with them, they are texts for performance yet have no audience. They are oral texts and yet they depend on movement, dance and physical contact of all kinds. They are owned exclusively by children and, in this case, by girls alone. They are spontaneous and unscheduled – events that fill in the increasingly few moments in the school day when children are temporarily freed from adult domination. On the school playground children have a certain amount of autonomy, of freedom and choice. In those very short spaces of time, sometimes as short as fifteen minutes, they may interact without adult intervention, make their own rules and behave with less inhibition. It can be seen as a time of festival or carnival, and is a brief period in which children participate in:

> cultural events with their own traditions, rule systems, sanctions, forms of periodicity and endurance, and spatial boundaries ... the school playground festival is one of the few places where a distant and non-intrusive supervision is possible, so that children's political rights can be guaranteed consistent with an adult concern with their safety. The school playground still provides the one assured festival in the lives of children.
>
> (Sutton-Smith 1990: 5–6)

In these moments then, it is perhaps surprising how many constraints and rules of a complex and predetermined nature the children inflict upon themselves. The self-regulation demanded by these 'unofficial' games, as the Opies call them (1969), provide well-defined and acceptable constraints. This framing and rule-making has long been evident and has been documented by folklorists and ethno-anthropologists (Opie 1985; Sluckin 1981; Sutton-Smith 1990). The textual nature of singing games, however, has received less attention; nevertheless, the games are particularly interesting because of their multifaceted nature. Knowing how to categorise and classify them is a problem for anyone attempting to go beyond the simple observation and recording of these events – how to describe their significance, indeed their existence. Susan Stewart's definition of children's games and folklore as a particular genre, as texts or speech events that operate as social events in a universe of discourse, provides a starting point (Stewart 1979). She enables us to see the texts of these games as having a constitutive function in a continuous process of making meaning. Play and metaphor can be seen as shaping activities which are capable of producing texts which stand in a paradoxical relation to common-sense texts and become a means of criticism and innovation. When the girls on the playground signal the start of a game they are 'exchanging one set of interpretive procedures for another' and recognising 'communication as communication, and behaviour as signification' (Stewart 1978: 30). The games as texts have their own grammar; the counting-out rhymes that precede almost any kind of game on the playground constitute an elaborate procedure which sets up and maintains the boundaries of the game that is to follow; the preparatory rhymes shift the players away from the discourse of everyday life and towards the discourse of the game: 'the text of the counting out rhyme is aligned according to the text of the game. The grammar of the verses is not the grammar of everyday talk that preceded them but the grammar of the game that follows' (Stewart 1978: 92). So when girls suddenly sit down in a circle, their feet touching, and lean forward to intone:

Ip dip sky blue
Who's it
Not you
Not because you're dirty
Not because you're clean
My mum says you're the fairy queen
So out you must go.

(Grugeon field notes 1995)

they are starting a process of shifting from the domain of the everyday world to another domain of reality. The counting-out rhyme becomes a form of meta-communication that signals the crossing of a ludic boundary (Sutton-Smith 1971).

Identifying a text: 'St Mary Anne'

I want to start by looking at the text of a game that has been very popular on local playgrounds since 1994. First, there is the problem of isolating a text, since it will exist simultaneously in a number of different forms. In response to the publication of Iona Opie's *People on the Playground* (1993), I asked student teachers I was working with to spend one morning playtime on local playgrounds and to record examples of games, jokes or stories in the time available: 'A remarkable number of games can be fitted into the fifteen minutes of playtime if they are minor transient games ... The children play these games rapidly, one after another, instant decisions being instantly translated into action' (Opie 1993: 4).

Students found that this was the case and returned with an impressive amount of evidence of a wide range of activities. This text, 'Marium' or 'St Mary Anne', was one of many that they had recorded. Two groups of students on different playgrounds had come upon versions of what was evidently the same game being played on the same day. Other versions of this were to come to light later.

One group observed a large number of girls playing a very coordinated clapping and singing game:

Group of approx 10 children form a large circle. When song begins first child claps the hand of the girl on her left, who in turn passes on the clap to the next in the circle and so on. The object of the game is that whoever makes contact (slaps the hand) of the person of the left after the final chant of the song (i.e. 123 – 3 is the number on which to try to slap the next person) is deemed as out. The chant continues until there is one winner.

(Student field notes 1994)

The student who transcribed the chant that accompanied the game was concerned that she had not transcribed it accurately:

> I asked the children what the words of the song meant or if they could spell them for me. None of the children knew either meaning or spelling but agreed that it sounded like that. They were unsure of the actual words involved:
>
> Marium marium marium
> sartorily macaroo macaroo
> Liar liar beep beep beep.

(Student field notes 1994)

On a nearby playground, a similar game was recorded:

> Most clapping games were done in pairs. This particular one was done in a group. Person who begins uses right hand to clap hand of person on the left. Continues around the circle. When singing the last line the person who will end on 'trois' withdraws her hand. If she doesn't she is out:
>
> St Maria, St Maria, St Maria,
> St Gloria, Gloria, Gloria,
> Send a letter,
> Beep, beep, beep
> Un deux trois.

(Student field notes 1994)

Three years later, on the same playground, this was still a very popular game, and another version was recorded:

> Saint Mary Ann, Mary Ann, Mary Ann
> Saint Gloria, Gloria, Gloria
> Laya, laya pee pee pee
> Laya laya pee pee pee
> Un deux trois.

(Student field notes 1997)

Another variation was recorded by a 10-year-old girl at the beginning of the summer term in 1997, in a collection of clapping rhymes that she and her friends had learnt from a new girl, who had recently arrived from South Africa. Jessica described this as a 'circle clapping game that sometimes loads of children play'. Like the texts above, it has a nonsense chant of four lines and a similar rhythmic refrain:

Derra derra ring ting ting
Derra derra ring ting ting
One two three.

(Jessica Smith audiotape transcript 1997)

It is evident that transcribing nonsense texts of this kind can only provide an approximate representation of the words that were being used. However, once a text has been identified it in this way, it can often be related to others. A musicologist at the University of Sydney recognised the version of 'St Marium' above as a game that she had recorded on a Sydney primary-school playground called 'Sar Macka Dora'. One of her versions seems very close to the versions recorded in the United Kingdom:

Son macaron
Son ferio, ferio, ferio
Leya, leya, tap tap tap
Leya, leya, tap tap tap
One two three.

(Marsh 1998)

She had collected thirty-five performances of this game on a single playground and wrote to me:

> this is different from the other games [that she had collected] largely because of the nonsense element of the text. The stable and defining element of this game is the movement formula. The text is highly variable but the movement elements and associated rhythmic features of music and text are what allow you to identify it. It is not possible to isolate text from performance.

(Marsh 1998)

She also provided another version collected in the United States:

I'm on my way to Tayo
On my way to
Tella tella ree see see
tella tella ree see
Un day twa.

(Harwood 1992)

I have chosen these examples to illustrate some of the difficulties involved in pinning down any definitive text and describe the mysterious universality of such texts. It would seem that the combination of meaningful and nonsensical verbal patterns with elaborate and highly patterned musical and movement routines in this game is typical of the games played by girls from the age of 5 to 12 all over the world.

The informal acquisition of linguistic competence

The Opies account for the tunes that accompany playground games as often no more than 'a kind of heightened speech ... they must be regarded as the wild flowers of music rather than its cultivated species, for children can preserve the tunes no more accurately than they can the words' (Opie 1985: vi). However, ethnomusicologist Hazel Hall considers playground rhymes and chants to be profoundly musical:

> The value of folklore in the creative development of children can be seen as young people explore through sound and movement the fundamental areas of music, language, poetry, dance and drama. In doing this, children are developing skills and knowledge in important areas of sensory communication: verbal, aural, visual, kinaesthetic and tactile ways of thinking and knowing.
>
> (Hall 1993: 262)

As they play, children are intoning texts at varying levels between speech and song: 'The way this music is intoned, the number of children participating, the accompanying text and the nature of the related activities are all integral to the performance' (Hall 1993: 257).

Looking at playground texts, she argues that they help children to explore the basic elements of language, music, poetry, drama and dance, and contribute to the way they are able to explore and experiment with different forms of intonation, patterns of rhythm 'in hand clapping rhymes the poetic and rhythmic match is perfect ... rhymes tend to be scanned in iambic feet, allowing the performers time to co-ordinate the hand clapping on the first stressed beat' (Hall 1993: 259). She illustrates the way the rhymes and games allow children to use tonal repetition and clusters, melodic motifs, rhyme, rhetorical devices and parody:

> The most common rhetorical devices in children's folklore are repetition of sounds (assonance, alliteration, onomatopoeia and rhyming), repetition of words, phrases, lines and verses, and concatenations; extra words, phrases, lists or whole rhymes may be appended to an existing rhyme like links in a chain.
>
> (Hall 1993: 29)

All these are commonly found in rhymes that require a physical challenge, skipping, counting out and hand clapping; all these features are elements of the phonological awareness that is seen to be a crucial requirement for success in learning to read.

A recent paper by John Widdowson offers an explanation for the continued existence of games like 'Marium', suggesting that childlore has an important role in the development of language and literacy in the primary-school years. He is concerned that ignorance of 'whatever goes on in the playground and/or in peer group interaction outside school hours' means that:

> for the most part teachers fail to capitalise on the wealth of material infor-
> mally learned by children within the traditional culture of the playground
> … at the end of playtime or lunch break this material is, as it were, left
> behind on the playground, and rarely crosses the threshold of the school
> building – a threshold which truly separates the informal and the formal
> worlds.
>
> (Widdowson 1998: 4–5)

He stresses that the linguistic competence and performance children have already acquired before they enter school have been 'imparted largely through an extensive range of traditional verbal interchanges between adults and children, often in a playful mode enjoyed by both' (1998: 6). This playful exchange of traditional language continues on the playground but becomes essentially a 'close knit and secretive' (1998: 8) exchange between peers, an experience 'shared and participated in by a group of children with diverse backgrounds and experiences of traditional forms'. The examples of games discussed here are just such texts; they give us a glimpse of the continuing process of informal language learning that takes place as children play together and participate in the traditional culture of the playground. Widdowson shows how young children's evident spontaneous delight in playing with rhyme, rhythm, metrical patterning and musical tunes contributes to their informal acquisition of syntax, semantics, figures of speech, rhetoric and the symbolic use of language (Widdowson 1998).

Girls reclaiming the playground?

The next text is not a singing game but, like 'St Mary Anne', involves a large group of players and was being played alongside it on the same playgrounds in 1997. It is interesting for a different reason: it may tell us something about how the players see themselves.

On a number of different playgrounds I had visited in the 1990s, Red Rover – a rather rough and boisterous game, classified as an 'Exerting game' (Opie and Opie 1969: 239) – was a favourite. In the summer of 1997, a game that was evidently as popular and seemed rather similar was called 'We are the Cow Girls'. This game was played most widely, enthusiastically and noisily. Examples could be seen on three different playgrounds from Year 2 to Year 4 during the same playtime. It has much in common with Red Rover: arms are linked to turn two opposing lines of players into a formidable barrage. It is aggressive but controlled; ritualistic high kicks are aimed but not delivered; it has elements of the chorus line. As it was being played on this occasion, it appeared to be a show of female solidarity and defiance, with the girls loudly proclaiming their presence. There were a number of versions taking place. In one, an advancing line of girls chanted:

> We are the tiger cubs
> Ready to fight you.
> (The opposing line retorted,)
> We are the Indians
> Coming to get you.
> (A girl from one side would then be nominated,)
> We want Sonia
> Ready to fight them.

This would be followed by a tug of war with the successful line, amidst great jubilation, gaining an extra person. And resumption of the game:

> We are the cowgirls
> Ready to fight them.
> Come and get it
> We want Esther …

Far from being marginalised on the periphery of the playground, in this game and others like it the girls assumed centre stage. Boys attempting to join in were ignored. On a video recording, boys resort to running the gauntlet between the advancing and retreating lines.

Another text takes me on to consider the gender issues that emerge as soon as we start looking at games played exclusively by girls. Since my first encounter with my daughter's repertoire at the age of 5, I have argued that these games can be construed as acts of defiance. Her repertoire included such rude clapping rhymes as 'My Friend Billy had a Ten Foot Willy' and 'My Boyfriend Gave me an Apple'. As I have noted elsewhere:

> These games can be seen as discursive practices through which children can become powerful. Rhymes can provide ammunition for resistance to the relations of power in the playground and are the means by which they [girls] may seize power in the discourse … Taboo rhymes are not childish acts of rebellion but tools of resistance and criticism in making boys, teacher, the school, the adult world, the powerless objects of their discourse.
>
> (Grugeon 1988: 167)

It was perhaps no coincidence, in the aftermath of the Spice Girls phenomenon, that one of the popular refrains on the playground was:

Girls go to Mars
to get more stars,
Boys go to Jupiter
to get more stupider.
Itsy bitsy lollipop
Itsy bitsy boo.

(Grugeon field notes 1997)

which is an adaptation of an earlier version using the words: 'Boys go to college/To get more knowledge/Girls go to Jupiter' ...

In the dynamic world of folklore, both the context and content of texts are always shifting. On the playground this is always the case; keeping up with change is a challenge. In the first months of 1998, a new phenomenon, the Teletubbies, arrived on two local playgrounds and it seems that they were to be found all over the country in a number of different versions. The following were being sung to the tune of 'Nick-Nack, Paddy-Whack':

I love you
You love me
Together we'll kill Dipsy
With a dagger through his heart
And a bullet through his head,
Sorry Laa-Laa, Dipsy's dead.

(Sung by 8-year-old)

Or, alternatively:

I hate Po,
Po hates me,
Tinky Winky killed Dipsy
With a kick up the bum
And a bullet through his head,
Sorry Laa-Laa, Dipsy's dead.

(Sung by two 11-year-old girls)

These examples are a reminder that the media, popular culture and current events very quickly become absorbed by children and reproduced in their play. There were many 'funeral' games following the death of Princess Diana in August 1997. A version of the *Neighbours* theme song, 'Neighbours, pick your nose and taste the flavours', very quickly appeared on playgrounds in the 1980s, and in the 1990s children were playing 'National Lottery' within weeks of its inauguration.

Powerful influences?

In the summer of 1997 another media event had invaded the playground – The Spice Girls, with their 'really, really want' mantra and their provocative dance routines, were alarming teachers and delighting children. On one playground the Spice Girls were banned. At a neighbouring school, the head thought the Spice Girls 'rather sweet'; the girls (6- and 7-year-olds) had asked for a 'Spice Girl corner' in their playground. In this school, the range of games the girls were playing seemed to reflect the exuberance and self-confidence expressed by the Spice Girls.

Observing these girls for only fifteen minutes, it was possible to chart the way they shifted from one kind of play to another; from dancing games parodying media events to traditional clapping and singing games. They spontaneously regrouped and moved from games in circles facing each other, intent on complex clapping routines, into a performance mode where they faced some imaginary audience engrossed by equally complex Spice Girls-type routines and then, as suddenly, switched back to a more traditional game. The two modes seemed quite interchangeable and evidently provided similar satisfaction and required as much energy. It was noticeable that the complex rules governed all these games and were closely adhered to.

There were many other examples of games that seemed to reflect the strong influence of the energy and bravado exhibited and promoted by the Spice Girls. There was evidence of a particular confidence and exuberance in the way the girls were playing, which could be a response to the role models offered by pop groups like the Spice Girls. The following text shares many of these features; the girls who played this game felt that it was definitely taboo as far as adults were concerned. It was accompanied by rather gross and comical mime as they acted out the text, and is a good example of one of the many rhymes, many with long ancestry, that allow girls to 'make fun of the still unknown and rather frightening state of adulthood' (Opie 1997: 210).

> We are the teenage girls
> We wear our hair in curls
> We wear our dungarees
> Down to our sexy knees
> I met a boy last night
> He gave me 50p
> To go behind a bush
> And have it off with me
> My mother was surprised
> To see my belly rise
> But daddy jumped for joy
> It was a baby boy
> My mother done the splits
> And had fifty fits.

What sort of text is this? Where has it come from?

As Iona Opie suggests, these mocking rhymes often have a long ancestry and this one certainly has an ancestry, if not a very long one. There is a version of 'We are the Teenage Girls' in *The Singing Game* that can be traced back to the 1970s:

> We are the Barbie girls
> We wear our hair in curls
> We wear our dungarees
> To hide our dirty knees
> We wear our father's shirt
> We wear our brother's tie
> And when we want a guy
> We simply wink the eye.

(Opie and Opie 1985: 478)

This rather innocent version is obviously a transatlantic import and was recorded in Glasgow in 1975, later appearing on a record of singing games in 1983. In 1985, the Opies relegated it to the end of their collection, in a section headed 'Twelve Less Popular Clapping Songs'. Perhaps they underestimated its potential, since it has survived into the 1990s in a more subversive version – which may reflect the more explicit knowledge that young children have access to, and the ambivalence of, the messages about their own sexuality that they are receiving from their culture.

The 9- and 10-year-old girls who were singing this version seemed confident and assertive:

LIZ GRUGEON How do you know these games??
CHILD 1 Oh we've been doing them since we …
CHILD 2 We made them up at school …
CHILDREN We made them up … we've been doing them …
CHILD 1 We've been making them up since we've been in the Four Plus Unit
CHILD 3 Ah we just made them up …
CHILD 1 Yeah.
CHILD 3 That rude one, um, I got it off my sister, though – told everyone else
     …
CHILD 4 I got it from my friend Jade
CHILD 2 and we put it all together
CHILD 1 we never tell the teachers
CHILD 4 we never do

Watching their play, it was interesting to speculate how much the 'girl power' of the 1990s is influencing their playground behaviour. Twelve years ago, when I first started to consider the reason for the continued existence and significance of these singing games for prepubescent girls, I argued that the texts of these games could be interpreted as subversive and resistant: songs that relished willies being shortened, balls becoming entangled in barbed wire, for instance, seemed to be making a statement from the young girl players' perspective. It could also be argued that many of the texts of singing games seem to predict a future of marriage, domesticity and childrearing and provide what James has called 'a cultural framing for gender during … childhood', which gives girls 'an opportunity to experiment with many different stereotypes of femaleness' (James 1993: 194). However, 'We are the Teenage Girls' seems far removed from the discourse of romantic love, and many of the singing games include painful episodes: 'boyfriends' are thrown downstairs, blown up and humiliated in a number of ways, and girls and women are active agents in this process. Despite the defiant tone and content of many of the songs they sang, however, the girls I recorded in the 1980s had seemed to be marginalised on the edges of the playground by boys who were monopolising centre stage, playing chasing games and football. This pattern seems to be changing.

What do they really, really want?

In the 1990s girls seem to occupy more playground space. The general postfeminist confidence which has invaded even the primary-school curriculum seems to have led to an awareness of equal opportunities and gender equality and has given rise to an explicit political correctness in texts and behaviour. Added to this, the media impact of groups like the Spice Girls seems more pronounced. On 6 April 1998, feminist critic Elaine Showalter was being interviewed on BBC Radio 4's *Start the Week* about her new book on 'heroines'. She described how she felt that she was writing this in response to women's desire for an 'epic' quality in their lives; women who exemplified this 'epic' quality would include the Spice Girls and Princess Diana; women who are 'larger than life' and whose epic lives are very largely a creation of the media. In these examples of girls' play, I want to suggest that there is evidence of young girls wanting to share in the possibility of a more 'epic' life and that the media continue to provide empowering role models for girls' playful exploration of the larger lives they may aspire to. It also allows an exploration of the darker and more fearful aspects of the world in which they are growing up. A version of the 'Teenage Girls' song, recorded in a secondary school and sung by teenage girls, deals quite explicitly with the taboo issue of incest and child abuse. However, at the age of 9, the girls themselves remind us where they see themselves. They ended their interview about the 'We are the Teenage Girls' song with a telling comment:

CHILD I Sometimes we dance around because we like singing the Spice Girl songs …
CHILDREN Yeah.
CHILD I and we like Tig and Stuck in the Mud.

For these 8- and 9-year-olds, the traditional texts of playground folklore are both empowering and reassuring; the culture of childhood allows them to explore dangerous adult themes while remaining children. In those carnivalesque moments at breaktime, largely out of earshot, young people have a unique opportunity to explore the boundaries of their experience within a safe and conservative environment. Riddles, puns, jokes and the nonsense rhymes that we have seen here challenge common-sense classification suggest that things are not always what they seem. Nonsense appropriates the forms and institutions of everyday life and rearranges them; play with taboo topics becomes possible precisely because nonsense introduces a state of anomaly and ambivalence. The girls create a context that can never be contextualised and never takes place in the real world. Thus the events that take place in the 'Cowgirls' game and the crude dramatisation of the 'Teenage Girls' song take their place alongside 'whopper-telling stories' and the use of extravaganza in speech and literature; the Rabelaisian humour to which Bakhtin refers (1976). Playground texts can be seen as part of an ongoing process of interpretation of different domains of discourse that have constantly shifting boundaries. On the playground these traditional games create a particular and unique context in which the 'metaphorical behaviour of nonsense, play and paradox is removed from everyday life, cut off from its reality-generating conversations and contexts, and limited to the "never-never land" context of playground, ritual and fiction' (Stewart 1979: 61).

Conclusion

In the first term at school, a young girl will learn, along with her peers and older girls, a number of playground texts that accompany complicated clapping, chanting or dancing routines (Grugeon 1993). The texts and routines will become more diverse and complex over the next few years. Some of the words will be traditional, passed down over many years and playgrounds; others will be instant borrowings or references from current media interests. The chants vary in different locations, but are held together by consistent rhythm and movement. Most participants acquire a considerable skill in coordinating words, intonation and movement.

The playground becomes a primary site for the informal acquisition of language skills, but also far more than that. It is the location for the ownership and creation of a young girl's culture, using a specific genre that is repeated, changed and recreated across the world. The texts emerge as part of a distinctive lore and language that is usually unnoticed by the adult world: mysterious, unwritten, unstable and ephemeral, merging words with movement (clap, skip, dance) and music in a rule-based carnival, celebrating nonsense and fun, often ribald, testing the boundaries of present and future roles and relationships. This chapter has considered a small fraction of playground lore, mostly gathered during one playtime. It suggests that the diversity and vitality of this culture and these texts are remarkable aspects of young girls' experience in their early school years.

Acknowledgements

I should like to acknowledge the work of many BEd students at De Montfort University who have contributed recordings and field notes to my studies.

References

Bakhtin, M.M. (1976) 'The Art of the Word and the Culture of Folk Humor', in Baran, H. (ed.), *Semiotics and Structuralism*, New York: International Arts and Sciences Press.

Grugeon, E. (1988) 'Children's Oral Culture: A Transitional Experience', in Maclure, M., Phillips, T. and Wilkinson, A. (eds), *Oracy Matters*, Milton Keynes: Open University Press.

——(1993) 'Gender Implications of Children's Playground Culture', in Woods, P. and Hammersley, M. (eds) *Gender and Ethnicity in Schools*, Milton Keynes: Open University Press.

Hall, H.S. (1993) 'Musical and Poetic Characteristics of Children's Folklore,' in Davey, G.B. and Seal, G. (eds) *The Oxford Companion to Australian Folklore*, Melbourne: Oxford University Press.

Harwood, Eve (1990) 'Girls' Hand Clapping Games: A Study in Oral Transmission', *Bulletin of the International Kodaly Society* 17(1): 19–25.

James, A. (1993) *Childhood Identities: Self and Social Relationships in the Experience of the Child*, Edinburgh: Edinburgh University Press.

Marsh, Kathryn (1998) The Influence of the Media, the Classroom and Immigrant Groups on Contemporary Children's Playground Singing Games in Australia. Unpublished paper at The State of Play Conference, University of Sheffield, 14–18 April 1998.

Opie, I. (1993) *People on the Playground* Oxford: Oxford University Press.

Opie, I. and Opie, P. (1969) *Children's Games in Street and Playground*, Oxford: Oxford University Press.

——(1985) *The Singing Game*, Oxford: Oxford University Press.

——(1997) *Children's Games with Things*, Oxford: Oxford University Press.

Sluckin, A. (1981) *Growing Up in the Playground: The Social Development of Children*, London: Routledge & Kegan Paul.

Stewart, S. (1979) *Nonsense: Aspects of Intertextuality in Folklore and Literature*, Baltimore: Johns Hopkins University Press.

Sutton-Smith, Brian (1990) 'School Playground as Festival', *Children's Environments Quarterly* 7(2): 3–7.

Sutton-Smith B. and Herron, R.E. (eds) (1971) *Child's Play*, Chichester: John Wiley & Sons.

Widdowson, John (1998) Childlore: Gateway to Language Skills. Unpublished paper at The State of Play conference, University of Sheffield, 14–18 April 1998.

Then it began to rain.
Rivers began to rise,
slowly at first and then faster.
Soon they became torrents:
they broke their banks;
they drowned the fields;
they poured into the towns;
nothing could stop them.

The Ark began to float;
it was carried away by the flood.
At first it was very rough,
then very calm.
Even the mountain tops had vanished
beneath the waves.
Only the Ark remained.

Plate 1 'Then it began to rain', from Antonia Barber (1997) *Noah and the Ark*, ill. Ian Beck, London: Transworld. Illustrations copyright © Ian Beck 1997. Text copyright © Antonia Barber 1997. All rights reserved.

And to this day,
when storm clouds fill the sky
and the rain seems unending,
the rainbow comes,
sudden and magical,
and makes the dark world
new again.

Then Noah thanked God
for keeping them all safe from the flood;
and God thanked Noah
for looking after the animals.
'It was a pleasure,' said Noah politely,
'but please don't do it again...
the flood, I mean.'

'Never again!' said God
and his moving finger passed across the heavens,
leaving behind a bright rainbow
to sign his promise.

Plate 2 'Then Noah thanked God', from Antonia Barber (1997) *Noah and the Ark*, ill. Ian Beck, London: Transworld. Illustrations copyright © Ian Beck 1997. Text copyright © Antonia Barber 1997. All rights reserved.

Plate 3 'Noah built the ark', from Heinz Janisch (1997) *Noah's Ark*, ill. Lisbeth
Zwerger, trans. Rosemary Lanning, Switzerland: North South Books. © 1997
Michael Neugebauer Verlag, Verlagsgruppe Nord-Süd Verlag AG, Switzerland.

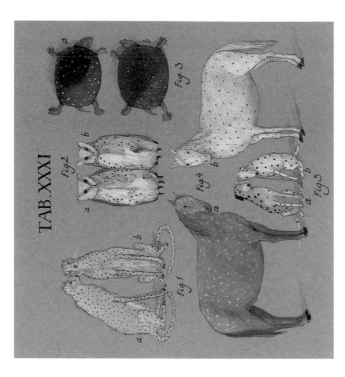

First they called the animals to the ark: two of each species that lived on earth, one male and one female of each kind. For God wished every species to live again after the flood.

Plate 4 'Two of each species', from Heinz Janisch (1997) *Noah's Ark*, ill. Lisbeth Zwerger, trans. Rosemary Lanning, Switzerland: North South Books. © 1997 Michael Neugebauer Verlag, Verlagsgruppe Nord-Süd Verlag AG, Switzerland.

Plate 5 'The animals streamed out', from Heinz Janisch (1997) *Noah's Ark*, ill. Lisbeth Zwerger, trans. Rosemary Lanning, Switzerland: North South Books. © 1997 Michael Neugebauer Verlag, Verlagsgruppe Nord-Süd Verlag AG, Switzerland.

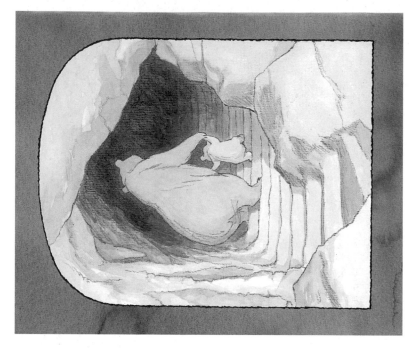

Plate 7 'Out into the darkness?', from Martin Waddell (1988)

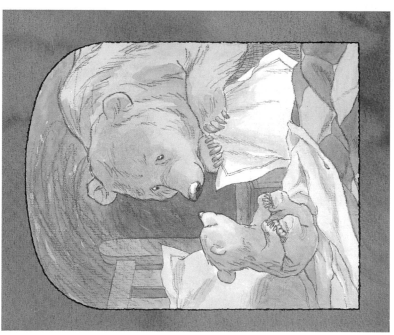

Plate 6 'I'm scared', from Martin Waddell (1988) *Can't You Sleep, Little Bear?*, ill. Barbara Firth, London: Walker Books.

Plate 8 'The bright yellow moon, and all the twinkly stars', from Martin Waddell (1988) *Can't You Sleep, Little Bear?*, ill. Barbara Firth, London: Walker Books.

Plate 9 'My babies are very good drivers', from Martin Waddell (1992) *Rosie's Babies*, ill. Penny Dale, London: Walker Books.

Chapter 8

Drama, literacies and difference

Helen Nicholson

Drama, as a particular mode of artistic representation, uses different forms of literacy to tell stories and communicate ideas. In the English curriculum, attention has been drawn to verbal qualities of drama, to the ways in which it encourages skills in speaking and listening, and the textual study of dramatic literature. However, as a cultural practice, drama includes more than verbal literacy; drama makes meanings through the languages of movement, visual images, sound and music as well as through the spoken word. Indeed, as a dynamic medium of social communication, drama is constantly changing, and the various ways in which experiences are presented and represented as dramatic texts reflect the complexity of the art form.

In contemporary theatre and dramatic practices, while the literary playscript has maintained an established place, drama that is created around visual images, sound and movement has become increasingly visible. The work of physical theatre companies, black and Asian practitioners and multimedia performance artists has led to debates about the representation of gender and ethnicity, for example, and to a renewed interest in how the body is portrayed and read. Supported by postmodern theories of representation and identity, in which it is acknowledged that selfhood is consciously constructed and interpretations of the body are culturally produced, artists and performers have reframed dramatic imagery, narrative and design. With a renewed interest in how the interplay between sound, word, movement and image creates dramatic meanings, contemporary dramatists have experimented with the juxtaposition of different artistic forms, and have made explicit references to the intertextuality of drama.[1]

Within this creative and intellectual climate, the idea that each drama is a cultural and social text has become widely accepted in educational discourse. The consequences of this shift in thinking is leading to a more inclusive model of drama education, where attention is paid to the various ways in which the dramatic form itself is interpreted, as well as the process of exploration of content or theme. In this context, a wide variety of dramatic styles are included in the curriculum, with attention drawn to the ways in which the content of the drama, the ideas expressed in it, are inseparable from the values associated with different dramatic practices and forms.

What is particularly interesting about the practice of drama, including the performance of more conventionally written playscripts, is that participants operate simultaneously on a number of levels – ideas, thoughts, feelings and values are created and represented in physical, verbal, aural, kinaesthetic and visual texts at one and the same time. Daphne Payne gives a description of the multiple texts that constitute drama practice:

> Drama is not speech, but action. It is a mode of expression which utilises a whole range of communication skills – words, certainly… but also facial expression, body language, mime, movement, dance – all those channels of communication of which the human body is capable in order to convey meaning.
>
> (Payne 1998)

How these different 'languages' of drama are combined, how the different textual elements interact, and how the semiotics of time, space, movement and gesture are created and read, is dependent on the particular ways in which ideas are symbolised and constructed, and the particular use made of dramatic genre, style and form. Drama draws on a complex web of different sign-systems which involve a range of physical senses; as practitioners young learners are invited to explore not only how drama is read, but how it is seen and heard.

In this chapter I shall argue that drama, as an intertextual art form, enables children to explore the multiple texts and textures implicit in a range of dramatic forms. I shall explore how learners might use and develop their abilities as encoders and decoders of visual images, aural texts, movement and literary forms to make drama which has personal and cultural significance. Indeed, it is precisely because dramatic texts are *multimodal* – combining the different textual modes of visual, aural, verbal and kinaesthetic languages – that drama develops a range of literacies, often ignored in a curriculum that has been traditionally dominated by written language.

Dramatic literacies

The term 'literacy' has not always been associated with drama education. Most usually it is identified with the written word, although an increased consciousness of the influence of new forms of cultural communication, particularly in media and electronic texts, has led to an awareness of the need to provide a wider description of what it means to be literate in today's technological society. In this context, literacy has gained a wider definition; the term is now variously applied to practices such as the ability to work with computers, to read and interpret a musical score, and to decode and compose visual images.

In this expanded definition of literacy, the emphasis is not only on the ability to *read* texts with a degree of competence, but to *practise* the skills and crafts associated with particular forms of literacy. For example, if I were to describe myself as computer-literate, it would be reasonable for you to expect me to work out how to use a computer program with some degree of proficiency. Similarly, it is difficult to imagine how someone might be described as musically literate if they have absolutely no ability to play an instrument or sing. Likewise, to be visually literate is usually understood to entail some knowledge of how images are composed. Literacy is not associated with passivity; it is an active process of interpretation and exploration. As Jane Gangi points out, 'literacy allows a kind of thinking that is reflective, interpretive and abstract, one which promotes questioning' (Gangi 1998: 53).

In this context, to speak of 'dramatic literacies' is to raise questions about the range of artistic practices involved in making drama. Literacy, in dramatic terms, is not primarily concerned with reading words on a page (although this may be part of the process); it includes an awareness of how different signifiers such as space, vocal colour, intonation, gesture, movement, design, costume, lighting combine to communicate in sound, image and movement. The practise of drama, in primary and secondary schools, from the most simple of classroom improvisations to the most complex professional productions, involves a synthesis of different semiotic vocabularies.

In the secondary-school curriculum, drama has a very particular place precisely because it encourages students to experiment with a wide range of artistic languages. As practitioners, students use the multimodality of drama to shape ideas, to explore situations, to represent experience. Described more simply, when students make drama they are putting together visual images, sounds, movement and speech in creative ways. As members of an audience, they not only take account of the action, but interpret such aesthetic qualities as the scenography, the use of space, the movement and aural elements of the drama. Making, performing and responding to drama does not imply that different semiotic vocabularies are isolated from each other. Rather, dramatic literacy entails a recognition of how the various textual elements included in dramatic practices are woven and integrated into a coherent whole.

In past practices, the tendency has been to offer students experience of drama in two quite separate ways. On the one hand, the drama curriculum has often focused on the exploration of ideas through role play and improvisation; while, on the other, there has been the reading of plays, most usually, in the secondary school, undertaken in English lessons. However, by placing an emphasis on the multitextuality of drama, I am suggesting that these two approaches to drama might be productively combined. The act of reading plays is itself a creative process, which involves an exploration of the ways in which visual, kinaesthetic and aural texts interact. Similarly, when students are creating improvised drama or role plays, their work is enriched by an explicit awareness of how the various textual elements of drama combine to make meanings. Furthermore, to return to Jane Gangi's definition of literacy, both sets of practices can be interrogative, reflexive and interpretive, particularly where they are taught with an explicit focus on the relationship between the content of the drama and the use of dramatic form. The following example, based on the teaching of a play-script, gives one illustration of how students might be encouraged to interpret and question the ways in which different elements of drama contribute to creating an atmosphere that illuminates the thematic content of the play.

A class of Year 7 students (aged 11 and 12) were reading Alistair Campbell's play, *Anansi*, in both their English and Drama lessons. The teacher aimed to encourage them to explore the play's thematic content of the slave trade and to develop an awareness of the effects of the play in performance. She divided the class into small groups, with each group taking responsibility for different aspects of play production, such as set, lighting and costume designers, sound technicians and directors. However, she also wanted the students to become aware of how the different aural, visual and kinaesthetic signifiers of theatre work together, and much of the work was undertaken collaboratively; the whole class were involved in acting the script, with time structured for the work of the specialist small groups. In one lesson, the class worked on the opening scenes of the play. It begins with a title and a stage direction:

The Good Ship Hope: West African Coast, 1791

Listen … hear the last sounds of a ship preparing for an Atlantic voyage. The Boy is seated at a desk, reading and writing. His father, the Captain, consults ledgers and maps.

(Campbell 1992: 2)

The play is set in three locations on a ship – the cabin, on deck and in the hold. However, the action moves between the ship, and 'a forest full of stories'. This presented the group of set designers with something of a problem. The teacher had given some guided questions to the group, anticipating their initial frustration with the constraints of small-scale theatre design and their preference for the resources of a major Hollywood film studio. Her questions asked the students to consider the practicalities of quick scene changes, the dramatic atmosphere they wanted to create, and how the actors might use the space. Similarly, the sound technicians were baffled by the stage direction, but quickly discovered their significance as creators of dramatic atmosphere. After some discussion, the groups shared their ideas. They discovered the necessity to invoke a similar dramatic atmosphere in different forms of design. As a starting point, they decided to create an atmosphere invoked by the word 'hopelessness'. It was an inversion of the ship's name, which the students recognised as dramatic irony, and which acknowledged the play's dramatic exploration of slavery. But 'hopelessness' is, in itself, too abstract a concept for designers to realise; it is difficult to give a literal portrayal of the word in sound or in furniture or props. A further brainstorm, in separate groups, made the idea more concrete. The visual design of the play took shape; hopelessness was symbolised by dark covers over wooden desks, tatty maps and ledgers, and the suggestion of claustrophobia through enclosing the stage space with beams that looked like stakes. The sound of the ship was created by rattling chains, a rhythmic sound-scape of chanting sailors pulling ropes, and an underscore of flapping sails, which, the students suggested, would continue through the dialogue of the opening scene.

In many ways, these highly creative and inventive designs were only realised because the teacher outlined specific constraints that accompany the processes of making theatre, and offered the students guidance in the form of structured questions that helped them solve the problems. However, as a result of this work, they were able to develop an understanding of the visual and aural quali-ties of a play-script which might have been overlooked if they had read the play as if it were a novel (focusing primarily on narrative and characterisation) and without considering the extra-dialogic features of the script. As Elaine Aston and George Savona point out, 'the habits of reading cannot be unproblemati-cally transposed across differential forms. The dramatic text must be read on its own terms' (Aston and Savona 1992: 72). And these terms include the visual, aural, kinaesthetic and verbal languages in the drama, without which the layers of symbolic meanings inherent in the play-script would remain unquestioned.

The concept of dramatic literacy is inclusive. It extends to drama practices that are primarily based on improvisation as well as those that are script-led. What all these practices share, when taught with cognisance of the range of languages that make up drama, is a sense of critical distance from the process of making meanings and communicating in and through drama. Indeed, dramatic literacy entails an ability to analyse the dramatic process, and reflect explicitly on how dramatic meanings are continually created, re-negotiated and redescribed. However, because drama is an art form that is physical as well as intellectual, dramatic literacy can be shown in the form itself, through creative use of the body as well as articulated in written or spoken language. This kind of open-ended learning invites speculation, reflexivity and questions, where it is recognised that drama offers a symbolic interpretation of experiences, thoughts, feelings and ideas, with all their contradictions and ambiguities.

Drama, differentiation and learning styles

The emphasis on learning in drama and the acquisition of a dramatic literacy has sometimes been criticised for taking an inadequate account of the individual needs of different children. Such a curriculum, it has been argued, is too prescrip-tive, too focused on learning outcomes, and overly preoccupied with meeting predetermined assessment criteria. Indeed, if drama lessons were so inflexible, and took no account of those delightfully unexpected moments of insight and creativity, it would indeed be a just criticism; planning for effective learning requires us, as teachers, to meet the needs of individual students. This entails careful consideration of the different ways in which individual children learn.

Theories of learning have emphasised that, unsurprisingly, students learn in a variety of ways. Drawing on psychological research, Michael Fielding has pointed out that students prefer to use different sensory channels to help them learn: some students have developed an ability to learn by using an auditory sense, while others are visual or kinaesthetic learners. He offers the following description of these learning styles.

> Auditory students prefer to learn mainly through talking or hearing ... Visual learners are helped most when they can see a visual equivalent or encounter the thing or process itself in a visual way ... Kinaesthetic learners have a need to touch and get physically involved in the work.
>
> (Fielding 1996: 88)

If students are to be supported in their learning, Fielding argues, there is a need to recognise the different ways individual children habitually learn, and to accommodate and extend their approaches to learning in classroom practice.

It is interesting that Fielding's description of different learning styles so closely mirrors the visual, aural, verbal and kinaesthetic languages of drama I identified earlier. What this suggests is that learning *in the dramatic form itself* inevitably includes a wider range of learning styles than many other subjects in the curriculum, and that this suits the abilities of a greater diversity of children. Perhaps this, too, explains the success of the methodology of drama practice to teach other curriculum areas, and accounts for why students who are labelled low achievers often appear to do rather well in drama. Because drama is multi-textual, the art form itself provides students with different points of entry into the work, and different ways of becoming involved.

Planning for differentiation in drama, therefore, takes account of the different ways individual students learn and includes a variety of dramatic forms, genres and styles. This extends to both the processes of making drama and the art form itself. For example, a Year 8 class (12- and 13-year-olds) were recently investigating the plight of World War II evacuees in their Drama lessons, where the teacher explicitly aimed to encourage the students to sustain roles, create a dramatic atmosphere and to use dramatic form to communicate with others. As a way of encouraging empathy, she showed the group pictures, which helped the visual learners; a soundtrack, which encouraged auditory learners to enter the drama; and asked the class to create a slow-motion mime, which appealed to those who were primarily kinaesthetic learners. The lesson was structured so that initially each element was explored separately: the children were invited to discuss the power of the image, the mood of the soundtrack and the dramatic effectiveness of their first attempts at the mime. Gradually, however, the teacher led the group in bringing these different activities together, and the class developed a mime that took account of the visual image (projected on to the studio wall), with the soundtrack playing in the background. It was a satisfying experience for the students, who used their particular abilities as learners to build on their understanding of role and situation and understood how different dramatic signifiers might be synthesised to create a strong dramatic atmosphere.

The range of teaching and learning strategies included in this lesson gave the children different points of entry into the drama. However, because all the students were involved in each activity, they were able to support each other both in developing a wider repertoire of learning styles and in gaining an explicit understanding of the effectiveness of dramatic convention and style. Experienced learners are able to use a variety of approaches to learning. In practice, while the recognition of different learning styles may be a useful way of identifying students' individual needs and structuring group work, any rigid categorisation of their abilities risks labelling children rather than enabling them. As teachers we have a responsibility to encourage students to develop a diversity of learning styles and, as teachers of drama we are entrusted with extending students' knowledge and understanding of dramatic art. Such an approach to teaching and learning has implications for progression and curriculum planning.

A fully differentiated drama curriculum takes account of students' individual needs by including a variety of learning styles, and supports them in tackling areas of difficulty. Furthermore, a curriculum that provides equality of opportunity will introduce students to a range of dramatic forms and styles and encourage them to interpret them inventively; in the Year 8 class I described, for example, there were two children with hearing impairments, who would have been excluded had the drama been dominated by spontaneous improvisation, and a child in a wheelchair, whose expressive use of gesture provided a focal point for the mime. As Michael Fielding points out, 'learning is about development, not stasis or dependency' (Fielding 1996: 90).

The process of becoming an independent learner involves the student recognising *what* they have learnt, and *how* they have acquired their knowledge, skills and understanding. According to drama educator Michael Fleming, 'progression towards increased independence in drama starts with both teacher and learner having a clear idea of what they are doing, knowing why they are doing it, and being able to assess to what extent the aims have been achieved when the activity is completed' (Fleming 1994: 135). In other words, if our students are to progress into independent learners, as teachers we need to make the aims of the work, the processes of learning and the assessment criteria explicit to them. However, when this is combined with an approach to dramatic literacy, this does not have to equate with rigidity or an overprescriptive and unimaginative approach to the subject. On the contrary, if progression in drama is linked to dramatic literacy, and if this involves questioning, invention, speculation and reflexivity, then this will be reflected in the aims of the drama curriculum. Such a drama curriculum will be structured with this in mind, enabling students to frame questions, to take account of the unexpected, and to evaluate and speculate within the dramatic form itself and as a critical response to the work of others. It is an approach to drama education which combines approaches to learning in the subject of drama with approaches to learning itself.

Communities of learners

Underpinning this argument lies the assumption that drama is a collective enterprise. Drama in schools is practised as a group activity, and this makes very specific demands on students and their teachers. The multitextual qualities of drama as an art form require students to produce a coherence in their work, where the visual, kinaesthetic, aural and verbal elements of the work complement and support each other. As individuals, students also need to find ways of working together to create drama that reflects their interpretations of the playscript or their shared understanding of the content or theme. This places specific demands on young people, particularly in an age when much social activity is influenced by the introspective and isolated pastimes associated with new technologies, and in an educational climate where individualised learning is valued above the achievements of a group.

In this context, the challenge to drama teachers is how to encourage the kind of collective classroom culture that is the prerequisite of good drama practices. Indeed, students themselves often cite the ability to cooperate (or otherwise) as one of the main reasons for the success or failure of their work in drama. The problem, it would appear, is not that students are unaware of the need to work together to create effective drama, but that they lack the skills and strategies to realise their good intentions. In this final section of the chapter, I shall focus on how an explicit recognition of the multimodality of drama can enable students to develop practices that foster successful learning communities.

As a drama teacher, one of my aims is to encourage students to make, perform and respond to drama in ways that have personal and cultural significance for them. In this context, there is a balance to be achieved between creating drama that has artistic integrity and accommodating the different ideas of individual members of the group. However, reader response theory suggests that the meanings of drama are subject to interpretation and reinterpretation; works of art contain, as Merleau-Ponty has described, not just ideas, but 'matrices of ideas' which are in themselves open to interrogation (Merleau-Ponty 1973: 90). This means in practice that drama often works best when it offers alternative perspectives and, rather than creating drama showing a single narrative viewpoint, leaves room for ambiguity, with some information withheld, and some questions unresolved and thus open to further interpretation.

Through the process of working, drama teachers can create a culture of collaborative learning that invites students to exchange ideas, to experiment with alternative perspectives and interpretations, to raise questions, to reflect and speculate. Dispelling the myth that cooperation always means agreement between individuals is both part of the process of creating a community of learners, and it is also integral to dramatic form itself. Indeed, experimenting with how visual, aural, verbal and kinaesthetic signifiers can be juxtaposed to create 'matrices of ideas' is a sophisticated skill, but one that students, by the age of 11–13, are well able to achieve. For example, if a situation seems to demand a sombre atmosphere, what happens if everyone is showing through facial expression or gesture that they are trying to be cheerful? What further questions does this raise? It is a process of opening questions, and finding modes of representation that, in themselves, invite further speculation and reflection. Within this climate, the intention is to demonstrate to students that tensions cannot always be resolved, that drama may be interpreted in different ways. Learning to live with ambiguity is both part of the process of working collaboratively and the process of making art.

A community of learners who work well together can live with and accommodate unresolved tensions. In practice, this requires teachers of drama to structure the process of working carefully, and to provide students with the apparent constraint of limited artistic choices. Imaginative work, as Sharon Bailin points out, is most likely to be achieved when students have access to the rules and conventions of dramatic form (Bailin 1998: 48). Indeed, it is only when students can understand and interpret dramatic conventions that they have the independence to break them. This requires learners to experiment with the different textual elements of drama, and find inventive ways of juxtaposing or contrasting the visual, aural, kinaesthetic and verbal qualities of the work. It is the kind of independence that comes from mutual respect and interdependence between individuals, where it is recognised that drama holds multiple viewpoints, multiple forms of representation and raises multiple questions. A community of learners, in the drama classroom, will learn to value difference.

Note

1 I am thinking here of the work of physical theatre companies such as V Tol and DV8, who incorporate filmic devices into their work, and of the experimental work of Trestle Theatre and Forced Entertainment.

References

Aston, E. and Savona, G. (1991) *Theatre as Sign System*, London: Routledge.
Bailin, S. (1998) 'Creativity in Context', in Hornbrook, D. (ed.), *On the Subject of Drama*, London: Routledge.
Campbell, A. (1992) *Anansi*, Walton-on-Thames: Thomas Nelson.
Fielding, M. (1996) 'Why and How Different Learning Styles Matter: Valuing Difference in Teachers and Learners', in Hart, S. (ed.), *Differentiation and the Secondary Curriculum: Debates and Dilemmas*, London: Routledge.
Fleming, M. (1994) *Starting Drama Teaching*, London: David Fulton Publishers.
Gangi, J. (1998) 'Making Sense of Drama in an Electronic Age', in Hornbrook, D. (ed.), *On the Subject of Drama*, London: Routledge.

Merleau-Ponty, M. (1973) *The Prose of the World*, trans. J. O'Neill, Evanston: Northwestern University Press.

Payne, D. (1998) No Sound, No Speech, No Drama?. Unpublished paper delivered at the National Drama Conference, April 1998.

Part III

In the picture: the meeting place for authors, illustrators and readers

Readers of picture books know the great pleasures to be gained from meeting picture-book makers, authors and illustrators. The spaces within the pictures, and between the pictorial texts and the words, invite the reader in and allow immediate entry into the many complex conversations echoing throughout the pages. The chapters in Part III introduce some of the myriad discourses communicating from the pages of picture books. Sometimes the voices of the picture-book makers are light-hearted, speaking to the reader/viewer of hope after trouble; sometimes they are more ambiguous and enigmatic; they may encourage the reader/viewer to enter the world of spiritual reflection or to face hard truths; they may teach – and preach. In Newbery's words, the encounters between all the contributors to reading a picture book offer opportunities for 'instruction and delight'.

Picture books are multilayered texts resonating with references to other texts. When children first meet picture books they may only be able to hear some of the 'many voices' – the heteroglossia of these texts. Bakhtin's metaphor for the textuality of the written word takes on greater potency, perhaps, when applied to multimodal texts. The inexperienced reader may not be able to recognise some of the languages spoken in the rich combination of picture, border, words, space and layout. As readers of picture books become more experienced, however, they come to have greater fluency with the 'languages' of the words, images and designs. With the greater fluency that comes from lengthy or more frequent meetings with these texts, it becomes increasingly possible to engage in dialogue. Even experienced readers sometimes have to pay careful attention, searching the pages for voices speaking in remembered cadences. Revisiting picture books means entering more conversations, recognising languages which were indistinguishable on first entering the text. Learning a new language means understanding something of the grammatical patterns used; becoming more fluent in an already recognisable language introduces some of the more sophisticated conventions and language systems used to make meaning. Current analyses of multimodal texts help reader/viewers to get to grips with the grammars of single-page images as well as the structures of whole texts. These insights remind us of the constructedness of picture books, honouring the complex meanings and textures of books where the makers have carefully combined words with images and space.

Jane Doonan analyses the grammar of the visual design of two contrasting books about Noah and the flood. She shows how knowledge of the systems of multimodal texts extends the scope for making meanings from pictures and the structure of the picture book as a whole. When we look at a picture, we may think we are viewing objectively, but what we are undergoing is a carefully contrived experience. Through contrasting texts about the same subject, Jane Doonan's chapter shows how rich the meetings between picture books and readers can be when informed by a developed understanding of the languages of the texts.

If meanings are constructed from juxtapositions of word and image, what happens when different illustrators work with the words of one author? Rich encounters are possible. Jacqueline Kirk uses Martin Waddell's books as a focus for considering the differences between picture books and 'illustrated' books. Waddell's insistence on the importance of the 'right artist', who adds something of her/himself to the story, also allows a more complex analysis of a multilayered text. When author and illustrator speak together, their voices combine in a harmony which brings out even more possible meanings than words or pictures alone could accomplish. When the reader joins in the conversation, meanings are extended even further; and, importantly, the companionable silences of the conversational encounter can be very powerful indeed.

Most very young children experience sharing that very arbitrary text, an ABC book, with parents or carers and teachers. It seems a 'natural' experience for young readers. To Anne Rowe, exploring the history of such books means encountering many changing attitudes to learning to read and the place of picture in that process. Alphabet books are texts that have been regularly rein-vented, testing the ingenuity of picture makers and the increasing sophistication of readers. They are, perhaps, some of the most intertextual texts children meet. Their history is a history of teaching reading. It is salutary to be reminded by John Locke, who represents some of the earliest attempts to formulate principles for teaching reading, that children should be taught to read 'without perceiving it to be anything but sport'. At present, the state of ABC books is very healthy, as many established artists have accepted the challenges of finding new ways to work with the age-old formula. In their contemporary form they are a place where didacticism and playfulness vie, merging instruction and delight in the balanced meeting of adult with child, reader and text.

Chapter 9

Show and tell

Perspectives on Noah's Ark[1]

Jane Doonan

In Jan Brueghel's painting, *The Entry of the Animals into Noah's Ark* (1613), along with many other creatures he shows a cat up in a tree after the birds, dogs chasing the ducks, tortoises going off in different directions, snarling lions and a jittery horse. A telling gap poses questions of how Noah is going to get these animals aboard, and then manage them: Noah's nightmare. This uncomfortably natural portrayal – the shock of the old – led me into looking at how the story is presented to children today in picture-book form. Of the many versions published recently, I have taken two with widely contrasting ways of reinterpreting the same story, and explored the texts, pictorial styles and visual design, looking for some of the possibilities open to the implied audience as its share of the creative process: finding answers to questions of what is going on, why the pictures look the way they do, how the words and pictures are functioning, the effects of the relationships between words and images, and what they tell us about our society – filling in different kinds of gaps. If you agree with the philosopher Anita Silvers that 'one of the major purposes of education is to engender the child's (or adult student's) development of concepts' (Silvers 1978: 46), then these two picture books will provide plenty of scope for practice. *Noah and the Ark*, retold by Antonia Barber and illustrated by Ian Beck (see Plates 1 and 2), floats on a mainstream of historical influences, and *Noah's Ark*, with a text by Heinz Janisch and illustrations by Lisbeth Zwerger (see Plates 3 to 5), navigates the choppy waters of metafiction. Both works stand in a special relationship to the Biblical pre-text, and in general relationship to other versions of the story and imagery as well as soft toys and models, all of which contribute meanings to the idea of the Ark.

Noah and the Ark: framing 'fearful symmetry'

Antonia Barber and Ian Beck bring a democratic impulse and generous spirit to the punitive and frightening story of how the wickedness of the world provoked God's wrath and caused the Flood. In *Noah and the Ark*, together they set up a number of involving strategies that draw us close and reassure.

Barber's retelling is shaped simultaneously to entertain a child with its subdued playfulness, and please an adult with its socialising impulse. The point of view and attitude throughout is that of a loving protective adult towards a young child. Her interpretation makes a significant change to the relationships between God, human beings and animals, in that there is a shared responsibility to put matters right with the stricken world. It is the Creatures who tell God that 'This Man you made was a mistake!'. And unlike the angry God of the Old Testament, this God sorrows and sighs before he comes up with the idea of saving the animals with Noah's assistance. Barber's text is in free verse, with echoes of the oral tradition in her fondness for alliteration and the narrator's direct address. She laces the poetry with artless asides, confiding detail and the occasional colloquialism. For example, Noah is astonished when God speaks to him and asks for guidance, 'never having seen an ark'. God dispenses with the tedium of giving dimensions, going straight to the needs of the matter – 'Make it VERY BIG and order A LOT OF FOOD'. Barber makes a little joke at God's expense. God tells Noah what to do; Noah delegates the manual work of construction and painting to his sons and daughters-in-law. Barber clears up mysteries like how Noah collected the animals – 'God spoke … /(They were less surprised,/being used to his voice.)/Each one turned at the whispered word'. As was to be expected, when the animals grew bored and restless 'Some of them mucked about'. At the conclusion both Noah and God remember their manners. Noah thanks God for keeping them safe, God thanks Noah for looking after the animals. ' "It was a pleasure," said Noah politely,/"but please don't do it again … /the flood, I mean." ' In the last verse, the narrator links events of the far past to the present day through the phenomenon of the rainbow: 'And to this day,/when storm clouds fill the sky/and the rain seems unending,/the rainbow comes,/sudden and magical,/and makes the dark world/new again'. The promise in Barber's words goes beyond simple reassurance about bad weather.

The pictorial sequence is designed with a high proportion of double-page pictures, which often show an unrestricted view of human represented participants who, within the size of the frame, are on a scale chosen to suggest 'close personal distance'. In camera terms this is closer than a medium shot but not as intimate as a close-up. The composition of the pictures give the beholder a sense of having access to events through logical progress across the picture field, to and from the farthest planes. The animals appeal to young children as each one looks like a (Western European) symbol, as seen in alphabet books, nursery friezes or in the form of soft toys: humanised, tamed, asking for a pat or a cuddle. Naming each one would present little difficulty for even the youngest observer.

Beck has made four particular stylistic choices for the visual interpretation, three of which grant his illustrations the gravitas and appearance of a record of a religious story. His drawing is given a particular and very unusual character; he uses decorative borders to frame the text; he adopts some of the pictorial conventions associated with artists of the Northern Romantic tradition for all but three of the compositions (which seem designed to evoke a different kind of response). For the latter, all sea settings, Beck treats the waves rather in the manner of Hokusai, a slant that affects interpretation. There is not, therefore, one totally unified style of representation.

As for the first of those stylistic choices, in the drawing process Beck seeks tactile surface effects akin to old engravings. The drawing is done in pencil, and mimics dry point, in which

> a steel needle replaces the burin, and held like a pencil, it throws up a burr of metal to the side of the furrow as it cuts into the metal plate. The burr is not scraped away and gives an added richness to the line.
>
> (James 1947: 67)

Beck shades and tones the drawings by hatching and crosshatching, with dots and flicks as seen in engraving. Colour, rich but muted, is stroked in with crayons which give a dry and grainy surface quality.

The layout is designed with sections of the text within a decorative border, superimposed (like labels) upon large pictures, one or two to each page opening. The decorative border serves various purposes. First, it embellishes the narrative line with small detail and contributes to the impression of the passage of time. For example, as the narrator speaks of the building and painting of the ark, the text is bordered by representations of small lengths of log which are not fully secured to each other. Over the page opening, the timber frame round the text, just like this stage of the story, is all neatly lashed into place.

Second, the border unifies the printed text with the pictorial matter. In pictures, frames act like pauses, and visual framing 'is a matter of degree: elements of the composition might be strongly or weakly framed' (Kress and Leeuwen 1996: 214). Taking in the picture plane as a whole, the decorative border – an element in itself – makes for a significant pause but a light one, as the audience reads the words within the label and sees the tiny details in the drawing. At the same time, the drawing style and colouring is uniform across border and main picture, so the abstract pattern they present is almost seamless. Perceptually, the framed section superimposed upon the main picture appears to float, this effect being intensified by the saturated white of its supporting paper which projects. The decorative border anchors the text-label while allowing the pictorialisation[2] to flow round and under it.

Last, the border lends what Kiefer calls 'cultural or historical authenticity' (Kiefer 1995: 111). Decorative borders allude to the illuminated manuscripts and books of the fifteenth century, particularly the beautiful Books of Hours, with their collections of psalms and prayers. Medieval art was doubtless William Blake's inspiration for his 'illuminations', including those for *Songs of Innocence*, in which tendrils of wandering vine leaves cling as borders to the pages. These associations with religion, and with a work of Blake's that concentrates on childhood, aptly suit the biblical matters and the intended audience of the Noah picture book. And, as we shall see, Blake's influence permeates well beyond the decorative borders, to matters of style and content.

Matters of style

The larger group of Beck's illustrations approach the intensity and conviction of the Northern Romantic artists, whose canvases from the late eighteenth and early nineteenth century transpose the experience of the supernatural from traditional religious imagery to nature. The iconographic vocabulary of Caspar David Friedrich, Philip Otto Runge, William Blake and Samuel Palmer includes miraculous details of nature as the reflection of divinity, in motifs of trees, flowers, sky and celestial bodies. These artists also show a preference for symmetrical compositions, an expressive factor in itself; such design is reminiscent of the hieratic form of early altarpieces. In the construction of individual compositions as well as their effect in the pictorial sequence and in his choice of motifs, Beck shows a kinship to William Blake and Samuel Palmer. Noah (according to Beck) is not unlike Blake's creation of God, with white beard and wind-blown hair and robes. Just as many of Blake's Bible illustrations 'represent the lineaments of some spiritual state' (Raine 1970: 18), so Beck's patriarch carries out God's will with shoulders back and upright carriage. Human-represented participants are placed in poses conveying more drama than naturalism. Blake regarded art, imagination and religion as synonymous, so his presence like a presiding genius over this modern version of the Flood story is fitting.

Following upon the title page, Beck opens with a sombre double-page picture reflecting on the narrator's words, which summarise the first chapter of Genesis and then God's anger at the fallen world. Beck fixes the mysteries in timeless symbols – the pale-faced moon, the great golden face of the sun, the ball of earth just coming into being, and all set in the starry heavens. Throughout the sequence Beck uses light falling upon animals and landscape to signify God. As the viewer crosses the picture field, the colours become increasingly desaturated. Beck exemplifies the realities of man's destruction of his habitat with images of smoking brick stacks belching pollution, which falls again in the far distance, as poisoned rain – oblique references to Blake's 'satanic mills' and a twentieth-century concern for environmental damage.

The major recurring motif in Beck's pictorialisation is that of the tree, which he uses to exemplify the destruction and rebirth of living things. This approach enables Beck to express suffering, but to avoid distressing his youngest viewers. In the very first page-opening bare-branched trees are buffeted by gales and seem to be clinging on for dear life to the edge of the world. On the next page-opening Beck depicts the elephant, giraffe, zebra and leopard in a grey landscape amidst more barren trees, which grow on the edge of a cliff. The animals are illuminated in shafts of God's light, as He ponders upon how to save His masterpieces. Elsewhere, anguished saplings are compressed into borders, and other trees are drowned by the rising water. The most poignant use of the symbol is on the seventh opening, the only one that bleeds on all four sides – the flood overflows into the real world beyond the edges of the paper. The picture shows a vista of water and ominous sky, with a leafless tree in the lower left foreground, and the ark, in the upper right background, on the horizon. A deluge falls directly upon the tree and, to apply Rosenblum's words about the Romantic extremes of empathy with nature, 'where branches almost appear to be the exposed nerves of a suffering creature' (Rosenblum 1975: 39). The use of the tree motif in landscape paintings, introducing an almost human element, can be seen in works by Caspar David Friedrich, John Constable and, in the nineteenth century, Van Gogh. Beck is taking and making the motif his own through using it as an extended metaphor.

The illustration of the animals leaving the ark is in the spirit of a pastoral picture by Samuel Palmer, who found deity in God's creation. They enter a world which is vibrant with fruit-bearing trees and meadow-carpets of flowers. The mountain peaks wear cypresses like feathers in their caps.

Preceding (as well as set among) these compositions are the three that carry the 'Japanese' treatment of water. On the title page clouds gather in the luminous yellow sky, the blue ocean heaves and swells and rises in waves that look like monsters capped in froth, chasing the red-roofed ark, which rides on the highest crest. Threatening in effect? No more than a playful game of Catch Me: the triad harmony of the primary tints have a direct appeal, the upward thrust of the hull exemplifies buoyancy. The second time we see the stylised seas they appear with a description of the drowning of the world. The chopping foaming waters present a fretted pattern of interlocking cool blues, greys and white so decorative, so beautiful in subtlety of tone and texture, as to distract attention from the dolour of the words. The third scene is a dove's-eye view of the ark. The noisy excitement seeping through the ark, as described by the narrator, is matched by the action of the waves, which are rippling diagonally across the picture field – a play of dancing shapes, lines of lace ruffles set upon transparencies of turquoise and cerulean.

Given that one of the functions of the design of pictures is to engage our attention, emotions and thoughts, how are we to make sense of the 'Hokusai' seas? Set within the *Noah and the Ark* pictorialisation, the sea settings draw attention to themselves through the semi-abstract treatment of the waves. Certainly one effect is to lessen the illusion that what we see is a realistic representation of the world. What we might mean by this is that within European culture images of the sea are represented by different conventions. The illustrations with the 'Hokusai' seas have, to borrow a term from linguistics, a lower modality than the other illustrations. Modality 'refers to the truth value or credibility of . . . statements about the world.' (Kress and Leeuwen 1996: 160). The concept of modality is equally essential in representation – as we scan an image we question its reliability within its given context. Most young viewers, bringing to their judgement familiarity with the style and appearance of similarly illustrated versions of biblical and traditional stories, will allow themselves to be convinced by the pictures, which have affinities with the Northern Romantic tradition. The lower modality of the sea scenes, with their decorative exuberance, works to advantage, given that Beck's aim is to shape his work for a young child. These waters, as agent of God's wrath, are no threat to this ark.

Closing the doors of the ark

Let the final double spread close the metaphorical doors. The 'fearful symmetry' of pictorial structure gives a sense of immutable order and promotes a numinous quality. Depth is created in a series of planes, each one favoured by a special object of interest for the viewer to explore, as the landscape recedes; foreground meadows, fields, orchards, a winding river, bosomy hills, and a distant mountain range. Symbolically, God, upper centre, is represented by golden pools and shimmers of light which fall upon this green and pleasant land. On a hierarchical scale Noah is positioned to the left, with most of the animals great and small to the right. Grey clouds are clearing the sky to either side. The distant mountains are framed with the perfect arc of the rainbow, which spans over three-quarters of the picture field. Upper left, the ark sits on the slope of Mount Ararat; upper right is the text label, behind which rises a large pear tree. The text-label lower left balances the larger animals, lower right. In the centre middle ground, the sons of Noah are shown, back view, gazing out over the landscape, while three giraffes make their own inspection. Structural linear emphases are curvular, the dominant shape is the circle: rolling hills, trees and bushes with foliage growing round as a ball, the faces of the animals full and benign – a shape which is repeated in small scale in the flowers. The tiger lies down with the lamb, an allusive nod to Edward Hicks' *Peaceable Kingdom* (1834).

The lion, bear, elephant and tiger gaze directly at the viewer. The gaze is a powerful graphic device for drawing the viewer into the fictive world. A direct contact is made, even if only on an imaginary level (Kress and Leeuwen 1996: 121–5). This is possible because as a viewer one 'becomes' two different people: a picture-viewer and a scene-viewer. The picture-viewer is the person in the real world, and the scene-viewer is created by the artist through the perspective which she/he chooses for the construction of the picture. In the illustrations, Beck has given us various positions to hold: we have seen the blighted earth through God's eyes, we have been the dove flying above the ark, a fish beneath the waters. But this time, with the direct gaze, a fiction is constructed that we stand, as our real selves, in the meadow. The gaze functions in pictures as it does in real life, when a person looks at us and demands some kind of response. The scene-viewer must interpret the gaze using pose and expression for guidance. In this particular instance the drama is over, the play is done and, like good actors everywhere, the animals seek our approval.

Noah's Ark: participants adrift on the flood

Noah's Ark is a metafictive version of the Flood story, made from Heinz Janisch's retelling and illustrated by Lisbeth Zwerger. The relationship between Janisch's text and the Bible is unproblematic; not so for Zwerger's interpretation. Her sequence is driven by modes of representation with which she experiments, so that *Noah's Ark* is as much about the way we construct the world through symbol and story as showing a given story. Questions of modality, what constitutes realism and how it may be inscribed, are foregrounded.

Janisch's text, translated by Rosemary Lanning, has direct detail and some of the resonance of a seventeenth-century Bible. The text opens at the beginning of Genesis 6.4, with reference to giants and the wickedness of men, and closes at the end of chapter 9, with the three sons leaving the ark to people the earth. The surface level of the text leads thus to closure, as God's command is fulfilled. The narrator's tone is formal. She/he describes how the Noah family 'made ready to go into the ark', there were 'plentiful supplies of food', and 'the floodgates of heaven closed' when God remembered the promise he had given to Noah. Janisch/Lanning (a matter of translation) could be almost quoting from the King James Bible when God says, 'Never again will I make a great flood to cover the whole earth. The seasons will return: seedtime and harvest, summer and winter.' As in the Bible, God is moved by anger to destroy His creation. He is not open to negotiation. Noah is voiceless and does as he is commanded. The text makes little concession to young listeners, but meanings are clear and, through its measured rhythms, rewarding to read aloud.

The picture book is large, with a square format. Layout is designed over a grid which brings the impression of unity to the turning of the pages. Each opening, with only one exception, shows the same pattern. On the verso is a section of the text together with a small illustration which varies in size, shape and style of communication – miniature paintings of narrative representations, some not much bigger than postage stamps, and others taking the form of spot paintings or cutouts. This material is framed by a fine line border, then by an outer frame of white, unworked page space. The recto carries a full-plate picture and white frame of matching dimensions. This pattern is broken only on the seventh opening, where there are two full plates. The formal layout harmonises with the formal character of the text.

Zwerger keeps her audience cross-referencing and hypothesising backwards and forwards across systems, painting styles, locations and the temporal span of the action. She is more concerned to move her audience speculatively than emotionally. As the title and the cover board picture indicate, the picture book is about the ark and the animals; we are not given any close-ups or full views of the faces of Noah and his family, so the illusion of 'knowing' them is denied. Visually we are in Zwerger-land, European but not datable, so there is no time frame in which to set the figures. As for the picture field, its most obvious characteristic is the artist's minimalist approach to settings and the sparseness of arrangement of forms on the paper. We have little sense of place. The lack of background detail denies a whole area of meaning because as viewers we make judgements from appearances, as we do in real life. This lack also undermines notions of scale.

Narrative representation

Zwerger uses two different structures for her pictorialisation and then plays variations on them. All but three of the large plates and their opposing text-page motifs are designed in narrative representation, unfolding actions and events – just what we would expect to find in a picture book. Zwerger's delicate pencil outline varying in hair-breadths of pressure conjures up the forms. Water-based paints are applied thinly, often with the texture of the supporting paper bringing a luminosity from beneath. Hues are subtle – tints of cerulean and sepia, greys warmed by copper or cooled by blue, rich muted green – and the boldest colour statement, a cadmium red, is carried by the ark.

The first full plate shows the huge black shadow (God's anger? Evil? A giant?) cast upon an arid landscape with three smoking towers, gigantic sword and axe, five scattered shinbones; the natural relationships between the scale of man-made things is destroyed. In the sky above fly graceful cranes. With great economy Zwerger exemplifies violent deeds in contrast to natural beauty: what needs to be destroyed, what needs to be saved. When God first speaks to Noah, the whole family is depicted in the centre of the picture plane, in His shadow and surrounded by space with just the barest indication of the ground plane beneath their feet: God's-eye view. They are set apart graphically as the agent of God's intention.

The emptiness, together with colour, also promote a surreal effect in several compositions. The building of the ark – watched by a curious centaur, an old woman walking her goat, and a young giant with a shaved head, takes place in a desert landscape bleached by the afternoon sunlight, under a midnight blue sky (see Plate 3).

Conceptual representation

The main narrative representation is suddenly interrupted on the fourth opening, by a change in structure, which holds for three openings in sequence. On the verso, the flow of the third-person narration continues, describing the arrival of the pairs of animals to the ark. This is accompanied by visual motifs. But on the recto, narrative representation is replaced by conceptual representation, a different system, and the artist's personal style replaced by depersonalised drawing with a greater degree of abstraction, representing participants in generalised terms. Zwerger presents, one after another, the facsimile of a page from a non-literary book: a tabular. The temporal dimension of the visual flow suffers a blackout as the audience asks what these pages mean or where they come from. There is no direct reference to them in the text. Who sees? Who knows?

The three successive pages might be extracts from Noah's 'manifest', or his identification guide. Zwerger designs the tabular pages to show a classification process using the images as denoting symbols. The first tabular page is headed 'TAB.XXXI' and five pairs of creatures are depicted in pastel and displayed upon a plain and neutral background of grey-sepia (see Plate 4). Depth is reduced, the angle is that which best suits the purpose of identification: frontal for owls, in profile for ponies, in plan for tortoises, and so on. The viewer must infer from the similarities perceived to exist between the five sets what constitutes the overarching category: a child can solve this one without any difficulty – spots. The next page comes from 'T.127' and the background is a pink-beige. The creatures here are categorised by having heads which are a different colour from their bodies. And the third tabular page, 'T.573' is on ribbed brown supporting paper. Creatures with long necks and long legs are neatly arranged for our inspection.

Encouraged to look again, a child-sharer will discover that there is more to make from these pages than animal categories. Inferencing begins with the two styles of tabular headings (which are not so immediately obvious in the picture-book sequence as they are in the above paragraph), then by questioning differences in the appearance of the supporting paper and the medium. Zwerger is creating the illusion that what we see are extracts from three different volumes inscribed by two different hands.

Playing between the designs

Staying with the tabular sequence, the spot paintings on the text pages show Zwerger playing *between* the two designs for visual communication – the conceptual and the narrative. They may be interpreted as a classification process and/or a narrative proposition. And for these small illustrations she also employs another variation in painterly style. The images are set on the paper without background, and on each page each group of animals is classified according to a system, just as conceptual representations might be, and drawn with detailed naturalism, denoting symbols of pictorial fidelity. However, they are placed upon the picture plane in a descending diagonal pattern on the first text page, in an apparently overall random pattern on the second text page, and in a horizontal left/right directional pattern on the third text page. These patterns would be meaningless without the accompanying verbal text, which explains what is not made clear visually. In their relationship with the words, all the creatures are making their way to the ark. They are moving on (imaginary) tracks or flightpaths and so are understood to be partaking in the narrative action.

The first set of spot paintings of insects and a pair of worms, looking like studies from a naturalist's notebook, analytical and full of life, are both beautiful to behold and an invitation for reflective scrutiny. They are in strong contrast to the static, objective images on the tabular pages, which are also presenting factual information and promote detached scrutiny; two different ways of showing, which require different responses and evoke different feelings in the viewer. However, over the three successive openings featuring the tabular pages, the images of the spot paintings and those of the tabular, though so different in style and denoting different overarching categories, have the same function when taken in relationship with the text: they serve as exemplifying symbols – a small sample of male, female, walking or flying, furred or feathered creatures 'from all corners of the earth.'

Zwerger's play upon classification takes another form when she places birds in pairs against the light ochre walls of the spacious aviary in the ark (at the same time subverting viewer's notions about what the interior of the ark might have looked like). She sets up a naming game at the same time as showing what taking God's word literally would look like – an excess of birds, including the dodo.

Looking for the rainbow

Generally, the image of the rainbow sets the final seal on illustrated versions of the ark story. Lisbeth Zwerger denies her audience the picture it expects to see. The small painting relating to the rainbow is sited at the bottom of the text page, and here she breaks with the text-page design and in effect merges real and fictional worlds. The image of Mount Ararat rises from the edge of the paper as if its foothills were in our own space, while the ark perches on its plateau, partaking of the biblical story of events. The rainbow is but a pale part-form in the sky.

Prominence is given to the exit of the animals from their restrictive quarters on the opposing full plate (see Plate 5). This shows a hurly burly of bodies, surging over the green mountain grass. The stag leaps in the air, and the fox is after it. The ostrich looks back for its mate, and the boar noses between the sheep. As in Beck's final illustration, we are given direct gazes from animals, but what a difference in their force! The hippo and the wolf eye us and we had best get out of the way. The animals travel across the picture field from right to left – in the opposite direction from the one we understand by convention to signify moving forwards both literally and metaphorically. They are not perceived as coming from anywhere or going anywhere; there is no order, and no sign of Noah. What are we to make of this tumultuous stream? It could be a pendant piece to Jan Brueghel's painting of *The Entry of the Animals into Noah's Ark*.

As a picture-book audience, Zwerger has treated us to narrative discontinuity, and to the shock effect of what Moss calls 'short circuitry' in that she exposes 'the conventional gap between the text and the world, between art and life' (Moss 1992: 58). Zwerger is quietly challenging her audience to make sense of the different styles and systems in which the animals are presented. How many ways are there for showing what is real or believable in visual terms? Real feral animals behave like those exemplified in the final narrative painting, but they don't look like that; animals as denoted in the tabular, are unconvincing except that they are real classifying signs. The spot paintings offer the most realistic represented participants, but they have no settings; only the shallowest implied space in which to exist. Zwerger might be making a point that all views are valid.

More gaps have to be filled in determining meaning through the relationships between the three sources of information the audience receives: the text and the two sources of visual communication – the mix of spot pictures and small complete pictures, together with the large plates. It is not always obvious. The viewer cannot always relate information coming from the words and images across the page opening; some relationships remain indeterminate or likely to be temporarily misinterpreted. Other variations in relationships show the text picture out of synchronisation with the main picture, or the text; individual illustrations act independently of one another or the text and even appear to contradict each other as well as the text.

Intertextuality

What is to be made from the relationship between *Noah's Ark* and its pre-text? As indicated earlier, there are strong biblical resonances in Janisch's account. For those who know the first nine chapters of Genesis, 'because of the co-existence within the one discourse space of pre-text and focused text the significance of the story will tend to be situated not in the focused text but in the process of interaction between the texts' (Stephens 1992: 88). After the Flood Noah planted a vineyard, and disgraced himself when drunk. Anyone with knowledge of this may be affected, when interpreting the final illustration in particular. Janisch closes with 'Noah went away from the ark, in hope and trust, and his offspring peopled the earth.' Zwerger ignores the human element, eschews visionary effects, and with her feral animals perhaps is hinting at the old world carried into the new.

In *Noah and the Ark*, Barber and Beck have reinterpreted the Old Testament for a New Testament – the idea of Man negotiating with God, of looking at the natural world to see its Divine Order with harmony and a pattern to everything. Theirs is the version of the world we like to give children, as adults projecting the desire of it being a happy place where virtue is rewarded, and faith and hope are guiding principles. *Noah's Ark*, through Zwerger's contribution, denies the kind of closure given by Barber and Beck, and might give rise to the question of whether it is truly intended for a young audience. Conventional picture-book versions of the Flood story are generally comforting and comfortable to behold. But the distancing effect of metafiction is not sufficient in itself to say that this picture book is too difficult for children. As Hunt has observed, 'it may be correct to assume that child-readers will not bring to the text a complete or sophisticated system of codes, but is this any reason to deny them access to texts with a potential of rich codes?' (Hunt 1990: 181). Young viewers with whom I have shared the picture book settle for the idea that they have seen Mr Noah's notebook, solved the mystery in the running story about the elephant's mate, spotted the dodos and the unicorn, and interpreted the final painting as meaning that the animals are glad to be off the ark. So be it.

In order to discover and make more – how in these picture books, the story,

designs and images exemplify the notions we employ to organise and understand the world – a child needs to know what else to look for, how to find it,
and needs to recognise the significance of what she/he already knows – that's
where adult mediators play their part. Take the covers off the ark. *This* voyage is
over.

Notes

1   This chapter is an edited and extended version of a paper read at the Children's
    Literature Association of America's annual conference in Paris, 1998.
2   I owe the term 'pictorialisation' to David Lewis, who prefers it to 'illustration' which
    suggests a hierarchical relationship – the pictures serve the words. I use both terms
    for the sake of variation only, preferring them to 'visual narrative' which throws
    emphasis on the narrativisation of pictures; Lewis, D. (1996) 'Going Along with Mr.
    Gumpy: Polystemy and Play in the Modern Picture Book', *Signal* 80 (May).

References

Antonia Barber (1997) *Noah and the Ark*, ill. Ian Beck, London: Transworld.

Hunt, P. (1991) *Theory and Children's Literature*, Oxford: Blackwell.

James, P. (1947) *English Book Illustration 1800–1900*, London: Penguin.

Heinz Janisch (1997) *Noah's Ark*, ill. Lisbeth Zwerger, trans. Rosemary Lanning, Switzerland: North South Books.

Kiefer, B.Z. (1995) *The Potential of Picturebooks*, NJ: Prentice-Hall, Inc.

Kress, G. and van Leeuwen, T. (1996) *Reading Images: The Grammar of Visual Design*,
London: Routledge.

Moss, G. (1992) 'Metafiction, Illustration, and the Poetics of Children's Literature', in
Hunt, P. (ed.), *Literature for Children, Contemporary Criticism*, London: Routledge, pp.
44–66.

Raine, K. (1970) *William Blake*, London: Thames and Hudson.

Rosenblum, R. (1975) *Modern Painting and the Northern Romantic Tradition, Friedrich to
Rothko*, London: Thames and Hudson.

Silvers, S. (1978) 'Show and Tell: The Arts, Cognition, and Basic Modes of Referring',
in Madeja, S. (ed.), *The Arts, Cognition, and Basic Skills*, St. Louis: CEMREL, pp.
31–50.

Stephens, J. (1992) *Language and Ideology in Children's Fiction*, London: Longman.

Chapter 10

New dimensions

Word and image in a selection of picture books written by Martin Waddell

Jacqueline Kirk

In an article for *Books for Keeps*, children's novelist and picture-book author Martin Waddell explained, 'When I write a picture book text I am just at the beginning of a long process, in which the whole structure and meaning of the story will be re-interpreted by someone else, an artist who deals in images' (Waddell 1991: 26). In the same article, and on the topic of the illustration of the characters in *The Hidden House* (1990), Waddell enthused, 'It is brilliant ... It is altogether different; it has a whole new dimension. It *works*' (Waddell 1991: 26). Picture books written by Martin Waddell have received less critical attention than they deserve, which is surprising when one considers the huge success of his work. For example, *Can't You Sleep, Little Bear?* (1988) now inspires readers in eighteen different languages (Nettell 1991: 17).

Before looking at Waddell's picture books in particular, it is worth distinguishing picture books from 'illustrated' books. David Lewis (1996) cites Whalley and Chester, who emphasise the 'balance' and 'integration' of written text and illustration in the former: '*the more rewarding examples of the [picture-book] genre show a complete integration of text and illustration*, the book shaped and designed as a whole, produced by a combination of *finely balanced verbal and visual qualities*' (Lewis 1996: 6–7, Lewis's emphases). Thus, Lewis suggests, 'the best picture books are those where pictures and words are woven together in some way to produce a composite form of text' (1996: 7).

In parallel with this definition, Waddell suggests that a picture book does not belong 'to either the writer or the artist, but both together, and *them* ... the people whose names are not on the cover: editor, designer ... all the people who ... make it work' (1991: 26). He makes clear that the relationship between word and image is more than '"A perfect blend" ... because blending conveys intermingling ... ' (1991: 27) Instead, he believes that a picture book grows in the process of illustration and he stresses the importance of the '*right* artist', who adds something of themselves to the story (1991: 27). He explains how 'My story became *our* book ... a picture book, not just a text' (1991: 26) The result was what Gomez-Reino would call 'an artistic whole' (1996: 70).

Implicit in Waddell's explanation is a notion of dynamic growth. He rejects the terms 'blending' or 'intermingling' because these are far too weak to encapsulate the achievement of the picture book. A picture book is a work of art, yielding its own unique energy. This energy derives from the successful relationship between word and image and, to this end, Waddell's insistence upon the 'right artist' is critical. Although Waddell's written text and the images are fine work in their own right, it is the successful union of both of them that is paramount.

How, then, does a picture-book text grow in the process of illustration? Martin Waddell finds 'the new dimensions' which Whalley identifies through 'complete integration of text and illustration' and 'finely balanced verbal and visual qualities'. First, the contents of the illustrations seize upon and powerfully extend those themes and meanings, which are pertinent to the written text. For, as Waddell reminds us, 'A really good picture book is a "big" story, written in very few words, often layered so that many meanings lie within it' (1991: 27). Second, the illustrations can extend the symbolic significance within a story, and this is particularly evident in *The Big Big Sea* (1994) and *Can't You Sleep, Little Bear?* Third, and perhaps one of the most exciting new dimensions in any picture book, is the illustrator's interpretation of the characters in the story. In the books discussed in this chapter, the most significant example is Barbara Firth's characterisation of Big Bear and Little Bear in *Can't You Sleep, Little Bear?* Finally, the composition and use of colour in the illustrations provide a rich, new dimension and invoke a sense of time and place. The elements of framing, scale and colour also extend the themes or layers within the stories.

While the growth of a picture book is engendered by the powerful relationship between the written and pictorial texts, it is also essential to remember the contribution of the reader. The reader extends the meaning of the story to make it personally relevant to them, because picture books 'are concerned with the moment-by-moment uncertainty of *making* your own meanings' (Watson and Styles 1996: 3). It is in these terms that critics talk of the 'readerly gap – that imaginative space that lies hidden somewhere between the words and the pictures, or in the mysterious syntax of the pictures themselves, or between the shifting perspectives and untrustworthy voices of the narratives' (Watson and Styles 1996: 2).

I propose to examine the relationship between word and image, and, through this, highlight the new possibilities for the reader, who generates an energy of their own. Within this context, the 'new dimensions' already outlined will provide a framework for a close reading of *Can't You Sleep, Little Bear?*, *The Big Big Sea* and *Rosie's Babies* (1992), and a brief reference to *The Hidden House*. In his comments quoted earlier, Waddell refers to the importance of a 'big' story. By 'big', he means '"... something-that-matters": ideas like the wheel of life' (1991: 27). The big stories in *Can't You Sleep, Little Bear?* are the fear of the dark or unknown, the warmth of the relationship between parent and child, reassurance and trust. It is to this book that I turn first.

Contrast and comparison

The written text in *Can't You Sleep, Little Bear?* is a perfect fusion of repetition and rhythm. One of the book's central attributes is the repetition of the language of comparison, 'big' and 'little'. The language of comparison is part of the theme of contrasts, together with *light* and *dark*, *inside* and *outside*. The diminutive draws attention to the character of Little Bear, with whom young readers are invited to identify. Waddell's written story pursues the language of comparison beyond the characters as well. In response to Little Bear's plea to light *all* areas of darkness in his bedroom, Big Bear reaches for the 'tiniest lantern', a 'bigger lantern' and the 'Biggest Lantern of Them All'. The intertextual references in this language of comparison echo *Goldilocks and the Three Bears*.

Through the scale and framing of the illustrations, Barbara Firth *extends* the notion of contrast. The first double-page spread portrays both Big and Little Bear in a vast, open space, in the forest outside their cave. The illustration bleeds to the edges of the pages, which Doonan would suggest has the effect of 'a life going on beyond the confines of the page … ' (1993: 81). In this story, the bleeding of the illustration serves to create a vast universe within which Little Bear, portrayed as a tiny figure, is a minute participant.

This composition adds new and greater dimensions to the terms 'big' and 'little'. It draws attention to the scale of the world *outside*, which helps the reader to sympathise with Little Bear's fear of venturing outside of the Bear Cave and into the dark, later in the story. The composition also contrasts with the framed illustrations of the Bear Cave itself, which suggest a warm and homely security *inside*.

A further layer to the book is the bear theme. As well as the two characters, the written text also refers to the 'Bear Chair' and the 'Bear Book'. Barbara Firth takes the former quite literally and portrays the arms and legs of the Bear Chair with paws! The Bear Book, which Big Bear is reading, is entitled *Ursus* (Latin for 'bear') in the illustration, and Firth adds a further dimension to the written text by depicting the Bear Book as the book of the story. The written narrative explains that Big Bear's book 'was just getting to the interesting part', and the fact that Firth has made this the book of the story suggests that Big Bear may already have a familiarity with the plot! On a first reading, the reader may imagine that Big Bear knows more than they do; it is exciting for the reader to be able to fill that 'gap'.

There is absolutely no doubt that Barbara Firth's most important challenge as illustrator of *Can't You Sleep, Little Bear?* is to characterise the two bears. It is her success in doing so that adds the greatest dimension of all to this enchanting book. In the written text, Waddell portrays Big Bear as an understanding parent, which is realised through his patient responses to Little Bear's fears. While Waddell humanises the bears through their ability to relate to and speak to each other, Firth creates a whole new world for them. By placing them inside a world of domesticity, illustrated in perfect detail, the humanisation of the characters becomes a visual reality. Their pictorial characterisation enables the reader to relate even further to other themes within the book, such as warmth, reassurance and trust.

The bear is possibly the most common animal in literature that is a 'symbol *of* [and a] metaphor *for* [the] integrated' self (Royall Newman 1987: 132): 'A strong sense of identity seems characteristic of bears; ... they are much like humans: they walk like people, ... assume different postures, can be comical or dignified, graceful or clumsy, contrary or loveable, ... similar enough for us to identify easily with them. But they trust their senses' (1987: 133–4). Royall Newman draws attention to the importance of the illustrations, which 'play a central role in extending and reinforcing the symbolic significance' (1987: 136).

So how do the images help us to identify with the central themes of the story? How is the bear a symbol *of* or a metaphor *for* the integrated human self in *Can't You Sleep, Little Bear?* First, there is the Bear Cave itself. On the wall of the lounge hangs a framed picture of two bears. On the mantelpiece is a bronze statuette of a bear, suggesting a pride in achievement, a particularly human characteristic. There is a baby's dummy, a pot of honey and a letter ready to post. On the door into another room are Little Bear's drawings, and the display of these makes it clear that his work is valued. Little Bear's bedroom is home to a cupboard full of toys, and in the bedside cabinet there is a book and an apple. Such domestic detail provides an environment in which the personal, warm, 'human' association between the two bears can take place.

The expressions and gestures of the characters in Firth's illustration represent more than any written word could define. A close up of both Big Bear and Little Bear, where their noses almost meet, is loaded with an intrinsic understanding and warmth (see Plate 6). When Big Bear leads Little Bear out of the cave, eventually to bring him 'the moon', the gesture expresses utter trust (see Plate 7). Firth has also composed the 'bright yellow moon' near the end of the story in such a way that it has the effect of a large halo over both of the bears (see Plate 8). The effect of this symbolism is to celebrate Big Bear's natural wisdom and trust and the acceptance of these qualities by Little Bear. It also extends the 'big' theme by affirming Little Bear's place in the huge universe *out there*.

The importance of composition cannot be overstated. As Shirley Hughes points out, 'We aim to lead the eye to the bit of the stage where the main action is taking place.' She continues to explain that this might be to 'highlight a telling gesture, a touching facial expression or an important detail tucked in somewhere which is a vital clue to the plot' (1996: 73). In reading/viewing *Can't You Sleep, Little Bear?*, the references to 'touching facial expression' and 'telling gesture' are especially pertinent.

Rhythm and movement

The Big Big Sea is very different from *Can't You Sleep, Little Bear?* and provides a spiritual and emotional adventure. The written text relates the story of a young girl and her mother, who walk down to the sea at night. A natural spontaneity is evident in the actions of the characters, which is apparent from the written text. For example, the beginning of the book reads:

> Mum said, 'Let's go!'
> So we went …

The freedom and tranquillity of the moonlit night arouse a sense of awe and wonder in the characters. Waddell draws attention to their joy of 'seeing' – the observation of the 'sea in the moonlight', the 'shiny bit' on the sea and the lights from the town. The written text has a poetic quality, which evolves from the rhythm and repetition of the language. One example is in the middle of the story, where the written text reads:

> And I ran
> and Mum ran.
> We ran and we ran
> straight through the puddles
> and out to the sea!

It appears that the illustrator, Jennifer Eachus, has interpreted the rhythm in the language as a metaphor for the rhythms of the natural world, and such an interpretation adds significant depth to this moving book. There are major recurring images in the illustrations that portray nature's own rhythm and movement – dark cloudscapes, misty blue waters, white ripplets and windswept, moonlit landscapes. Doonan calls such recurring images 'expressive, exemplifying symbols' (1993: 46). They signify the dominant layers or themes of the book – that is, nature, freedom and preservation of spiritual harmony with the world. The full double-page illustration near the beginning of the book bleeds to all sides of both pages. The effect of this is to create a moment in time, a pause for the reader to interpret the event, to appreciate, to feel the chill of the wind, as the character is doing. The character of the little girl gazes at the moon, in harmony with nature, a subtle contrast to a previous page, where she looked slightly anxiously away from it.

The defining sentences in the book have an emotionally vibrant weight and much potential for the reader:

> 'Remember this time.
> It's the way life should be.'

One interpretation of this is that the emotional attachment with nature is a means from which the characters (and reader/viewer) can escape from a present life situation, which is *not* how they want life to be. However, since the book is multilayered and has potentially many meanings the reader fills the gaps to make her/his own meaning. The fact that the character of the little girl remains nameless adds to the mystery and freedom of the story. By focusing on events associated with the characters rather than the characters themselves, it allows readers to engage in and reflect on the experience more freely, drawing themselves into the illustrations.

My own reading of this book invites me first to infer a celebration of the natural world, a celebration that forsakes the material. In the pictorial text this is symbolised by the illustration of the *unnatural* lights from the town. It is significant that these lights do not distract the two characters away from the sea, where they choose to stay. The story also celebrates spiritual harmony and the loving relationship between mother and daughter. This picture book is one, like many others, that can address 'powerful issues and probe difficult areas of life' (Styles 1996: 28). It is not easy to describe a spiritual encounter, but *The Big Big Sea* allows the reader to experience one for her/himself.

Composition and colour

The big story in *Rosie's Babies*, portrayed most subtly, concerns sibling rivalry. As Rosie discusses her own 'babies' – a rabbit and a bear – she seeks her mother's attention. She receives it at the end of the story, when Rosie, alone with her mother, asks to talk about 'ME!'. Rosie does not appreciate that she has received her mother's attention throughout!

Significant to this picture book as an artistic whole is its composition. Illustrator Penny Dale depicts Rosie, her mother and the real baby together, on each lefthand page. Subtle facial expressions and gentle manoeuvres in posture contrast with Rosie's imagination, depicted on the right-hand pages. The effect of this is to provide an exciting new dimension, where a relationship exists between the two pictorial narratives, as well as between word and image.

Waddell's written text contains subtleties that characterise Rosie's need to assert her importance. For example, repudiating her mother's suggestion that she is a 'baby', Rosie replies, 'I'm not a baby, I'm four years old.' Later in the story, Rosie explains that 'My babies know I will look after them ... I'm their mum.' Near the beginning of the book, Rosie states that her 'own' babies 'sometimes ... make me cross!' A sophisticated reader might equate this with Rosie's sibling jealousy and therefore her need to assert her importance. Throughout the book, the right-hand images extend the subtleties present in the written text in a way that highlights Rosie's need to assert her significance. For example, where Rosie's imaginative adventures are at the height of their action, the right-hand images of Rosie particularly highlight her need to be involved (see Plate 9). In the written text, Rosie proudly states, 'My babies drive cars that are *real* ones ... ' (my emphasis). The cars are 'real'; Rosie is important, she is part of the action and *her* babies need *her* company. Line effects create a sense of speed for the car, and a fractured layout provides 'runs of sequence' (Rowe 1996: 227) and a sense of events passing time. The reader is inspired to 'fill in the gaps', or to make 'invisible pictures' (Pullman, cited in Rowe 1996: 227). They can decide how much time has passed and how the events might interlink.

Dale portrays a distinctive maternal importance in her illustration of Rosie supervising her babies in the park. In the written text, Rosie makes clear that 'there are no mums and dads … only me!' Dale depicts Rosie with an 'adult' posture, reading a book and tending to her bag. However, the large dog behind the seat reminds us that this is a small, imaginary world. On the next page, Rosie tries to frighten the dog away, since her 'babies' are scared. The dog looks out at the reader, expressing a look that suggests that it is anything less than frightened! While amusing, this suggests that Rosie is trying too hard to assert herself. She has her mother's attention but she just fails to realise it.

As Rosie asserts her importance in her imagination, she subtly assumes a new posture in the left-hand illustrations. As the action is at its peak – when Rosie and her babies drive 'cars … lorries and dumpers and boats' – Rosie makes eye contact with her brother or sister for the first time. As the book progresses from here to its conclusion, Rosie's attention turns increasingly to her sibling and eventually the baby touches Rosie's nose.

As she gradually turns her attention to her brother or sister in the left-hand illustrations, Rosie becomes less involved with the babies in her imagination. It is interesting to note that, where the baby reaches out to touch Rosie's nose, the written text reads: 'My babies make their own pies.' Dale extends the significance of this by portraying Rosie making pies independently of her own 'babies'. On the next page, too, Rosie picks apples by herself. There is notably less action in the things that Rosie and her babies do as the story reaches its conclusion. Rosie accepts her sibling, and her need to assert her importance through her active imagination is no longer necessary.

In the final double-page spread, the left-hand illustration depicts Rosie leaving her sibling's room, having put the baby to bed. A pair of rabbit ears can be seen in the background. This touching conclusion draws together Rosie's real world and her imaginary world, where her brother or sister now has the 'privilege' of sleeping in the same place as her own 'babies'. The unity shown in the illustration makes clear to the reader that Rosie is both happy and content.

Throughout *Rosie's Babies*, colour adds a new dimension to the story. A nursery colour theme is pertinent to the book. Endpapers are baby pink and baby blue, and a pastel colourwash is evident throughout the left-hand illustrations. However, a contrast is apparent in the illustrations that depict Rosie's active imagination: there is an increase in saturated colour and there are bolder hues, for example, in Rosie's red coat and the yellow truck. The effect of this is to suggest vitality, action and importance.

In *The Hidden House*, colour is a metaphor for the big theme in the story – the wheel of life and death. Waddell's written text tells the story of Bruno, who makes three wooden dolls to keep him company. However Bruno goes away and does not come back. At the beginning of the book, when Bruno has gone, the images of his house are washed with muted greys, browns and greens. These colours have an association with loneliness and sadness. When a new family arrive, a double-page spread, vibrant with primary colours, shows a large vase of flowers and a number of kittens, representing new life. The final illustration is full of blooming flowers, saturated with hues of yellow and red – colours associated with warmth and sunshine. The winter in the Hidden House is over.

Conclusion

The purpose of this chapter has been to examine and honour how word and image work together, in order to create new dimensions and an artistic whole. It has also celebrated the significance and contribution of the reader. Clearly, Waddell's insistence on the 'right artist' is of paramount importance. Firth's characterisation of Big and Little Bear and their home reinforces their symbolic significance and the major themes in *Can't You Sleep, Little Bear?* and creates a whole new world for them. Dale's composition in *Rosie's Babies* challenges the reader to relate not only word and image, but to engage with two sets of images that work subtly together. Colour and recurring image provide a rich new dimension in *The Big Big Sea*, and colour is a metaphor for life and death in *The Hidden House*. These texts, I am sure, will continue to challenge and delight both adults and children in many generations to come. This opportunity exists because the dynamics and interrelationship between word, image and reader offer far-reaching possibilities. Together, they *work*.

References

Doonan, J. (1993) *Looking at Pictures in Picture Books*, Stroud: Glos. Thimble Press.
Gomez-Reino, H. (1996) 'Reading Picture Books with an Artist's Eye', in Watson, V. and Styles, M. (eds), *Talking Pictures*, London: Hodder and Stoughton.
Hughes, S. (1996) 'Getting into the Picture', in Watson, V. and Styles, M. (eds), *Talking Pictures*, London: Hodder and Stoughton.
Lewis, D. (1996) 'Pop-Ups and Fingle-Fangles: The History of the Picture Book', in Watson, V. and Styles, M. (eds), *Talking Pictures*, London: Hodder and Stoughton.
Nettell, S. (1991) 'Authorgraph No. 68 – Barbara Firth', *Books for Keeps* 68: 16–17.
Rowe, A. (1996) 'Voices Off – Reading Wordless Picture Books', in Styles, M., Bearne, E. and Watson, V. (eds.) *Voices Off – Texts, Contexts and Readers*, London: Cassell.
Royall Newman, A. (1987) 'Images of the Bear in Children's Literature', *Children's Literature in Education* 18(3): 131–8.
Styles, M (1996) 'Inside the Tunnel: A Radical Kind of Reading – Picture Books, Pupils and Post-Modernism', in Watson, V. and Styles, M. (eds), *Talking Pictures*, London: Hodder and Stoughton.
Waddell, M. (1988) *Can't You Sleep, Little Bear?*, ill. B. Firth, London: Walker Books.
——(1990) *The Hidden House*, ill. A Barrett, London: Walker Books.
——(1991) 'Writing Texts for Picture Books' in *Books for Keeps* 68: 26–7.

——(1992) *Rosie's Babies*, ill. P. Dale, London: Walker Books.
——(1994)*The Big Big Sea*, ill. J. Eachus, London: Walker Books.
Watson, V. and Styles, M. (1996) 'Introduction – A Variety of Voices', *Talking Pictures*, London: Hodder and Stoughton.

Chapter 11

Learning the letters

Anne Rowe

> By 'children's books' I mean printed works produced ostensibly to give chil-
> dren spontaneous pleasure, and not primarily to teach them, nor solely to
> make them good, nor keep them profitably quiet. I shall therefore exclude ...
> almost all alphabets, primers and spelling books.
>
> (Harvey Darton 1932: 1)

Two ABC books stood side by side on the 'recent publications' shelf in a well-
known children's book shop in Oxford: Michael Roberts' *Jungle ABC* (1998)
and *Alfie's Alphabet* by Shirley Hughes (1998). They make interesting reading.
Although the pairing is total serendipity, each in their own way highlights the
distance run by the ABC formula. Both books illustrate the delights of dwelling
within a book and the pleasure of exploration.

Roberts' creation is highly stylised and is a challenge to all readers with its
bold collage designs. Each letter has its own double spread, the single capital
letter set in an expanse of matt black while the other page vibrates with busy or
teasing designs that suggest animation. You recognise the letter because you
know it and the picture offers a sophisticated image to decode and so make the
connections. Indeed a book for readers of all ages. Shirley Hughes slips her new
alphabet exploration into the whole world of Alfie and his family. Each page
presents us with the familiar world beautifully detailed, each a small anecdote
waiting to be realised along with the recognition of other well-known Alfie
stories, for example *Alfie Gives a Hand* and *Alfie's Feet*. It's a complex, multilayered working, complete with intertextual reference for the emergent reader,
which comes alive in its sharing.

It seems appropriate here, before stepping back to review the development of
alphabet books, to make a general point that in the range of ABC books there
are: texts containing alphabets; those that use the alphabet as an ordering
device; and books that are alphabets. Each is included here.

To consider the development of the alphabet book is to witness the journey
that has taken place in understanding the nature of reading. Ideas have shifted
from viewing reading as 'simply' phonic recognition to the appreciation that it
is a complicated, multilayered exploration involving a range of knowledges

about print and its contexts, engaging the reader as an active participant with the book, previous experiences, and often the responses of another sharer. Certainly children need to know their letters: the alphabet is a basic building block for both learning to read and the acquisition of spelling and this was the view of the early texts. Contemporary alphabet books demand much deeper responses in an effort to create meanings. Originally, the alphabet was presented as stark print, but the alphabet book today, as a picture book, brings the subtleties of the visual image to those images embedded in the verbal text, where the slippery linguistic possibilities of both pictorial and verbal text challenge and delight young readers. Matters were somewhat different in the earliest kind of alphabet given to learners: the horn-book.

Horn-books

The horn-book or criss-cross-row was used commonly during the sixteenth to eighteenth centuries. The term 'criss-cross-row' may refer to the cross that headed the text or to an earlier arrangement of letters strung on wire in a cruciform. Andrew Tuer has written the authoritative history of the horn-book (Tuer 1971). He notes Shakespeare's references to the use of horn-books, for example in *Love's Labour's Lost*, where in Act V, scene i the page boy Moth says of the pedant Holofernes, 'Yes yes he teaches boys the hornbook'. Tuer also quotes Dr Johnson's comment that the horn-book was 'the first book of children, covered with horn to keep it unsoiled' (1971: 2). These literary details and a fascinating array of illustration (paintings, prints and artefacts) all underline the widespread use of the horn-book in teaching the young to read.

The horn-book was usually made of oak, flat, bat-like in shape, with a convenient handle, which was often pierced so the aid could be attached to the learner's belt. A printed sheet of paper was pasted on to the board and covered with a thin sheet of horn in order to avoid unnecessary wear and tear. The text contained the alphabet in capital and small letters, some in black letter (Gothic) script, though later (and more usually) in roman type. There was also a syllabarium (common blends of vowel and consonants) and such texts that readers would know by heart, such as the Lord's Prayer and sometimes grace. Some texts included the nine digits. Pat Garratt makes an interesting comment on the syllabarium in noting the connection between it and the giant's cry in *Jack and the Beanstalk*. On detecting fresh meat close by, the giant (in Joseph Jacob's version) says 'Fee-Fi-Fo-Fum/I smell the blood of an Englishman ... ' (Garratt 1994: 4). Children with experience of the horn-book would have made the link between their rote chanting and the literacy level of Jack's opponent, perhaps?

To underline the unvarying nature of the text and its longevity, Tuer quotes from the autobiography of John Britton (published in 1850) concerning his memories of the Dame school in Kingston St Michael, Wiltshire:

Here I learned the Criss-Cross Row ... from a Horn-book on which were the alphabet in large and small letters and the nine figures in Roman and Arabic numerals. The Horn-book is now a rarity.

(Tuer 1971: 8–9)

This last comment struck home to Tuer, who searched in vain for a genuine example of a horn-book only to conclude that those on display in collections are rarely genuine. The physical disappearance of horn-books is easy to understand when one considers their constant use, and possible misuse, and the spread of cheap alternatives. On the other hand, these horn-books had been produced in large numbers and were widely used in both Britain and America. Margaret Spufford comments on an example at the end of the seventeenth century of a Staffordshire village shop owned by Jeffrey Snelson, a mercer, whose stock books show a large number of horn-books. (Spufford 1997: 4-62). As she rightly suggests, there must have been a ready market for them, otherwise why stock them? Perhaps in the early nineteenth century these, by then deemed very old-fashioned teaching aids of the Dame school, fed the turtle stoves close to the teacher's desk .

The horn-book had various nicknames: 'jim-crack' (indicating that the bat could be used in other ways to drive home the lesson), 'battledore-book' and 'hornbat'. Battledore was an eighteenth-century invention of an enterprising Salisbury printer, Benjamin Collins, who was a business colleague of John Newbery. A battledore had the horn-book texts in another guise, now mainly printed on card, approximately 20cm by 13cm in size, and folded into a book shape.

Later battledores could simply be a bold presentation of the letters, as in *Martin's Nursery Battledore* (c.1820, Opie Collection of children's books, Bodleian Library, Oxford), which contained only the capital letters in large ornate print. Obviously the publishers did not think that the rococo flourishes would hinder recognition. However, most battledores differed in one important way from horn-books: they were usually illustrated with woodcuts, as in *Gaffer Goodman's Picture Horn Book No. 1: The Alphabet and Words of Two Letters*, published by Chapman and Hall, but with no date (Opie Collection). One side was divided into four large and four small pictures, with captions. The larger pictures showed a cow and milkman, a duck, a horse and rider, and a swan, while a lamb, a goat, a chicken and a robin filled in the smaller. On one side the flap stated that this was a progressive series and, on the other, printed instructions to the teacher recommended the small amount of learning required of the pupil in this particular battledore. The task would not be intimidating, unlike many others, which presented a daunting array of work requiring several years' persistence to master. This battledore should detain them but days. The writer recognised the excitement children felt when they got a new card, and so advised the teacher to ensure that each was thoroughly learnt before the next one was presented. He also suggested that words be sounded out and named, not spelt out, and that this work should be tackled in short bursts so as to avoid boring the young learner.

The obverse of the card was shared between an introduction to the letters and a recapitulation and extension of them. There was a picture-captioned alphabet of mainly common things e.g. 'Aa' with 'ass', 'Bb' with 'bed', along with 'cat', 'dog', 'egg', 'fox', 'gun', etc. with the inevitable 'xerxes' (sic) for 'Xx'. The 'Vv' is curious in that it is 'V' for 'van', a coach with seats down the sides with a postilion riding beside the driver. On the other half the letters were presented unadorned with a section of disordered letters to be used to test the pupil, a simple syllabarium section and a series of sentences illustrating all the problems of restricted vocabulary: 'Do go', 'We do go', 'Go ye as we', 'He or I do go'.

Alongside the horn-book and battledore, we need to consider the needle-work sampler, so beautifully and diligently stitched, which uses the well-known horn-book composition of the alphabet, digits and pious text and, like the battledore, also contains illustrations.

Early primers

There were other, perhaps supplementary, publications that taught the alphabet: primers. Possibly the earliest is *The BAC [sic] Bothe in Latyn and in Englysshe*, printed by Thomas Petyt around 1538. However, as Pat Garratt notes, it is not a true primer in that it only has a selection of the material commonly found in the primer (Garratt 1994: 5). It can still be seen in the library of Emmanuel College, Cambridge. Like the horn-books, primers contained, along with the alphabet, such texts as the Ten Commandments and well-known prayers for use in church devotions and daily life. They were designed to be slipped into prayer books, thus making the important connection between learning to read and religion. This is underlined in the definition of primer given in the *Shorter Oxford Dictionary*: '1 A prayer book, or devotional manual for the use of the laity, before, and sometime after the Reformation.' The second definition indicates that a shift in meaning has taken place: '2 An elementary school book for teaching children to read.' Both aspects are worth attention.

In his complex manoeuvres with Rome, Henry VIII saw encouraging the vernacular as a popular move, which could also be an advantage to his cause. He devoted 'some of his attention to the preparation of standard manuals for education. These included first a grammar, second an ABC book and lastly a new primer' (Garratt 1994: 7). Protestants wanted to do away with a priest as a necessary intermediary between the individual and God, and that meant that being able to read the Bible was essential. In the hands of the Puritans, early primers became fearful propaganda, teaching people to read, but in the additional texts preaching 'Reading to Live'. Books thus displayed the way to heaven, usually along the path to martyrdom.

John Bunyan is the best-known of the Puritan writers who produced work for children. Of his *A Book for Boys and Girls or Country Rhymes for Children*, published in 1686, Percy Muir comments that 'The title of the book is the best thing about it' (Muir 1954: 29). It has the Puritan ethic set out in the preface, 'to show how each fingle-fangle/On which they doting are, their souls entangle' (1954: 29). The inclusion of the Ten Commandments, the creed, the Lord's Prayer – in verse – as well as an alphabet with lessons in reading and arithmetic, and a spelling list to be learnt, shows all the hallmarks of a primer lurking behind Bunyan's encouraging title.

Some primers were very long-lived; others were long-lived and much-travelled. The *New England Primer* was well-known both in America and Britain (Meigs *et al.* 1969: 110-19). It was based on *The Protestant Tutor for Youth*, which had been published by the London printer Benjamin Harris who, having fallen foul of the law for another publication, went to Boston, New England, where he set up again as a printer. In the late 1680s he printed *The New England Primer*, which was simply the *Tutor* under another name. The contents included the familiar capital and small letter alphabets and pages of syllables to be learnt by rote. It included the Lord's Prayer, the creed and the Ten Commandments, and an account of the execution by burning of the Reverend John Rogers for his religious beliefs. There was a frontispiece depicting Rogers at the stake attended by his wife and nine children, one of them a babe in arms, and it concluded with Rogers' poem written to his children just before his death. Strong meat for young minds.

The New England Primer contained a rhyming alphabet, the verse being an aid to memory, and it was illustrated by small woodcuts (Opie Collection). Meigs points out how a number of the verses needed to be amended over the years, a nice insight to the times: the opening 'In Adam's fall/we sinned all' is constant, but the earlier 'The cat doth play/And later slay' and 'The dog will bite/The thief in the night' were considered too secular, and were replaced by 'Christ crucified/For sinners died' and 'The deluge drowned/the earth around' (Meigs *et al.* 1969: 113). Similarly, there was a problem with the verse for U, which used David's lust for Uriah's wife. Later U was simply omitted, not an uncommon form of censorship, and 'Vashti for pride/Was set aside' solved the problem. The perennial difficulty with the letter X was solved, as so often before and since, by pressing Xerxes into service. This primer was in use for over a hundred years but, as religious fervour cooled, so other texts were deemed more appropriate as introductions to reading and the secondary meaning of primer took over, to flourish in the nineteenth century.

Passing pleasures

A Little Book for Little Children heralded an awareness of the need to provide pleasure in learning such arbitrary information as the alphabet. The remaining copy, now in the British Library, is two books bound together, possibly because of a mistaken idea that they were by the same hand: that 'T.W.' was Thomas White. The Thomas White section was published possibly around 1703, while the T.W. section is dated later (internal evidence suggests nearer 1712). The Thomas White section continued the Puritan approach to childhood but, as Muir argues, the T.W. book, for all that it was didactic and full of traditional material, for the first time approached learning from the child's point of view. The T.W. version of A Little Book contains an illustrated alphabet. From the evidence of the extract printed in Muir's book, the cuts are from different sources, by different hands. For example, the rudimentary turnip for T contrasts with the well-executed Xerxes and Zeno (Muir 1954: 38). This practice was commonplace. The Little Book also contains the first appearance of the well-known rhyme 'A Was an Archer', a feature that recurs in different forms in later alphabets.

In 1742 Mary Cooper, a London publisher, brought out The Child's New Plaything. Cooper was among the first to have a separate children's book list and she valued the notions of pleasure and playfulness. The Plaything was subtitled 'a spelling book intended to make learning to read a diversion not a task' (Cooper, Opie Collection). As well as alphabetical pictures, it contained a fold-out sheet headed 'This Alphabet is to be cut into single squares for children to play with'. Each square had a capital and small letter and decorated borders. Above the letters were captions of names and common objects; for example, 'Abraham/Apples', 'Edward/Ears', 'Obadiah/Orange', and for X the anticipated 'Xerxes' with 'Xercise'.

Pat Garratt notes that in recent times a similar game was found in a loft in Maine (Garratt 1994: 12). It had been published in 1743/4 by Benjamin Collins, the battledore inventor. It was printed on paper stuck to card, displayed capital and small letters and includes one of the many parodies of 'A Was an Archer', in this case 'A Was an Admiral'. A booklet was also found outlining the use of the squares, and the author comments on the influence of the writings of John Locke in devising this teaching game. Locke was not alone at this time in advocating the importance of pleasure in learning, but he is probably the best known. Thoughts Concerning Education was published in 1693 and went to many reprints during the eigtheenth century. Collins' game reflects Locke's suggestion of using such things as 'dice and playthings, with the Letters on them, to teach the children the Alphabet by playing'. He declared that children should be 'cozened into knowledge of their letters, be taught to read, without perceiving it to be anything but sport and play themselves into that which others are whipped for', and that he wanted 'easy pleasant books' for learners (Locke 1693: Preface).

John Newbery (1713–67) was another publisher strongly influenced by Locke, and among the long list of books he published there was an important section devoted to children. As noted at the opening of this chapter, Harvey Darton begins his Children's Books in England with the publication of A Little Pretty Pocket Book. (Harvey Darton 1932). (Oxford University Press published a facsimile edition of it in 1966.) The Pocket Book, subtitled 'Instruction with Delight', could be purchased on its own for sixpence or with a ball or pincushion for eight pence. Newbery emphasised the importance of play, but also showed a keen entrepreneurial spirit, a forerunner of the book-related marketing so common today. The *Pocket Book* makes use of alphabetical listing: 'The Great A Play' occupies one side of a double spread with 'The Little a Play' on the other. Each page has its woodcut illustrating a common game: great A shows Chuck-Farthing, whilst little a illustrates Flying a Kite; each has a verse concerning the skills involved with a Moral or a Rule of Life tagged to it.

'Pretty' became a catchword for Newbery and he published books such as *Pretty Poems*, *Pretty Book of Pictures*, *Pretty Plaything* and *A Pretty Book for Children*, which is a veritable compendium of alphabets (Opie Collection). It contains, for example, an alphabet in 'Easy verse for children to learn by Heart', alphabets in different typefaces: Gothic, roman and italic type, an alphabet on squares with a version of 'A Was an Archer' – 'A was an Angler and he caught a fish, B was a Brazier and he made a dish' (X this time was *Xantippe that errant old scold*) and an alphabet with cuts to 'A Was an Admiral'. Added to these were a simple syllabarium, acrostic alphabets of moral sentences and proverbial sentences with even an advanced syllabarium organised alphabetically. It concluded with a retelling of *Reynard the Fox*, a story commended by Locke as suitable for the young, and a version of *Cinderella* – at last some narrative as a prize for all that hard work. It also contained prayers and graces.

In *A Pretty Book for Children* there are elements of the primer side by side with the alphabet that later became an independent book and, importantly, the use of the alphabet to organise thematic material. Publishers following Newbery's lead were to find a ready market for each of these elements, especially with the growth of primary education in the nineteenth century.

Early reading books

The primer translated itself into the early reading book. Some were progressive in that they presented a part of the reading curriculum and often addressed the reader directly, as in *Mrs. Lovechild's Golden Present* printed by J. Kendrew of York but undated (Opie Collection). The frontispiece shows a Dame school with a teacher looking remarkably like Mrs Punch. The receiver of the book was told that learning to read was the golden present and that it was better than earthly treasures. The alphabet was presented with 'engravings' and rhyming couplets. The children were then tested to prove their attentiveness to these lessons by tackling the letters without the illustration, those pictures 'which the engraver has charged me so much money for'. There were lessons in word-building and it concluded with the Lord's Prayer and an uplifting story, *The Virtue of a Rod or The History of a Naughty Boy*, most likely a story to be read to the children as evidence of the golden present that will be theirs – some day.

My First Lesson Book to Teach Me Spelling And Reading, published by Thomas H. Keble around 1850, tried to imply by its title that this was produced directly for the the child (Opie Collection). It had sixteen pages and boasted forty engravings, although the connection between text and picture was not always obvious. An early syllabarium page shows the two letter sounds illustrated by a naval officer reading a sextant, a jewellery box, a rather grand teapot, and a heron on the edge of a pool. These pictures would have come from a common pool of blocks, used because they were there, rather than for their appropriateness as an aid to decoding. But, like *Gaffer Goodman's Horn-Book*, it could be argued that this format did not overwhelm the learner.

This could not be said for many other primers, which were substantial books, published most likely with the teachers in mind and containing a complete course in reading. The *English Primer or the Child's First Book*, sold by J.G. Rusher for sixpence, contained fifty-four pages (Opie Collection). Barnicott's *Improved Reading Made Easy*, at the same price, contained eighty-eight pages (Opie Collection). How daunting! *Rusher's Primer* informed the child that 'He who ne'er learns his A B C/For ever will a Blockhead be.' It begins with letter recognition of both capital and small letters, presenting these at first as white images on black, and then in both roman and italic script along with the test sections, before launching into an alphabet section of rhyming captions on the lines of 'A was an Acorn that grew on an oak/B was a boy who delights in his book'. Xerxes, it was noted, 'was well known in his day', although perhaps not as well-known as he became because of the growth of alphabet books. The syllabarium here also contains that line of 'fe, fi, fo, fu' in one column. It progresses through simple statements to a connected passage acrostically, if meaninglessly, arranged to use the alphabet: 'As I am to go on, so I do;/Be ye as I am, so do ye:/C is as he is, as so as am I/Do as we do, to be in it'. There were few pictures and little memorable text. It displayed its origins with the inclusion of the Ten Commandments and 'Our duty towards God and our Neighbours'.

The independent alphabet book

Pat Garratt notes the early appearance of *The History of A Apple-Pye* in 1671 and its consistent popularity, suggesting that it may well be 'the most famous and familiar alphabet rhyme' (Garratt 1994: 9). John Harris, who took over Newbery's business, published one such in 1808. There was a wide continuum in these books, from the cheap chap books at one end – which were more simplified initial primers without the syllabarium, and concentrating on words set to an image – to those destined for the nurseries of the middle classes, finely produced, with hand-coloured engravings. *The Juvenile Alphabet or A.B.C. of Birds and Flowers* (n.d., n.p.; Opie Collection) is an example of the former, with three pictures and three letters per page; for example, 'Aa' with a picture of an anemone, just to confuse the sounder-out, accompanied by the words 'Ass', 'Apple', 'Arrow' and 'Arch'. The X words are 'Xema Ridibundas' or 'Laughing Gull' as depicted, and 'Xenophon', 'Xipias', 'Xebeck' and 'Xotics' for exemplars. Despite the inclusion of the pictures to attract the pupil, the emphasis was still firmly on the words. The illustration was merely appropriate decoration.

John Harris, better known for publishing *The Butterfly's Ball*, included alphabets of the higher quality in his lists. The *Alphabet of Goody Two Shoes* (1808) and *An Alphabetical Arrangement of Animals for Little Naturalists* (1812) are both fine examples (Osborne Collection) (see Figure 11.1). With *Goody Two Shoes*, Harris was building on the popularity of a character introduced by John Newbery. Goody Two Shoes appears on the title page pointing at a building, the ABC College. The text is a series of verses linking two letters on a page. It begins with 'A was an Apple/And put in a pie' – a neat intertextual reference illustrated with all the details of pie-making, with Goody Two Shoes making a direct appeal to the reader, holding up an apple for inspection. The pictures integrate the information conveyed in the verbal text, and for some letters the picture takes over the double spread. There is humour in both word and picture, and for modern readers much fascinating detail with the depiction of 'Ralph with his Raree-show' or travelling peepshow and the Dancing Master 'N., Mr. Nobody,/Just come from France', sporting his tiny violin, while here Xantippe repeats her shrewish appearance. Most importantly, however, it is the colour and its subtlety that is pleasing and surprising; all the more surprising, since it is literally the handiwork of child workers, each in charge of a particular colour and area to paint. It is perhaps difficult for us to appreciate fully the impact of colour when we take it much for granted these days.

By now, the emphasis had moved to the picture, whether on the part of artists, who took a greater interest in the form, or book-makers, who devised thematic books. They either used existing pictures or commissioned new ones, using the alphabet to organise the given information. The art was to find a new tag for these books, which appeared with flowers, birds, animals, common objects, the farmyard, the railway, Londoners, etc. as their theme, or took an amusing, historical, scriptural, classical or modern approach. There was even a *Peace Alphabet*, celebrating the end of the Crimean War in 1865 with, of course, 'N for Miss Nightingale with her famous band'. There was an alphabet for those who wished to display their Greek, the *Aldiborontiphosskyphoniiiostikos*, with an *Arabian Nights* theme. There were comic alphabets: Master Punch produced one, as did George Cruikshank and Richard Cruikshank, and Edward Lear. There was even an alphabet of Christian morals (Opie Collection).

The desire to exploit new printing techniques, including colour printing, involved using talented artists who could exploit these inventions and so produce a quality product at a cost that most could afford. This resulted in the publishing of 'toy books', which flourished, for example, in the hands of Edmund Evans, a London printer of the last quarter of the nineteenth century. He printed alphabet books by both Walter Crane and Kate Greenaway. Kate Greenaway's work included her version of *A Apple Pie* (reprinted 1979) and an alphabetically organised *Illuminated Language of Flowers* (reprinted 1978). Crane's books include *The Railway Alphabet*, *The Farmyard Alphabet*, *The Baby's Own Alphabet*, *Noah's Ark Alphabet*, *An Alphabet of Old Friends* and *The Absurd Alphabet* (the last two reprinted together in 1981). The Crane listing underlines

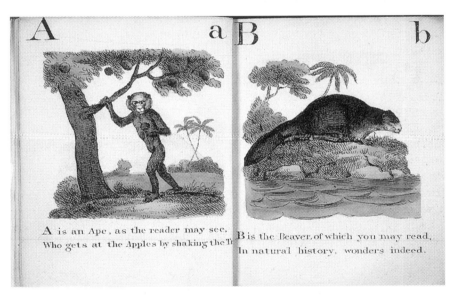

Figure 11.1 Frontispiece, title page and first page-opening from *An Alphabetical Arrangement of Animals for Little Naturalists* (1821), London: Harris & Son. Reproduced with the permission of the British Library (7207 a 11).

not only that such books were popular with the Christmas trade and important financially, but that the form challenged the artist – something that continues to be true as seen in the flourishing alphabet lists available today.

Alphabetical order

To look through a modern collection of these delights is to see how well-known picture-makers still are challenged to produce their version – Quentin Blake, Shirley Hughes, Satoshi Kitamura, Helen Oxenbury and Brian Wildsmith, to name but a very selective handful (Blake 1989; Hughes 1984; Kitamura 1991; Oxenbury 1971; Wildsmith 1962). Playing with the form is another aspect, building it into a story; for example, as Dragonwagon does with *Alligator Arrived with Apples: A Potluck Alphabetical Feast*, with its delicious alliteration (1987), or the element of intrigue in *Eye Spy*, which plays a game of puns, with an American accent: 'ant/Aunt' (Bourke 1991). There are books from other countries: for example, *Whatley's Quest*, an Australian publication (Whatley and Smith 1994) and *A is for Africa*, which explores life in Nigeria (Onyefulu 1994), or the *African Animals ABC* (Browne 1995). Robert Crowther took the alphabet into paper technology with *The Most Amazing Hide and Seek Alphabet Book*, with flaps to pull and lift (1977).

Many of the texts produced for young readers require or encourage the sharing of the book with an adult or experienced reader. With certain recent alphabets, it is difficult for the child to get a look in at all. *Animalia* by Graeme Base (1986) is one such, but by its title alone *The Ultimate Alphabet* by Mike Wilks (1986) earns the final comment (see Figure 11.2). In his introduction, he talks of the journey he has undertaken in its making, a journey without landscape through the English language with twenty-six stops. He sets up endless explorations for the reader, through complex collations of knowledge, identifying and making connections between 7777 seemingly disparate objects. He aims to make us believe that 'a marvel has happened there before our very eyes' – a long way from the minimalism of the horn-book (1986: i).

Conclusion

Arguments about the nature of reading, and the best (some say the *only*) way of teaching it, still dominate and divide. One aspect highlighted by the development of the alphabet book is the transference of focus from 'it' – the act of reading, seen as linear and sequential, to 'them' – the readers, their needs and interests. Modern alphabet books recognise the wide range of skills that even the youngest reader brings to the task of making meanings, which goes beyond mere sounds. These books also suggest that, because reading is more organic than linear, the visual and verbal skills of mature readers can be challenged. These complex readings are perhaps more like building the new three-dimensinal jigsaws – bits are added idiosyncratically and their full import is not

Figure 11.2 From Mike Wilks (1986) *The Ultimate Alphabet*, London: Walker Books.

always realised until other connecting pieces are in place. The challenge, to those who regularly share print with young readers, is to be aware of just what pieces are in place and, like all those educators of the past, to consider how to help young readers to recognise and acquire those as-yet-unrealised knowledges and connections that will help to put the rest in place. We need to be in command of all the complex mapping that makes up the process of reading, but we also need to keep our focus on individual readers as they begin to deal with the complexities of the meanings they are making.

References

Base, G. (1986) *Animalia* London: Macmillan.

Blake, Q. (1989) *Quentin Blake's A.B.C.*, London: Jonathan Cape.

Bourke, L. (1991) *Eye Spy a Mysterious Alphabet*, San Francisco, CA: Chronicle Books.

Browne, P.-A. (1995) *African Animals ABC*, Bath: Barefoot Books.

Crane, W. (1981 reprint) *An Alphabet of Old Friends* and *The Absurd Alphabet*, London: The Metropolitan Museum of Art/Thames and Hudson.

Crowther, R. (1977) *The Most Amazing Hide and Seek Alphabet*, London: Viking.

Dragonwagon, C. (1987) *Alligators Arrived with Apples: A Potluck Alphabet Feast*, ill. J. Aruego and A. Dewey, London: Julia MacRae Books.

Garratt, P. (1994) *After Henry*, London: Children's Books History Society.

Greenaway, K. (1987 reprint) *The Illuminated Language of Flowers*, London: Rinehart and Winston.

——(1884) *The Language of Flowers*, London: Derrydale Books.

Harvey Darton, F.J. (1932) *Children's Books in England: Five Centuries of Social Life*, Cambridge: Cambridge University Press.

Hilton, M., Styles, M. and Watson, V. (eds) (1997) *Opening the Nursery Door*, London: Routledge.

Hughes, S. (1984) *Lucy and Tom's a.b.c.* London: Victor Gollancz.

—— (1998) *Alfie's Alphabet*, London: Bodley Head.

Kitamura, S. (1991) *From Acorn to Zoo*, London: Andersen Press.

Locke, J. (1693) *Thoughts Concerning Education*, in J. L. Axtell (ed.) (1968) *Educational Writings of John Locke*, Cambridge: Cambridge University Press.

Meigs, C., Thaxter Eaton, A., Nesbitt, E. and Hill Viguers, R. (revised 1969) *The New England Primer*, London: Macmillan.

Muir, P. (1954) *English Children's Books 1600 to 1900*, London: Batsford.

Onyefulu, I. (1994) *A is for Africa*, London: Frances Lincoln.

Oxenbury, H. (1971) *Helen Oxenbury's A.B.C. of Things*, London: Fontana.

Roberts, M. (1998) *The Jungle ABC*, London: Thames and Hudson.

Spufford, M. (1997) 'Women teaching reading to poor children in the sixteenth and seventeenth centuries', in Wilks, M., Styles, M. and Watson, V. (eds) *Opening the Nursery Door*, London: Routledge.

Tuer, A. (1971 reprint) *The History of the Horn-Book*, Amsterdam: S. Emmering, The Usbourne Collection; noted in Catalogue.

Whatley, B. and Smith, R. (1994) *Whatley's Quest*, Sydney: Angus and Robertson.

Wildsmith, B. (1962) *Wildsmith's A.B.C.* Oxford: Oxford University Press.

Wilks, M. (1986) *The Ultimate Alphabet*, London: Pavilion.

Part IV

Meetings in imaginative spaces

In a recent review of the writings of Jorge Luis Borges, Michael Wood draws attention to 'the criss-crossing complicity of reality and fantasy'.[1] He points to the interconnectedness of the two, 'because fantasy is so rooted in reality that it always returns, like a boomerang, to the scene it meant to abandon'. The contributors to Part IV examine the relationship between reality and fantasy – the world of reason and the world of the imagination. When it comes to providing narratives for children, there are some highly charged and divergent views about the texts which should be on offer. Some commentators feel that in children's literature there has been too much emphasis on issues of modern life – drugs, divorce, violence – which drives children into the realities of adulthood too soon. For such critics of texts for children the world of the imagination is starved by such an emphasis. For others, the fantasy worlds of film and television seem to deny children the nourishment of creating their own imaginative narratives. Or, worse, they fear that children watching such fantasies might be driven to enact some of the more excessive and violent acts depicted in popular culture.

Jenny Daniels looks at some of the 'gritty realism' of Burgess, Walsh and Swindells, as well as the fantasy worlds of Pullman and Le Guin, arguing for a less definite distinction between fantasy and realism. Daniels points out that it is worth re-examining our views of what 'being a child' actually means. Perhaps adults avoid confronting the kinds of realities young people face in their everyday lives in a kind of nostalgic urge to protect them. The more responsible view would be not only to recognise that fantasy narratives can give difficult messages about how life might be lived and that tough, realistic stories can offer food for the imagination, but to acknowledge that children need both. The books she describes 'acknowledge the pain and pleasure of living' and 'signal the price which has to be paid if citizenship and commonality are abandoned'. David Whitley outlines his ideas of 'first age' and 'wisdom' fantasies, looking at popular culture as well as Garner and Le Guin to develop his view that fantasy narratives can 'engage seriously with key issues in contemporary culture'. Commercial interests may offer fantasies of the first age, whose optimism can hit a discordant note; wisdom fantasies suggest that 'within images of a distant past we can become alive to the horror and the wonder of the world'. Such literature, he asserts, may address itself to 'unacknowledged voids in modern culture'.

In an exploration of myth and legend, culture and morality, Eve Bearne argues that, because neither the morality nor the narratives themselves are stable, they demand that children weigh up issues of morality and become active readers and producers of texts and meanings, making some tough decisions as they go. Mythic stories help children to confront difference and sameness and to see that it may not be necessary to reconcile such opposites, but to acknowledge their coexistence. Not only do children gain from reading about people diversely represented and behaving towards each other in different ways, they also need to become producers of their own fantasies, retelling and talking about the stories, engaging in tricky matters of choice as they grow in interpretation of their expanding worlds.

Part IV ends, then, with imagination that allows us, as Ursula le Guin says, to 'get ... out of the bind of the eternal present', but also demands that we take risks in exploring the relationship between lived and imaginative worlds. Children can do this if we trust them to do so and help them to learn how to ask and to begin to answer some of the important questions.

Note

1   Michael Wood (1999) 'Productive Mischief', *London Review of Books*, 4 February.

Chapter 12

'Harming young minds'
Moral dilemmas and cultural concerns

Jenny Daniels

In May 1997, the *Guardian* newspaper featured two articles in the Home News section. The headline 'Child books on bullying and drugs "could harm young minds"' drew the reader's attention to issues found in recent fiction for children. The page included a large colour photograph of Anne Fine clutching her entry for the Carnegie medal, *The Tulip Touch* (Fine 1997). Other pictorial insets included Jacqueline Wilson, Arthur Ransome and C.S. Lewis. The article by Kaye Watson-Smyth set out the concerns expressed by a number of representatives about the short list for the Carnegie. All the books were 'controversial', covering topics such as teenage heroin addiction, arson, bullying and thieving. Nick Seaton from the Campaign for Real Education echoed the feelings of many parents when he said, 'The judges should be looking for books that present the happier side of life. I do not think it is idealistic to want to shield children from issues like drug abuse and bullying'. Later in the article, Philip Pullman retorts: 'you cannot ringfence childhood. Children should have a dose of artistic truthfulness, and some of these books are educational' (Pullman 1997).

The second article on that particular page carried the headline 'Nurses union urges action against "thin and beautiful body" adverts as survey shows children's worries over weight' (Watson-Smyth 1997). A recent survey showed that one in four children aged 11 are worried about being overweight and the figure rises to half sharing this fear by the time they are 16. Christine Hancock from the Royal College of Nursing said, in the same article,

> Our survey shows that the insecurities that children can feel about the way they look, from teenage spots to severe eating disorders because of worries about weight. It is all too easy to forget what it feels like to be young and insecure about your looks and appearance.

One very simple message is clear from reading this edition of a popular newspaper. It is not easy being a child in the late twentieth century! The juxtaposition of these articles has the coincidental effect of highlighting the tensions inherent in constructions of childhood. Some commentators feel that the world of fiction should be protected and protective; the 'real world' encourages children to feel unhappy about their bodies, to strive for the 'perfect shape'. It is only one example of the many concerns that children can internalise from their agency within the culture. Both articles carry a number of comments from professional bodies – or their representatives. Again, children's welfare, whether physical or emotional, provides a focus for public debate. This reflects an increasing concern from a large number of professional bodies as well as parents. In the current climate, it almost rises to a note of panic. From such highly charged issues comes moral confusion.

What is possible?

We called the conference 'Where Texts and Children Meet' held at Homerton College in September 1998, when most of the chapters here were first presented as papers, addresses, etc. The term 'text' was deliberate – we wanted to acknowledge and include a range of forms that give children access to what Bruner has called 'possible worlds' (Bruner 1986). We wanted to know what children themselves thought about the world they live in – and, more specifically, how they use texts of all kinds to enter both the 'possible worlds' and to deal with their existing worlds. How do they engage with the multitudinous amount of information with which they are bombarded on an average day? How do they select and reject? Do they understand the difference between fantasy and realism? Are such terms in themselves helpful? I cannot hope to answer such enormous questions – but it was fascinating to hear the views expressed at the conference. Neither am I solely interested in the debate triggered by the Carnegie award, but it does frame some of the argument. My texts in this chapter are three books: one written by a Carnegie winner, one by a 'new' writer and one by an established author. I want to demonstrate how valuable a work of fiction can be precisely because it does allow for the child reader to select and reject – indeed it would be a failure if thinking and decision-making were not inherent in the reading process. I argue that even the youngest reader has the power of discrimination and that, for young adults, fiction has never been so challenging and exciting.

The three books I focus on in this chapter are: Melvin Burgess's *The Baby and Fly-Pie* (1993), *Northern Lights* by Philip Pullman (1995) and *The Farthest Shore*, the third book from Ursula Le Guin's *Earthsea Quartet* (1972). Two of the writers have achieved notoriety through award-winning books. Burgess, in particular, has championed the right for younger readers to read about drug addiction and the sordid realities of living with heroin. His novel *Junk* (1997) won the Carnegie medal amidst a storm of media hype in 1997. It draws on social realism in dramatic and compelling ways – causing a similar effect to the film of Irvine Welsh's *Trainspotting* (1993), which was released in 1996. Welsh and Burgess are writers taking readers and viewers into new areas of experience: their knowledge of drug use and addiction is used to create a highly moral story – even if the detail can be disturbing. It is, of course, the drug issue which becomes sensationalised. What is more dramatic is the social world these writers describe. Their protagonists (it would be unfair to call them heroes/heroines) inhabit parts of our cities that we dare not venture into. We keep well away from the dangerous parts of town, we would not want to live next door to a squat. They belong to a statistic which is to be read about, moralised over and socially concerned about, but we never want to get too close. It is a dangerous world and one that is the result of crippling social policy over a long period of time. Can these writers be accused of voyeurism? They describe themselves as 'working-class' but their professional work excites the interest of middle-class liberals.

Yet it is perhaps less to do with old-fashioned concepts of class than a subtle set of social negotiations happening at a moment of historical circumstance. Robert Swindells, angered by insensitive comments from a Tory MP about the homeless, went to live on the streets in order to know what street life was like. The experience gave added depth to his *Stone Cold* (1993), but the real chill factor was the horrific account of the Rosemary West trial and the events in Cromwell Road. For anyone who had read *Stone Cold*, fact and fiction blurred, echoed and resonated in minds and imaginations in a disturbing pattern.

Burgess's *Junk* operated in a similar way. The media regularly reports on different solvents and pills used by young people. We read about deaths from Ecstasy tablets, particularly moved by the Leah Betts tragedy. It is the stuff of parent nightmares. We agonise about teenage children and the possibility of what might happen to them away from the safety/control of home. Burgess is not trying to shock us in his story of Tar and Gemma; they are, after all, two young people who try and work out a life together against a backdrop of adult indifference and social negligence. Burgess merely tells it how it is – that all kinds of drugs are available in every part of England and that young people (like many older ones) are attracted to a lifestyle and set of feelings denied them by everyday life. He certainly does not advocate drug use in the book. It might, as Burgess himself said, 'help a generation of drug abusers to pull back from the brink' (1997). Like *Trainspotting*, the open acknowledgement of an underclass, a number of people living among us, there, but invisible, is shaming and illuminating. It is also a far cry from Arthur Ransome or Enid Blyton – a safer and cosier world for children to make into 'possible worlds'.

Pullman is less controversial as a writer for children, but I would argue that his fantasies in *Northern Lights* have equally chilling connections with a form of social realism. Drawing on Greek mythology, the book is a well-written travel story or, more accurately, a quest. It, too, won the Carnegie medal, but with much less contention. Critics and literary pundits were probably relieved to award the prize for what could clearly be defined as the book's literary merit. *Northern Lights* is set in a hypothetical future and as readers we need not, initially, be concerned about down-and-outs, drug-abuse, social problems. The first few chapters are set in an Oxbridge College – surely the most reassuring scenario for literary critics! Yet, like Burgess, Pullman goes on to present a world that is grotesque in its social infrastructure. In *Northern Lights* there are several levels of alienated and disenfranchised groups. They are vulnerable and, when organised, clearly represent a threat to the government. State machinery moves in to control and destroy when necessary. This is not a childish fantasy – the book has Orwellian overtones and is just as disturbing, and possibly more chilling, than the books of so-called 'social realism'.

Ursula Le Guin is the most established and respectable author for children. *The Earthsea Trilogy* (now a quartet) delighted young readers for over thirty years: the series was timeless in feel, and the writing had an enduring quality. It is usually classified as fantasy and indeed much of the narrative is fantastical. Yet it also operates in a frame of realism, the language soars but the issues are firmly rooted in moral decision-making and realistic choices. And therein lies the rub. By looking at these books in more detail, I hope to show how inadequate the terms 'realism' and 'fantasy' actually are.

Denying humanity

Melvin Burgess's *The Baby and Fly-Pie* (1993) tells the story of a brother and sister, Davey and Jane, and their friend Sham. Set in a metropolis, the children live on the Tips, eking out an existence by going through rubbish and living off other people's waste. Burgess gives no indication as to how this came to be – the voice of Fly is ingenuous in tone but secretive in content. This has the effect of making the reader constantly ask questions and try to put together parts of the narrative deliberately omitted by Burgess. We do not know how the city has come to be a divided and totalitarian regime – but it has overtones of cities we read about, particularly large cities in South America. Davey and Sham work the tips for 'Mother', as members of a gang she 'protects' in exchange for salvaged goods. Davey is at pains to point out the advantage of being a 'rubbish kid'.

> We're the rubbish kids, Mother's boys and girls. Everyday we went out to the Tip to sort through the rubbish for Mother Shelly – all the metal here, all the furniture there, all the wood and all the paper in separate heaps for her to sell on as salvage. The Tips gave the Mothers a good living but we were always hungry. We didn't complain. We were orphans and losers and if it wasn't for Mother we'd be on the street. Some kids thought it was a laugh to run wild but they were the ones with someone to go back to when they needed them, the part timers. We'd have been proper street kids, the real thing, the ones who say, 'My Mother is the street, my Father shoots.' What they mean is there are only two things interested in them – the street, and the Death Squads.
> That's another thing about the Tips – no one tries to kill you.
> Me and my sister Jane used to be street kids before she got us out. On the street you have to beg and steal for pennies. Street kids sleep in shop

doorways or down subways and during the day they drift about like litter. You see them everywhere, skinny and ill and dirty and cold, cluttering the place up. Street kids are rubbish – real rubbish, not like Tip rubbish because that's useful.

When the streets get too messy they clean them up. They take you away and no one ever sees you go. People pretend that they take you to nice villages and towns where you have a proper life but we know better than that. The kids see everything.

(Burgess 1993: 6)

In this extract we can see Burgess operating at his best. The information is shocking, but the matter-of-fact tone of Davey's speech places the reader in a dilemma. We have to assimilate the cruelty of their existence, and at the same time accept it as part of the narrator's truth. Yet our moral faculties (for want of a better word) are actively questioning and rejecting the horror of children forced to live in such a way. Like Jonathan Swift before him, Burgess is prepared to vex us, to make us 'deny our humanity in order to provoke it' (Swift 1729). There is no sentiment in Davey's words – and Burgess is not seeking any. He merely 'tells it how it is' and Davey expects the reader to accept the inevitability of his life. Burgess, however, is the real authorial voice and we are enmeshed into a complicated and highly moral set of decisions by reading the book.

Burgess, like Swift, uses language for powerful effect. The leader of the protection racket is called Mother – a travesty of the usual connotations. Powerful, ruthless and an extortionist, she has no maternal characteristics and one suspects Burgess of having a little fun with gender/feminist issues. It is Mother who names Davey 'Fly-Pie' when he prepares a cake for her which, accidentally, contains a bluebottle. The tone of Davey/Fly's language is conversational and open. He speaks directly to the reader and the situation is explained in neutral tones. Burgess also uses dialogue to good effect and this makes the narrative accessible to a less experienced reader. Both of these serve to make the horror of the situation less dramatic.

Working the Tips one day, Fly and Sham discover a gunman hiding in a cardboard den. The man is wounded and still armed but the most startling fact is that the gunman has taken a baby as a hostage. The baby is distressed; hungry, filthy, and taped at the mouth to keep it quiet. Again, the reader is moved by the situation, a mixture of fear for the boys, compassion for the child and anger at the gunman. It is a gripping and chilling moment, charged with intense emotion. The boys are ordered to bring food and medicine back to the cardboard den. They agree, tempted by the large amount of money offered and genuine concern for the state of the baby.

Sham tore the strip of tape off the baby's mouth.

The baby gasped. It hurt. She stared at Sham. You could see how filthy she was – her mouth was white and red where the tape had been the rest of her was nearly black. Then she opened her mouth for the biggest loudest howl she had ever made. Sham stuck the bottle in.

The milk was cold, just out of the fridge in the shop. But she didn't care. She gargled and glugged for a second, seeing what it was. Then she wrapped her little hands around the bottle, curled up her legs, as if she wanted to wrap her whole self right around the bottle, and sucked and sucked and sucked ...

(Burgess 1993: 25)

Burgess conveys beautifully the baby's movements and the boy's tenderness. The primal need for food becomes the starting point for Fly's responsibility for the baby. It is a responsibility that will lead him into danger and even threaten his life. His commitment to the baby is heroic but never sentimental. The quest to return the baby to its parents becomes fraught with difficulties. Jane is involved in the quest and the subtle relations between the three young people is described with sensitivity and clear-sightedness; at no point does Burgess patronise or condescend. The subsequent reaction from the police and authorities is frightening in the extreme. At every point, the trio experience hostility, suspicion and very genuine fear, both physical and emotional. As readers, we are caught up in their plight, we begin to have some understanding of what it is to be an outcast, to be hunted, to have no one to trust. The climax of the novel is incredibly moving and sad. Hunted down and the baby returned, Fly and Jane face each other on the hillside:

Behind us were more sirens. Jane pulled a face. They've got their precious baby back, haven't they, what more do they want? She sniffed. They don't need to bother with us. A pair of rubbish kids we are ... She looked at me and pulled a face. You better get going. Don't worry about me. They'll lock me up. Plenty to eat and drink and all the rest and I'll talk and tell them what – you know me. They ought to know, didn't they? You run for it.

We hugged. Jane said, We just wanted a life, didn't we Dave? Then I left her. She was sitting back down on that heap of stones with her hands in her lap when I ran off, looking back the way they'd come.

(Burgess 1993: 189)

In simple words, Burgess makes such a powerful point about the right of any individual, whatever their background or status, to have a decent life. Jane is 'disposed of' a page later as the police and authorities find her still sitting on the pile of stones. Her resigned comment, 'they ought to know', is a sad indictment that, in this novel at least, most of the adults in positions of authority are at best indifferent, at worst cruel, to the plight of children, especially those who might be at risk. A natural sense of justice fuels the angry response to Jane's summary execution. It is a stark form of realism, but one that alerts the reader to the dangers of both ignorance and apathy.

Transforming ordinary experience

Northern Lights (1995) is also set in a hypothetical future, but it is a society which has a tighter structure and a clearer explanation of its history. Philip Pullman draws on an Homeric tradition of storytelling to write this first book of the Trilogy *Dark Materials* and, as the author himself describes the book, 'it is set in a universe like ours, but different in many ways'. We are introduced to Lyra, the heroine of the story, in a candid and straightforward manner. Lyra lives in Jordan College, cared for by the academic community. Like many children, she is fascinated by the forbidden – in this case the Master's study. Lyra, driven by curiosity, enters the room and explores the desk, portraits and artefacts. When the Master arrives, she is forced to hide behind a sofa, where she sees the Master pour a sachet of powder into a glass being prepared for a guest. The name of the visitor arouses Lyra's curiosity further, and she hides in a old wardrobe to await developments. Such a narrative, although well-written, is hardly original. What makes it memorable is the daemon on Lyra's shoulder. The idea of a physically separate consciousness/emotionality embodied in a living creature is an imaginative construction. The ability of the daemon then to change itself in direct relation to, in this case, Lyra's emotional response, makes the reader intrigued and curious. What kind of society is this? While the opening seems very conventional and reassuring, Pullman is at the same time subverting all our expectations, causing us to question. In the act of questioning, we are drawn from the sofa into Lyra's view of the world, and at the same time privileged to know exactly what she is feeling from the behaviour of her daemon Pantalaimon. As a narrative device, it is inspired: we not only have a direct line to Lyra's subconscious, hence making explicit the moral dilemmas which she confronts, but the dialogue between the two gives tremendous drama and tension to the events. Not surprisingly, the book was celebrated by several awards, including the Carnegie.

This early introduction of the daemon signals the difference to which Pullman alludes. It is particularly difficult to categorise this book into any one genre, least of all realist or fantasy. The subtle interplay between both is exploited to excellent effect. For example, just after the episode in the study Pullman describes Lyra:

> In many ways Lyra was a barbarian. What she liked best was clambering over the college roofs with Roger, the kitchen boy who was her particular friend, to spit plum stones on the heads of the passing Scholars or to hoot like owls outside a window where a tutorial was going on; or racing through the narrow streets, or stealing apples from the market or waging war.
>
> (Pullman 1995: 36)

In the tradition of great literature, Pullman could be describing the youthful Catherine Morland in Jane Austen's *Northanger Abbey* (Austen 1818). Unlike

Catherine, however, Lyra has a rather more important conquest to undertake than one of mere romantic conventions. She has been chosen to fulfil a particular destiny – one which will take her to uncharted territory and make her a prey to danger and evil. The Master of the College explains:

> 'Yes, Lyra has apart to play in all this, and a major one. The irony is that she must do it all without realising what she's doing. She can be helped, though, and if my plan with the Tokay had succeeded she would have been safer for a little longer. I would have liked to spare her a journey to the North. I wish above all things that I were able to explain it to her … '
> 'She wouldn't listen,' the librarian said. 'I know her ways only too well. Try to tell her anything serious and she'll half listen for five minutes and then start fidgeting. And quiz her about it the next time and she'll have completely forgotten.'
> 'If I talked to her about the dust? You don't think she'd listen to that?'
> The Librarian made a noise to indicate how unlikely he thought that was. 'Why on earth should she?' he said. 'Why should a distant theological riddle interest a healthy, thoughtless child?'
> 'Because of what she must experience. Part of that includes a great betrayal …
>
> (Pullman 1995: 33)

With such language Pullman draws on religious and grand narratives in what starts out to be a book for children. As with all good stories this is not exclusive to where texts and children meet – this is a book 'that all may read' (Blake 1789: 'Introduction'). The future is as bleak in this novel as it is in Burgess's work. Pullman develops the story as a quest in the fashion of Greek stories, so that the structure is strangely familiar even when the content disturbs. The book is full of magical allusions and a deep consciousness of otherworldliness. His skill as a writer is borne out by the seamless way in which these narratives blend into the more predictable adventure and excitement. But there is real energy in his writing, a muscular strength that comes from a writer who knows the craft of writing and the engagement of reading:

> Iorek Byrnson's paws made hardly any sound as they padded through the snow. The trees were thin and stunted here, for they were on the edge of the tundra, but there were brambles and snagging bushes in the path. The bear ripped through them as if they were cobwebs.
> They climbed the low ridge, among the outcrop of black rock, and were soon out of sight of the party behind them. Lyra wanted to talk to the bear, and if he had been human she would already be on familiar terms with him; but he was strange and wild and cold that she was shy, almost for the first time in her life. So he loped along, his great legs swinging tirelessly, she sat with the movement and said nothing. Perhaps she preferred it that anyway,

she thought; she must seem like a little prattling cub, only just beyond babyhood, in the eyes of the armoured bear.

(Pullman 1995: 209)

Pullman is able to conjure a style of writing that draws on the reader's memory, physical sensations of the present, Lyra's way of seeing the world and the topographical location of the action. Phrases like 'ripped through them as if they were cobwebs' bring to life the very vivid sensation of an ordinary experience transformed into a wonderfully powerful metaphor. Again, it would be limiting to ascribe this book to any particular genre. While it recognises and works within the real world, it is precisely the language that makes it different; different, that is, to the known universe. As readers we are trapped and enchanted by the possibilities of this 'possible world', content to suspend credibility in favour of a richer experience.

Fantastic and familiar

The third book I want to look at briefly is from the *Earthsea Trilogy* (now a quartet) by Ursula Le Guin. This is by far the most fantastic of the three/four books in that the normal triggers of social realism are difficult to find. Earthsea is a different land with its own map (helpfully provided in the frontispiece) and, for readers of the earlier books, a return to known characters and conflicts. There is an archaic feel to the story, but the writing bristles with tension and excitement. Again the effect of the classics can be noted in Le Guin's construction of the narrative and the characterisation in the novel. But it is the quality of the writing that demands attention.

The Farthest Shore (1972) tells the story of Prince Arren, accompanied by the Archmage, and their bid to save Earthsea from a nameless evil. The quest takes the young prince through a number of dangerous trials, always protected by Sparrowhawk. In the following sequence, Arren is with the raft people as they dance on the shortest night of the year.

> Arren danced with them, for the Long dance is held on every isle of the Archipelago, though the steps and songs may vary. But as the night drew on and many dancers dropped out and settled down to watch or doze, and the voices of the chanters grew husky, he came with a group of high leaping lads to the chief's raft, and there stopped while they went on. Sparrowhawk sat with the chief and the chief's three wives, near the temple. Between the carven whales that made its doorway sat a chanter whose high voice had not flagged all night long. Tireless he sang, tapping his hands on the wooden deck to keep time.
>
> 'What does he sing of?' Arren asked the Mage, for he could not follow the words, which were all held long with trills and strange catches on the notes.

'Of the grey whales and and the albatross, and the storm … They do not know the songs of the heroes and the kings. They do not know the name of Erreth-Akebe. Earlier he sang of Segoy, how he established the lands amid the sea. That much they remember; the lore of men. But the rest is all of the sea.'

(Le Guin 1974: 141)

The mythical quality of Le Guin's writing is evident. While the action is made explicit, the subject matter is written with the knowledge of another mystical universe. The language is rich and dramatic, the sentence constructions are strange. We can visualise the scene and that helps us to understand the metaphorical allusions in the text. Yet they are difficult to put into words. Le Guin, although an expert in the use of words and language, recognises that words also have the power to defy any crude form of analysis. We are swept into the story yet never left to flounder. Such is her skill that, as with poetry, we suspend belief and enjoy the thrill of the ride. Some readers actively dislike Le Guin, possibly because they are unable to tolerate ambiguities, to surrender to the control of an imaginative writer. Yet her writing is rooted in realism and the conflation of Earthsea with a more familiar world is constantly in tension. The beauty of the language to do this and create its own identity is a particular gift. She presents a realism which is inexorable – the realism of error, arrogance, fear, hope, betrayal and redemption – through language which is both strange and familiar.

Conclusion

I started this chapter with the premise that children at the end of the twentieth century are bombarded with all kinds of difficulties and concerns that exist as part of normal living. Perhaps every generation has had to face difficulties; one could argue that children are much more vulnerable, for example, in times of war. But there is a pernicious element to modern childhood. The very fact that childhood itself is under question, the recognition that children can, and do, commit murder has resulted in uneasy relationships, particularly from professional associations concerned with children. And the children themselves? How do they start to define themselves against a culture that sends out such conflicting messages and no clear idea of what 'being a child' actually is?

In these grey areas, it seems to me that the kind of books discussed here play an invaluable role. They are not conduct books: the writers themselves are anxious to distance themselves from such a position. But they all acknowledge the pain and pleasure of living, the courage it takes to make the right decisions, the difficulty of making personal ambitions commensurate with wider social demands. All three of the books cited here, in their different ways, also signal the price that has to be paid if citizenship and communality are abandoned. In the ever-increasing isolationism of individuals at the end of the millennium, such warnings should not be ignored. As Pullman said, 'we cannot ringfence childhood', and it is the role of literature to throw light and understanding on the deeper issues at work in ourselves and society. Literature may not be our salvation, but it does help us all, whether child or adult readers, to recognise the agencies at work within our society, and to reflect on our responsibilities. Jerome Bruner puts it succinctly:

> Literature subjunctivizes, makes strange, renders the obvious less so, the unknowable less so as well, matters of value more open to reason and intuition. Literature in this spirit is an instrument of freedom, lightness and imagination, and yes, reason. It is our only hope against the long, gray night.
>
> (Bruner 1986: 17)

References

Austen, J. (1818) *Northanger Abbey*, Harmondsworth: Penguin.

Blake, W. (1789) *Songs of Innocence and Experience*, Harmondsworth: Penguin.

Bruner, J. (1986) *Actual Minds, Possible Worlds*, Cambridge, MA: Harvard University Press.

Burgess, M. (1993) *The Baby and Fly-Pie*, Harmondsworth: Penguin.

——(1997) *Junk*, London, Andersen Press.

Fine, A. (1997) *The Tulip Touch*, Harmondsworth: Puffin.

Le Guin, U. (1972) *The Farthest Shore*, London, Victor Gollancz.

Pullman, P (1995) *Northern Lights*, London, Scholastic Children's Books.

Swift, J. (1729) Letter to Pope, 29th September, 1725. Taken from Williams, H. (1963) *The Correspondence of Jonathan Swift*, London: Clarendon Press.

Swindells, R (1993) *Stone Cold*, London, Hamish Hamilton.

Watson-Smyth, K. (1997) 'Child books on bullying and drugs "could harm young minds"', *Guardian*, 7 May 1997, p. 7.

Welsh, I. (1993) *Trainspotting*, London: Minerva Press.

Chapter 13

Fantasy narratives and growing up

David Whitley

> First there's the children's house of make believe,
> Some shattered dishes underneath a pine,
> The playthings in the playhouse of the children.
> Weep for what little things could make them glad.
>
> (Robert Frost, 'Directive')

In our culture the link between the 'other world' of make-believe and childhood is extremely strong; fantasy is the very starting point of narrative, its first 'house'. And the loss of that house is recalled, almost universally, with a sense of plangent sorrow: 'Weep for what little things could make them glad'. The inference would seem to be that children grow out of their need for make-believe as they mature, and that their ability to recreate the world afresh from its small particulars, once lost, is in some profound sense irrecoverable.

Yet even a nodding acquaintance with the canon of Western literature would seem to throw this view into doubt. Taken in its broadest sense, much of what has been most enduring in the writing of Chaucer, Malory, Spenser, Swift, Cervantes, Rabelais, not to mention the Romantic poets, could be taken to reside within the realm of fantasy. Even Dante, Milton and Shakespeare (at least in some of the comedies and romances) could be deemed to have written epic or dramatic fantasies. Fantasy in this wider sense is not a specialism; its forms may vary from age to age, but the alternative to mimetic art, the urge to draw on an imaginative realm that goes beyond the claims of ordinary experience and the strictly plausible, has always existed as a counterpart to realism in the making of stories.

Here, then, is a seeming contradiction. On the one hand fantasy is a timeless mode, inflected within various forms within different cultures and at different historical phases, but as central to adult as to child experience. From another perspective, though, fantasy narratives are affiliated to childhood, particularly early childhood. In this latter sense they would seem to contain something which we believe we must give up as we mature into adulthood, a Neverland in which only lost boys (and girls!) are allowed endlessly to defy death and the claims of experience over an ultimately triumphant optimism. In what follows, I would like to consider this seeming contradiction in more depth.

Two types of fantasy

Many fantasy narratives attempt to distil experience into the interplay of fixed dualities (good/evil, light/dark, and so on) and in a similar interpretive spirit I would like to propose two main kinds of fantasy itself. These relate partly to different stages of development, but they are also distinct 'types' of fantasy narrative in their own right.

The first type I shall call 'fantasies of the first age', a title derived from what is surely one of the great fantasies of early literature, *Sir Gawain and the Green Knight*. King Arthur's court in this story is described as being all 'in their first age' and the action that follows could be taken as a searching test of the quality of idealism in youth. Fantasies of the first age, more generally, seem to be conceived in a spirit of optimism. They may take on hard conflicts, but they tend to ride out the vicissitudes and uncertainties of life with a zestful pleasure. For all the ups and downs of the narrative, there is an underlying confidence that things will sort themselves out in a satisfying way, which leaves the spirit of joy intact. A good model for fantasy of the first age stories is perhaps Shakespeare's *A Midsummer Night's Dream*: the presiding spirit is the anarchic Puck, and the moonlight that constitutes the play's aura casts no shadows so harsh as to counteract its youthful energies.

In contrast stands a second type of narrative which, for neatness' sake, one might call 'fantasy of the second age', though in fact I prefer the term 'wisdom fantasy', since this suggests a relationship with the ancient 'wisdom' literature of proverb, fable, prophecy and riddle. In this second type of fantasy narrative, the presiding spirit is age rather than youth, even though the protagonists may themselves be young. The stories may end on a positive note, having harmonised conflicting forces in a manner that appears superficially similar to that of fantasies of the first age, but the tone and thematic emphasis will be different. Wisdom fantasies tend to focus centrally on the theme of death; the struggle of their protagonists is likely to involve an effort of immense self-control, an inner discipline. The exuberant and expressive delight of fantasies of the first age is countered by more sobre forces of containment: a measured, weighty sense of the cost of experience and loss. If you compare Shakespeare's *The Tempest* with *A Midsummer Night's Dream*, you may get some feeling for the distance, as well as potential overlap, between the two forms.

I am not proposing that these two types of narrative form any absolute opposition. I think of them as functioning rather more like what William Blake called 'contraries'. Indeed, within their contrasting forms one might well detect something analogous to the contraries Blake himself formulated and explored through the concepts of 'innocence' and 'experience'. There are echoes, too, perhaps, of some of the opposing categories Freud used to characterise the inner drama of the mind: 'id' versus 'superego'; or (even more pertinently from Freud's later thinking) 'thanatos' – the death instinct – opposed to the life force, 'eros'. Many fantasy narratives are likely to have some features relating to both the 'types' I have sketched above. Even what could be taken to be the archetypal fantasy of the first age within children's literature – Barrie's *Peter Pan* – is made more moving and complex through shading its central preoccupation with adventures within the realm of eternal youth with viewpoints deriving from the second type of narrative I have termed wisdom fantasy:

> Peter was not quite like other boys but he was afraid at last. A tremor ran through him, like a shudder passing over the sea; but on the sea one shudder follows another till there are hundreds of them, and Peter felt just the one. Next moment he was standing erect on the rock again, with that smile on his face and a drum beating within him. It was saying, 'To die will be an awfully big adventure'.
>
> (Barrie 1988 [1906]: 11)

The shock of mortality touches even Peter Pan momentarily.

Narratives intended for very young children are, perhaps naturally, most infused with qualities associated with 'fantasies of the first age'. Stories as different as Shirley Hughes' *Up and Up* (1979), Mick Inkpen's *The Blue Balloon* (1989) or John Burningham's *Where's Julius?* (1986) share an irreverent sense that the disturbances created within their magically implausible plot lines are pleasurable and life-enhancing. Hughes and Inkpen allow the reader to follow their fantasies through with unrestrained exuberance, whereas writer/illustrators such as Maurice Sendak, in *Where the Wild Things Are* (1967), may enclose the wildness and freedom of child fantasy subtly within a boundary of adult consciousness. But in each case the free play of the imaginative realm is endorsed, albeit tempered to different degrees by adult realism.

Blurring the boundaries

Some recent writers for children – Anthony Browne is perhaps the most complex and accomplished recent example – have figured child characters in their stories who are no longer free to enjoy the fictive world they inhabit on the pleasurable terms that 'first-age fantasies' largely offer. Browne's child characters often struggle or are oppressed by their environments, in challenging ways that seem more consonant with realist writing for older children than the optimistic fantasy narratives of 'early years' authors. His stories do not generally fit the terms of 'first age fantasies': it is almost as though, within the contemporary culture of childhood, the story must set itself against conditions which oppress in order to release – once more – the energies of lighter, more innocent pleasure. Browne's stories tend to be more parables of emotional regeneration than tales within which youthful energies are available intact, to be acted out and tested within the world. In *Gorilla* (1983), for instance, the young girl protagonist is portrayed as emotionally starved, her father's energies drained by the work culture within which he is immersed. The gorilla in the story – a father-substitute fantasy – is a kind of missing link with a more natural and spontaneous past. It is also a subtle but mordant critique of certain aspects of contemporary work culture and their effects. The emptiness of the child's world (expressed most poignantly through the illustrations) and the critique of adult values (which borders on social satire) are darker tones than 'first age fantasy' normally admits. Browne, like William Blake, seems to work with a powerful sense of the 'mind forged manacles' that operate even within the terrain of innocence to which childhood is affiliated.

Anthony Browne's books are perhaps liminal, in this respect. They operate on an intermediate terrain between first age and wisdom fantasies. In writing for older children, and in longer, more developed forms of fantasy narrative, the issue of what checks the flow of 'energy as delight' becomes increasingly critical. Good fantasy writing is not really a retreat from the difficulties of the world into an imaginative safe haven, even though the wish-fulfilment elements of many fantasy narratives may act with restorative power. Rather the selection of events that run counter to the terms of ordinary human experience must be justified. The inventiveness of fantasy becomes empty if it is merely self-serving, but rich and interesting if it allows identifiable human dilemmas to be explored from new angles. Since fantasy invokes the possibility of living under different terms and conditions, the new world it activates inevitably invites comparison with our own. For this reason it is often claimed that fantasy writing is more Utopian than its realist counterpart, though at certain periods the dystopian elements have been just as strong and have sometimes predominated. From the point of view of the present argument, though, we need to be aware of the way fantasy can engage with experience in this world, even as invention flies from it. The wish-fulfilment it offers needs to be grounded in something substantial if it is to become fully satisfying. In a society that constantly draws on fantasy to stimulate our desires as consumers, this latter consideration is likely to be particularly critical and complex. This is especially true within the realm of popular culture, where the pleasure principle operates with most immediacy and force.

Consider, for example, George Lucas's original *Star Wars* trilogy. Here the ballast to the special-effects thrills of the space adventure yarn is supplied by mythic elements in the plot structure. Lucas has acknowledged that he drew, loosely and imaginatively, on his memories of Arthurian literature. The familial plot, with its discoveries and climax in a struggle to the death between father and son, also has loose affinities to a number of classical myths. More pertinently in the present context, the films appear to centre on some of the key themes and motifs of 'wisdom fantasies'. Luke Skywalker's quest to become a Jedi knight is imbued with the characteristics of the mage/warrior's training and self-discipline, while the philosophical colouring given to the classic conflict between good and evil – the 'force' – is similar in some respects to Eastern religious concepts such as the Tao. Discipline, understanding and inner balance are required to use the power, which accrues from knowledge successfully. Yet, for all these trappings, *Star Wars* remains essentially a 'fantasy of the first age', full of comic inventiveness, light in tone, and allowing the youthful optimism of its protagonists full play within the realms of adventure and spectacle. It is well-executed entertainment: its weightier elements are not designed to be taken too seriously but to give it balance – and perhaps commercially to promote its cult status.

Within contemporary culture it is difficult for popular narrative forms to embrace the concerns of wisdom fantasies with any great seriousness, even though the prevalence of gestures towards these areas may imply recognition of a growing need in young adults. The playfulness with which *Star Wars* incorporates the fake gravitas of its cosmic philosophy is matched in the 1990s spate of *Batman* films by a characteristically modern (or perhaps postmodern) tone of self-conscious mockery. Each time the script's exploration of Batman's sense of responsibility and need for control starts to get too sententious, there is a swerve into comedy or an action sequence drawing in his sidekick Robin's youthful, less disciplined energies. In *Batman Forever*, Batman's commitment to his superhero quest is rationalised as a kind of psychopathology: the half-buried memory of having witnessed – helplessly – his parents death as a child is offered as the traumatic inspiration for Batman's one-man crusade. Batman's mission to protect the world from evil is then projected not as simply noble: it is as much neurotic, even disturbed, as it is idealistic. This pop psychoanalysis, though not terribly convincing in itself, feeds into a modern scepticism about the roots of altruism as well as skewing the film's masculinist power fantasy into a parodic form, more palatable to postfeminist audiences of the 1990s. But the tongue-in-cheek play with the quest motif so fundamental to wisdom fantasies alters the terms on which we engage with the story. At their best, wisdom fantasies provoke in us an acute sense of our mortal being. The *Batman* films deal largely in pastiche and convention, archly ironised. The dark visual aura created within the films, the focus on an intensely self-contained central character enigmatically leached of emotional affect, serves to heighten our awareness not of mortality but of perversity. It is the grotesque world inhabited by Batman's extravagantly weird enemies and the perverse, often eroticised instincts given full expression there that attract viewers. This is not so much the terrain of wisdom fantasy as of a special kind of urban neo-Gothic.

Wisdom fantasy and politics

Some of the most popular fantasies devised for older children take on the motifs and colouring of second age wisdom fantasies, then, but they do not engage their audience in the same way. Although they must tell a story which is gripping, novelists who use fantasy forms are perhaps freer to adopt a more serious attitude to their material and to exploit its speculative potential more fully.

Obviously, the secondary worlds in which such writers situate their plots remain highly selective. Fantasy writers tend to turn to the past to get their bearings and the quasi-feudal pastoral settings of much conventional fantasy fiction seem particularly to exclude consideration of political dimensions of characters' lives in any very relevant modern sense. We live in a century intensely aware of political meanings, of course (even if many perceive themselves as alienated from conventional politics). In this context, the great fantasy writers of our age – J.R.R. Tolkien, C.S. Lewis. Mervyn Peake, Ursula Le Guin – may appear escapist in their evocation of worlds so distant from our own, however intensely realised. A writer such as Alan Garner, who works on a borderline between social realism and fantasy, is able to inflect his fiction with a subtle yet powerful sense of class and regional struggles embedded within the communities he writes about. More characteristically, though, fantasy literature simplifies social and even moral structures in order to heighten a sense of the underlying spiritual dimensions. The wisdom in wisdom fantasies takes symbolic forms: the adventure or quest leads it into a realm more grounded in metaphysical speculation and existential crisis than in any directly political agenda.

One might speculate that for many young adults the need for fictional forms that embody both these elements is especially crucial. Within our largely secular culture most adults feel insecure or even embarrassed about engaging in metaphysical discussions with young people as they move beyond the charmed circle of childhood. Even sex is an easier topic. Likewise, the deeply held convictions and values which should bring political debate to life can seem locked into the ritualised attachments of adulthood in ways that alienate young people. Yet bringing these elements together in fictional forms is in many ways a daunting challenge and it is perhaps not surprising that, in the past, fantasy narratives have been most compelling when they have excluded both sex and politics from significant consideration. Taking out the great preoccupations of the late twentieth century can allow some strange and original visions: the chasteness and purity of impulse found in fantasy forms of writing often constitutes part of their power and attraction.

Of course, not all fantasy writers have accepted this embargo, however. The sections of Alan Garner's *Red Shift* (1973) that are set in the present, for instance, focus centrally on a young male's difficulties in coming to terms with his sexuality. Yet the fantasy element of the story relies on a device relating the present, intensively but also mysteriously, to a pattern of events from key moments in the past. Garner's evocation of what it means to grow up in 1970s Britain is not overtly political, though it does offer trenchant observations on consumer culture from the outsider's viewpoint of those with little or no money. But the fantasy device of asserting the centrality of certain nodal points from the past within the experience of the present is *implicitly* highly charged with political significance. Garner's decision to layer contemporary experience with violent, graphic scenes from struggles for power during the English civil war and the period of Roman occupation embeds the central narrative within both conflict generated through radically opposed political ideals and the bloody realpolitik of colonial occupation. In writing that asserts a cyclical view of history there is always some danger that any critical sense of human responsibility and agency in the present may seem to be overpowered by irrevocable, mysterious and largely unconscious patterns from the past. Few readers will, however, leave Garner's *Red Shift* without being stung into a painful, if unresolved, sense of the symbolic connectedness of sexual and political experience at its widest reaches. In offering this connectedness in such a hard-edged and austere manner (albeit tempered with a strong sense of the redemptive power of love) Garner is aligned with narratives of growing up that I have termed wisdom narratives. His young male protagonist's exuberant wordiness, wit and keen sense of irony are playful in ways that only superficially resemble fantasies of the first age. The undertone is continually grave, serious, potentially tragic.

Garner's use of fantasy to establish correspondences between past and present may run the risk of reducing the complexity of current conflicts to violent archetypes associated mythically with particular places and times in history. Yet the gain is a terrific sense of imaginative extension, a break with the potential parochialism of the present and, implicitly, a revaluation of both past and present perspectives. For writers whose narratives remain within the sphere of their secondary other worlds, the problems (and dangers) are somewhat different. In these more 'classic' fantasy narratives the other world is deliberately distanced from contemporary concerns and features. Yet, in the finest of these narratives, this isolation is used, paradoxically, to intensify a particular form of engagement with aspects of contemporary experience. J.R.R. Tolkien. for instance, claimed that even that most medieval of fantasies, *Lord of the Rings* (1954–5), emerged partly from fears generated through the rise of fascism in mid-century Europe. Subsequent fantasy writers of quality have wrestled with a dialectic in which escape from the politicised culture of the late twentieth century allows an alternative perspective on contemporary issues to emerge. Ursula Le Guin's *Earthsea Quartet* (1993) is perhaps one of the finest examples of this tendency.

Making strange: the politics of other worlds

Le Guin is a magnificent storyteller. Her plots are largely linear; they tend to work through events sequentially and from a single perspective, the apparently simple narrative structure being matched by a sense of having pared down the constituents of experience to those elements which really matter. There is thus a sustained seriousness of tone, which in lesser writers could become overbearing or monotonous, but which in the *Quartet* remains gripping. In part this is because the spare, weighty style is so perfectly suited to the subject matter of the stories, in which the hero's quest for knowledge and power as a mage necessitates shedding every trace of vain ambition and moving beyond ordinary human needs. To make this *via negativa*, whose dominant tone is muscularly ascetic, into a compelling, even exhilarating adventure is the work of great craftsmanship and imagination. The use of material found frequently in wisdom fantasies – the hero's apprenticeship to a mage who will define his task, the images embodying evil, the struggles with forces representing the abuse of power and the paradoxes of death and life – all these are handled with a depth and range that makes *Star Wars* seem trivial by comparison.

Yet there are problems. The series was first conceived as a trilogy. The middle book, *The Tombs of Atuan* (1971), could be read as a kind of liberation narrative as well as quest: in it, a young high priestess, Tenar, begins to question her role within the sacred mysteries of ancient catacombs requiring human sacrifice. She is eventually rescued by the hero, Ged. This sounds a conventional enough formula, but Le Guin develops her material with searching acuity. She allows the central images to become suggestive of a wide range of meanings – anthropological and social, as well as moral, emotional, psychological – so that the dramatic focus of the 'tombs' ends up as rich in implication as the imaginative set pieces on which Spenser worked such evocative spells in *The Faerie Queene*. Le Guin's work, indeed, seems to me to have more in common with the old masters of allegorical romance than is often recognised.

Among the themes worked with in this section are the gendered roles assigned to men and women with their different drives, social positioning and destinies. Although this is contained within the traditional narrative framework of 'hero rescuing distressed lady', the result is less clichéd and more open to questions than this framework might imply. In the last novel, *Tehanu* (the fourth book in the series, first published in 1990, some seventeen years after the trilogy was completed), Tenar asks challengingly, 'Which of us saved the other from the Labyrinth, Ged?' (Le Guin 1993: 522). The question of women's power, as well as men's, has been made explicit.

Although the central book in the trilogy is concerned with women's power as well as men's, the narrative is aware but not driven by its sense of gendered difference or inequality. In *Tehanu*, however, the plot turns explicitly on the issue of inequality and social change. Here the fantasy novel has become fully political. For all the medieval trappings, Le Guin's reprise to the *Earthsea Trilogy* stakes its claim clearly within the modern ideological terrain of feminism. The plot turns on a profound sense of change within the Earthsea universe, focusing ultimately on the resistance, fear and hope engendered by the idea of woman as spiritual leader – the 'archmage'. Tehanu, the figure who is ultimately revealed as the hero Ged's successor, is a living emblem of the most extreme manifestations of male oppression. Abused and raped as a child, her face is hideously scarred by the burning inflicted as punishment for her 'crime' in having endured this male cruelty. The novel is full of reflections on the profound differences between men and women and climaxes in the defeat of an evil wizard, who represents the hatred of intense misogyny.

This sketch of the contents of the trilogy/quartet is designed to give a sense of the degree to which the novel is ideologically focused, but (again) can give little insight into what Le Guin does with her material. In many ways she is at full stretch in terms of craftsmanship in deploying her power as a novelist. The material is as coherently, imaginatively and intelligently worked with as in the best of her fiction. Yet there is a greater risk in colonising such explicitly ideological ground. This risk lies not so much in anything so banal as that ideas are allowed to dominate over plot, or character development or subtlety of design. Le Guin has too strong a sense of the art in her creations to allow any such crude propagandist substitutions to take effect. The risk lies rather within the nature of the wisdom fantasy form within which she has chosen to work. In order to invest that form with the ideological cutting edge of feminism, she must make its grasp of the constituents of ordinary, day-to-day, mundane reality register more strongly than is usually the case. Feminism's distinction is to put domestic, as well as political and economic, concerns at the centre of its agenda. To do so seriously Le Guin's novel must stoop to consider the implications of the hero's aptitude for tidying up and doing the dishes, alongside the grand theme of despair after sacrificing his magical powers. Tenar's feelings about her humdrum role as wife and mother must be pitched against the heroic caste of her identity shaped in *The Tombs of Atuan*. To attempt not just to mix but to use these contrasting spheres of experience dialectically – each serving to challenge and re-evaluate the terms of the other – is supremely difficult. At a stroke pathos may come to seem more like bathos, and wonder and grandeur collapse into banality. Moreover, the writer must take risks with the language, as well as content of her chosen form.

To take one example from many possible, consider Tenar's assessment of the new redeemer King Lebannen of Enlad, after she has been rescued by him:

> His hair was dark and soft, his skin a clear bronze-red; he was dressed well and plainly, with no chain or ring or outward mark of authority, but he looked the way a king should look she thought ...
>
> (Le Guin 1993: 603)

and later, concluding their discussion:

> He rose at once. 'Lady Tenar, you say you fled from one enemy and found another; but I came seeking a friend, and found another.' She smiled at his wit and kindness. What a nice boy he is, she thought.
>
> (Le Guin 1993: 605)

'What a nice boy he is': Le Guin counterpoints the dominant tone of gravity and decorum in speech here with the unselfconscious homeliness of the language within which Tenar's reflection is couched. You get a measure of the risk such a linguistic experiment takes if you consider the effect of one of the apostles pausing to reflect 'what a nice boy' Christ was after some uncommon gesture of sympathy in the Gospels. The homely phrasing punctures the high seriousness of the tone, and potentially undermines the reader's commitment to perceiving the male figure as hero. Superficially this looks similar to the kind of self-conscious parodying of the masculinist heroic ideal that takes place in popular contemporary action films such as *Batman*. But I would argue there is a critical difference. The self-conscious play with gendered images that takes place in popular films is generally designed to make earlier conventions palatable to sophisticated modern audiences. The pleasure the film offers is its licence, within the terms of ironic play, to enjoy the contradiction of both traditional masculinist ideal *and* its feminist counterchallenge. Audiences are not put under any pressure to resolve this contradiction: it is simply part of a postmodern recycling of older forms, a commercially orientated repackaging through irony of the pleasures associated with traditional heroic exploits. The context in *Tehanu* is quite different. Here the ironic, homely phrasing emphasises the point that Tenar has opted out of the masculine versions of the quest for ultimate knowledge and humane power, centring herself, with strength, in a more limited, mundane world. We are not invited to participate in an easy resolution or pleasurable enjoyment of contradiction. The text has an uncomfortable, more challenging edge; it refuses to lose touch with the personal cost of social change, and remains a wisdom fantasy in a much more full-bodied sense.

Ursula Le Guin's *Earthsea Quartet* suggests that we do indeed have to give up something when we follow the fantasy mode through within its most fully realised forms. What we give up, though, is not the urge, the fundamental drive, towards fantasy itself. *Tehanu* finishes with an image of the female will to power, within the figure of the new mage in the making, which is every bit as fantastical as the male versions that have preceded it. Clearly profound questions are opened up in this process, but what readers have to give up, more specifically, is their allegiance to a form of authority and way of seeing that is invested in a single, central character. Ged's authority and heroic stature is essentially broken, and then remade, in different forms and with different sources of power. One should not underestimate the sense of loss involved in this process: it is this, I think, rather than the more explicit political dimensions, that results in some readers feeling disappointed by *Tehanu*, the last novel in the quartet. But this loss is also essential to the process of growing up, of moving beyond the control (if not the love) of parental figures, and of dealing with the process of change which includes death. It may even be, as some have argued, that all fantasy narratives are, in this profound sense, about the process of growing up; though some are obviously more successful than others in embodying this grand theme. If the distinction I have argued for between fantasies of the first age and wisdom fantasies is useful, it is partly because it offers to differentiate some of the more subtle shadings of tone and approach within stories whose starting point is almost invariably youthful.

I have argued that fantasy narratives can engage seriously with key issues within contemporary culture. Despite this, however, the fantasy novel remains rooted in a sense of strangeness which is not just the licence to move beyond the plausible. It is also its assertion of the challenge of the past, in terms of both its wisdom and intractability. Alan Garner's novels tend to be set in the present, but the fantasy element within them allows access to a often terrifying connectedness with the past that, nevertheless, opens the possibility of awakening to fuller consciousness. Le Guin's *Earthsea Quartet* remains much more fully contained within the rhythms, forms and social structures of imagined preindustrial societies. Yet here, too, current concerns – with ecology, with feminism, power and responsibility – are engaged with centrally. It is in the dialogue between past and present that the best fantasy writing is forged, the strange worlds that ensue allowing both a different quality of connections and a – paradoxically escapist – reassertion of fundamental terror, beauty and power in the universe. Growing up in a world where commercial interests promote the optimism and irreverent energy of 'fantasies of the first age' as a source of continual pleasure, a false note can be sounded. Wisdom fantasies, at their best, provide a check to the promotion of false optimism within youth culture. They offer an alternative to the often bleak discordances of realism and a sense that within images of a distant past we can become alive to both the horror and the wonder of the world in ways it is now hard to recover. At difficult stages of growing up, young people often need what their grandparents can tell them more than their parents. Yet those voices from the past are not always available to them in forms to which they can relate. It may be that fantasy literature addresses itself to such unacknowledged voids in modern culture.

References

Barrie, J.M. (1988) *Peter Pan*, London: Viking Kestrel. First published 1906.
Browne, A. (1983) *Gorilla*, London: Julia MacRae.
Burningham, J. (1986) *Where's Julius?*, London: Jonathan Cape.
Garner, A. (1973) *Red Shift*, London,: Collins.
Hughes, S. (1979) *Up and Up*, London: The Bodley Head.
Inkpen, M. (1989) *The Blue Balloon*, Sevenoaks, Kent: Hodder and Stoughton.
Le Guin (1993) *The Earthsea Quartet*, Harmondsworth: Penguin.
Sendak, M. (1967) *Where the Wild Things Are*, London: The Bodley Head.
Tolkien, J.R.R. (1974) *The Lord of the Rings*, London: George Allen & Unwin.

Chapter 14

Myth, legend, culture and morality

Eve Bearne

Families, schools and communities all bear responsibility for encouraging children to behave according to agreed practices of justice, tolerance, fairness, respect, honour. Even if the concept of 'honour' might vary from culture to culture, there is nevertheless a charge on the older members of the society to develop the acceptable behaviours of the group. In any society there are implicit and often explicit expectations about how older people, children, men and women should be treated and should behave. Even Governments (in the United Kingdom, through the Office for Standards in Education, or OFSTED) now have powers to check on the ways schools foster spiritual and moral development. All this adds up to a drive towards agreed rule-following. At the same time, most communities want to foster independence, innovation and imagination. Stories offer meeting places for these different cultural imperatives. When we tell stories to children we want to enthral and transport them into the world of the imagination, but we also want them to learn about how life should be lived. Children's stories are expected both to instruct and delight. Instruction-through-story is a tradition in all cultures and in most families, from the everyday anecdote to the well-formed and often-repeated fable, teaching story or parable. And many of the kinds of stories used to teach moral truths are myths, legends or folk tales, orally told and passed on through cultures and communities.

In this chapter I want to look at myth and legend as vehicles for moral teaching. However, while these tales are very much part of the canon of 'children's literature' they present some problems. In the first place they were not, at first, 'literature', but sprang from oral cultures. They were not told for children, but for adults (although no doubt some children might have been around at the time). And if they are meant to teach, their morality is sometimes highly ambiguous. This raises questions about whether these stories ought to be seen as 'suitable' for instructing children, particularly since neither morality nor traditional narratives themselves are stable; they both change according to cultural context. A European notion of honour may not match that of honour enacted in Southeast Asia, for example. One religion's view of reaching heaven through hard work and diligence may not necessarily be matched by other religious beliefs; virtue and spirituality may not always be seen to reside in deeds. Equally, tales that carry moral and spiritual messages change according to who is telling them.

Shifting the blame

Many people reading this will be familiar with the Pandora story; a woman, instructed not to open a box, is overcome by curiosity, gives in to temptation and releases wickedness into the world. This has echoes, of course, of Eve's temptation of Adam. Even modern versions place the blame firmly with Pandora who was seduced:

> And Pandora did try. She really did. But one day when Epimetheus was out, she just could not forget about the chest and somehow she found herself standing right beside it.
>
> 'No!' she told herself. 'I expect it's full of cloth – or dishes – or papers. Something dull.' She bustled about the house. She tried to read. Then …
>
> '*Let us out!*'
>
> 'Who said that?'
>
> 'Do let us out, Pandora!'
>
> Pandora looked out of the window. But in her heart of hearts she knew that the voice was coming from the chest. She pulled back the blanket with finger and thumb. The voice was louder now: 'Please, please *do* let us out, Pandora!'
>
> 'I can't. I mustn't.' She crouched down beside the chest.
>
> 'Oh, but you *have* to. We *want* you to. We *need* you to, Pandora!'
>
> 'But I promised!' Her fingers stroked the latch.
>
> 'It's easy. The key's in the lock,' said a little voice – a purring little voice. It was. A big golden key.
>
> 'No. No, I mustn't,' she told herself.
>
> 'But you do *want* to, Pandora. And why shouldn't you? It was your wedding present, too, wasn't it? … Oh, all right, don't let us out. Just peep inside. What harm can that do?'
>
> Pandora's heart beat faster.
>
> *Click*. The key turned.
>
> *Clack. Clack.* The latches were unlatched.
>
> BANG!
>
> The lid flew back and Pandora was knocked over by an icy wind full of grit. It filled the room with howling. It tore the curtains and stained them brown. And after the wind came slimy things, growling snarling things, claws and snouts, revolting things too nasty to look at, all slithering out of the chest.
>
> (McCaughrean 1992: 10–11)

Not only does this story teach us that disobedience and succumbing to tempta-tion are wrong, but that it is all the woman's fault.

An African story tells it differently, however. Nyachero was daughter of a star who was courted and married by an earthly king. When her first baby was due she returned to her parents' home, as was the custom, accompanied by twelve armed men. When they arrived at the country of the stars there was no one there to greet them so Nyachero left the warriors in a comfortable room but warned them not to touch any of the three large pots in the room:

> After waiting for some hours, the men grew hungry and began to wonder what the three pots might contain. They argued amongst themselves but at last one man lifted the cover from a pot and peered inside. No sooner had he lifted the lid than a cloud of mosquitoes flew out, whining around them and stinging them everywhere. The men beat the insects off with their hands and sat miserably, scratching their skin.
>
> However, it was not long before they grew hungry again and someone opened the second jar. Out came a cloud of locusts which flew in their faces and in their hair, crawling over their bodies so thickly that they almost smothered them. Again, the men beat them off and sat down more miser-able than before.
>
> Hours later, when dawn was clouding the sky and there was still no sign of Nyachero or her people, another hungry man lifted the lid from a third jar. Out came a cloud of flies which swarmed around them smelling the blood which the mosquitoes had drawn.
>
> (Knappert 1986: 52)

Is hunger an excuse? Or should they have learnt the first time not to open the next pot? Whatever the moral message, this alternative explanation from a different culture shows just how effectively myths shift their shapes according to time, place and culture.

Tracing a single story through different versions can show just how varied the interpretive weight of morality can be. Theseus, for example, can be seen as arch betrayer or classic hero, and Ariadne as wet and wimpish or resourceful and cunning. In a version written in the 1890s, Ariadne is described as 'a beau-tiful, tender-hearted girl' who looked at Theseus 'with blushing cheeks and a beating heart'; Theseus is 'brave and strong' and there is no mention of the betrayal on Naxos (Kupfer 1897: 136–7). In a version by Tony Robinson and Richard Curtis a hundred years later, however,

Ariadne led Theseus back to his cell.
'Good luck tomorrow,' she said. 'Are you frightened?'
'No!' replied Theseus stoutly. 'Well ... a bit.'
'No need. You'll be all right,' said Ariadne and she kissed him.
(Robinson and Curtis 1988: 69)

Here, Ariadne is a no-nonsense practical young woman, who thinks further than just killing the Minotaur and so gives Theseus the thread to get him out of trouble. At the end of this story, Theseus is revealed as weak and deceitful. In another modern version, Ariadne is the king's 'plain little daughter', and when she gives Theseus the thread he replies: 'Excellent! ... I could marry a girl as clever as you!' (McCaughrean 1992: 64). When he has safely returned from the labyrinth, however, and Ariadne claims him as husband: 'He suddenly realised that just because Ariadne had saved his life, she expected to marry him! He studied her face. That nose was *very* big. And those eyebrows were *very* thick' (McCaughrean 1992: 65).

On his way home he sends Ariadne off to get supplies on Naxos and abandons her:

'When I marry,' he thought, 'it will be to a beautiful queen or a goddess.' He was in such a hurry to get away that he quite forgot to change the black sail for a white one.
(McCaughrean 1992: 65)

And so his shallowness and treachery were his undoing. But in this 1990s version it was desire for beauty that was his downfall rather than his lack of honourable gratitude for his life.

These different versions point not only to the instability of the narratives and their morals, but also to the paradox of presenting classical myths, for instance, as suitable material for children's hearing and reading. The Ariadne story of love and betrayal can be overlooked in the retelling of a daring quest against a monster. Even a very cursory look into Greek, Roman and Norse myth strongly suggests that these stories would be remarkably unsuitable for the young, yet they have remained popular with children and with the adults who make choices on behalf of children about what texts they should read. A brief reminder of the origins of the gods of Greek myth illustrates just how dubious these stories might be for a young audience: the world was created out of Chaos, which gave birth to Gaea, the Earth, who in turn gave birth to Uranus. Together they produced the Titans, the Cyclopes and the Hecatoncheires. Uranus tried to destroy his children and only Kronos was brave enough to attack his father. He castrated him and married Rhea, fathering many children. However, since these were destined to destroy him he swallowed each one as it was born until Rhea saved one, Zeus, by trickery. In time, Zeus gave Kronos a potion which made him vomit up the other gods and goddesses, and then began a long battle against the Titans. Eventually, Zeus and the other deities succeeded and established a stronghold on Mount Olympus.

Similarly, in Norse mythology the world was created from a great void when Odin and his brothers killed the Frost Giant Ymir and it will end when the Giants kill Odin and his comrades in battle. Fighting is a central element in the stories and is the way a warrior can die nobly and reach the warriors' paradise, Valhalla. Nevertheless, as with Greek and Roman myths, although life might be, in Hobbes' terms, 'nasty, brutish and short', there is a good deal of drinking, eating, lovemaking, trickery, friendship, treachery and revenge to be got through before attaining paradise. This is not the stuff of children's literature as many people would understand it. Life as reflected in these stories is perilous and so is taken on with verve, energy and an element of cunning. However, it may well be that because of the elemental and fundamental issues which myth presents, the stories recommend themselves to readers who are, like the mythic figures they read about, shaping and facing up to their growing experience of everyday reality. In myth, imagination is mingled with fact. And the relative power of the divine and the human is a central thread. For children, this is highly relevant as they grapple with their own responsibilities and rights within their communities and social groups.

Contradictions and oppositions

The appeal of myth for young readers is remarkable, since the content of the stories is very much related to the adult world, but this paradox is just the first in a number of tensions and conflicts surrounding myth as a form of literature. One of the most appealing aspects of myth is that it refuses to be pinned down. Many writers and thinkers over the ages have tried to define myth and its relationship with people, societies and cultures. However, scholarship tries to define or interpret myths, they seem to defy explanation and in chasing interpretations there may be a risk of missing the potency of the stories themselves.

As stories which have been transmitted throughout generations they have also been transformed through those retellings. It is possibly because of their origins in oral tellings that myths offer such rich and multi-faceted possibilities for readers and tellers. They deal with the large matters of life and death, the soul and the afterlife, power and powerlessness, courage and fear, and the force of the passions – love, lust, anger, retribution, revenge. Symbol, metaphor, imagery, oblique meanings abound as the myths give shape to the big matters of existence. They tackle important questions of morality, although that morality may sometimes seem ambiguous or questionable to different cultures. Myths offer possibilities of sharing experiences which can sometimes be terrifying; in forming these experiences into crafted stories, potentially devastating forces are contained and controlled. By making art from the raw material of knowledge of a violent and threatening universe, myths create a fine thread between acknowledging fearful realities and transforming them into fantasy to make them more manageable.

Mythic stories are threaded with contradictions and oppositions: the golden age of innocence balanced against the responsibilities of knowledge; the power of deities and the vulnerability of humankind. In standing up to the gods and goddesses of classical mythological tales, men and women showed inventiveness, cleverness, bravery, craft and cunning. The actions of the central characters are often selfish, foolhardy, ignoble according to Western views of morality, and downright stupid, yet they are heroic. They undertake difficult journeys and overcome hazards. In some cases they are aided by divine powers and magic; in others they are punished for seeming to challenge that power in acts of hubris. They tell of individuals who have thoughts and feelings just like you or me, who, through metaphorical transformation, experience more than the here-and-now; they place those individuals in settings with all the tensions, contradictions and passions engendered within families and social groups, but offer the possibilities of magically transporting the courageous individual from that setting. If the content – rape, incest, murder and mayhem – is not what would conventionally be encouraged for young readers, then the struggles against adversity, the journeys and tests of strength do have resonance for children growing in understanding of themselves and the world. The particular power of myth lies in its ability to offer something both specific and general in stories that are permeated with the dualities and paradoxes of human experience.

One of the paradoxes is that, while mythic stories take the imagination soaring, they are also familiar and so, in a sense, secure. In her novel *The God of Small Things*, Arundhati Roy describes a character watching a Kathakali Man – a dancer who depicts the traditional Indian stories of heroes and gods. The stories are well-known yet the performance is riveting:

> The Great Stories are the ones you have heard and want to hear again. The ones you can enter anywhere and inhabit comfortably. They don't deceive you with thrills and trick endings. They don't surprise you with the unforeseen. They are as familiar as the house you live in. You know how they end yet you listen as though you don't ... in the Great Stories you know who lives, who dies, who finds love, who doesn't – and yet you want to know again. *That* is their mystery and their magic.
>
> (Roy 1997: 229–30)

These great stories somehow allow the hearer/reader to handle difference and sameness. Bakhtin describes language as pulling in two directions: centripetally towards the centre, identified as a 'unitary' language, and centrifugally, reaching outwards to the various languages that make up that apparent but false unity (1981: 272). These various languages are what Bakhtin terms 'heteroglossia'. Bakhtin's ideas offer a potent way of understanding myth and legend, texts which speak with many voices throughout the ages of their tellings and retellings. In terms of morality and the education of the group, traditional tales operate with the centripetal forces of conformity to norms and standards in constant tension with the centrifugal pull of difference and cultural diversity. As an experience for the individual hearer/reader, the stories are held together by the centrifugal force of identification with the dilemmas and conflicts presented to the protagonists balanced by the centripetal forces of those things which threaten to fragment life. Children acutely experience these forces – the urge to conform and the urge to rebel; the awareness of the responsibilities of being part of a community in tension with the urge to go beyond its bounds.

Play and morality

I want to argue that children handle these things through play – and particularly through the play of the imagination. I wish to assert that children are not only capable of moral thinking but that they are often prevented from discussing difficult moral issues through the concern of adults to protect them from harm.

Let me first say a thing or two about play and story. In his novel *The Dumas Club* Arturo Perez-Reverte uses one of his characters to argue that:

> Children are the perfect players and readers: they do everything with the utmost seriousness. In essence, games are the only universally serious activity. They leave no room for scepticism ... However incredulous or doubting one might be, if one wants to play one has no choice but to follow the rules ... Reading a book is the same: one has to accept the plot and the characters to enjoy the story.
>
> (Perez Reverte 1993: 283)

There is a lot in the above, but I'd like to push it further. I want to consider the role of fantasy and imagination – those aspects of inner play which use the conventions of story and of games to go beyond the rules – and, in doing this, I want to look at modern mythic stories as depicted on television, video and comics or the new graphic novels. Perez-Reverte argues:

> a novel or a film made for pure consumption can turn into an exquisite work, from The Pickwick Papers to Casablanca and Goldfinger ... Audiences turn to these stories full of archetypes to enjoy, whether consciously or unconsciously, the device of repeated story lines with small variations ... And what is the television serial if not an updated version of a classic tragedy, a great romantic drama or the Dumas novel?
>
> (Perez Reverte 1993: 293)

But it is the modern media of television, video and comics that seem to have awakened once again adult fears about children's moral development. There seems to be a clash between reason and desire – children's desires and adults' rationality.

In her book *Kid Culture*, Kathleen McDonnell cites research that suggests children who cannot fantasise – and so learn the boundaries between reality and fantasy – are those who are most at risk from their TV- and video-watching. She points out, however, that adult concerns about children's corruption by story in various forms is a recurrent cultural fear. Plato thought that stories were bad for the young, and people have been attempting to ban stories or sanitise them for children ever since. She points out that these fears are founded on certain common fears:

> They certainly share some basic assumptions, chief among them being that any endeavour children engage in should serve some higher moral purpose – should, in a word, be educational. This is a burden placed on children's play as well as all their forms of entertainment and is a bias every bit as strong today as it was in the nineteenth century, when children's books were supposed to give moral guidance and 'build character'. Today, of course, we use a different terminology. We speak of 'positive role models' and 'quality' (meaning educational) programming. But the underlying sentiment is basically the same. Kids' programs without any obvious educational intent are automatically considered junk and garbage, while 'quality' children's programs are supposed to be tasteful, not loud and brash – rather like a well-behaved child.
>
> (McDonnell 1994: 113)

She draws a distinction between these adult judgements and adults' own desires:

> It's interesting that we adults don't put this burden of being educational on our own entertainment. We acknowledge that we have a range of tastes, moods and interests. We accept that we often turn to so-called 'low' culture to feed our desires of the moment.
>
> (McDonnell 1994: 114)

She goes on to suggest that part of the contrast in attitude lies in the subversive nature of much of children's chosen viewing, challenging adult authority over children. I would argue, however, that the mythic tales – *Power Rangers*, *Teenage Ninja Mutant Turtles* or whatever – are far from subversive of society's urge towards cohesion and consensus. All myth establishes the notion of powerful deities and the struggles of people in their encounters with that power. These stories are inherently conservative; good usually triumphs and virtue is rewarded. It may be that such very simple moral messages, borne by 'fantasies of the first age' as David Whitley puts it (see p. 172–82) mean that these popular cultural stories do not endure; every few years a new 'mythic' fashion emerges.

Nevertheless, they allow children to play with some of the difficult ideas carried by myth and legend.

Stephen's story

I'd like to use a story that combines two 'mythic' icons of popular culture which have been seen as 'bad' for children, one for negative gendered images and the other for the promotion of violence – Barbie and Action Man – and look at what one child did with them.

Stephen was 9 when he wrote this picture book for his younger sister (aged 4), who asked for a story about Barbie.[1] He was not happy about this. His transformation and subversion of his sister's original request, and of the popular cultural characters he uses for his narrative, give an example of just how children can play with ideas to make their own narrative – and moral – choices. Looked at in terms of interest, this picture book carries complex meanings (see Figure 14.1). Ostensibly about Barbie, it is a story about Action Man, yet although Action Man dominates the verbal text, much of the interest for Stephen lies in the technical elements of his pictorial narrative – the Action Base and the aeroplane. It is a story of power: men's power over Barbie and the power of the *Eagle* (aeroplane) representing Action Man's power over Doctor X. The grammar of the text follows the epic form: it begins in the middle of the action and has as its focus a weak person who needs to be rescued by a hero or a superhero who can leap off very high buildings without endangering himself. The hero has to overcome a villain, and the divine intervention to help the hero comes in the shape, first of all of a computer map, then as a soaring machine. The characters are marked out by symbolic features – Barbie's bra, the henchmen's guns and Action Man's bandolier, and the initials on the front of his combat clothes. Although the villain does not appear, he is referred to as 'Doctor', as in many James Bond-like films and stories, the title suggesting scientific (magical) powers. Added to this, he is a predator, living in a lair. In line with myth- and legend-type stories, this narrative begins on the ground, moves into the sky as the adventure develops, then ends firmly grounded again. The layout of the pictorial text echoes that journey, with the emergence into two double-page spreads in the middle of the narrative, then a return to single pages at the end. In his robust but spare verbal narrative, Stephen gives the bare bones of the traditional quest to eliminate the villain who has captured the heroine:

Barbie gets attacked by doctor X's men
Action Man saves Barbie.
Action Man takes Barbie to his base.
Action Man takes Barbie to the Eagle the Airoplane.
Action Man takes Barbie to the Action Zone Dr X Base.

Barbie stays in the airoplane but after a while she got kidnapped.
Action Man kills Dr X and saves Barbie after that they got married.
Then Action Man makes Barbie into Action Woman.

It follows the power journey motif of many epics, and ends with the introduction into a new family – 'they got married' – in accord with the closure of
traditional tales. The pictorial narrative tells us more: it places Barbie at first in
a very 'pinned-down' position on the left of the pictures. Action Man is
depicted as above her in a more powerful position and the guards keep her in
her place – at the left-hand inactive part of the image. She is mostly seen in
profile throughout, making no contact with the reader until the very last
picture, where she is transformed into a much more powerful figure, equal in
stature – and attire! – to Action Man, and facing us, demanding our attention.

I was intrigued about the choices Stephen had made in his story. He told me
that it was 'all about toys'. He had asked his sister, 'Do you want a romantic
story about Ken and Barbie or an action story comedy with Action Man and
Ken?' She had decided she wanted an action story because they had a lot of
Action Man toys at the time, but he explained: 'In every other story Action
Man falls in love with the heroine so I decided to have Action Man married to
Barbie.' However, Stephen extends the narrative and subverts the usual
grammar by adding a postscript – the final page, added as an afterthought after
he had 'completed' the story – where the formerly weak and helpless female
victim is given equal (perhaps) powers with the hero. Their next adventure may
not follow the same traditional grammar – or will it?

The endpapers of Stephen's book indicate further adventures in the modern
mythic form, involving a whole range of popular toys:

Action Man And Barbie
Are Back But they've
Got New Friends.

Characters: Action Man,
Barbie, Sindy and Ken and
Dr X's twin Brother.

Title: TOY STORY 3
Author: Stephen Edmonds
Illustrater: Stephen Edmonds

The difference between this and some of the television versions or the Perseus-
like models of classical myth lies in Stephen's decision to recreate Barbie as a

more equal companion to Action Man. When we were talking about the story, he could not account for this, and I didn't push him; he may have been drawing again on superhero texts of popular culture where women are given a more central position in the heroic structure. Wherever his story choices came from, I want to acknowledge the imaginative reconstruction which Stephen has done as a variation on a well-known theme. I would not like to read into this narrative any more than is there, but it seems to me that by playing with a range of different voices drawn from popular story forms, Stephen has stamped his work with a range of choices – including making the *Eagle*, the aeroplane, his central interest. He has certainly made his own statement about his view of romance and companionable adventuring.

As he has grown older, Stephen has chosen to read some of the more demanding quest narratives, including Tolkien's *Lord of the Rings*, while still enjoying film and television popular myths. Although adults may have reservations about encouraging popular mythic cultural forms, these may be a bridge to some of the more genuinely tough tales of traditional myth and legend. Or, simply, as Kathleen McDonnell (1994) points out, perhaps all of us need a variety of stories – soft-edged and 'first age', as well as demanding 'wisdom narratives' (see pp. 172–82).

Figure 14.1 Stephen's story: Barbie and Action Man. Stephen Edmonds was in Year 5 at St Philip's Community CE school when he wrote this piece.

Figure 14.1 (_continued_) Stephen's story: Barbie and Action Man.

Barbie stays in the atroplane but after a while She got Kiddnapped

Action Man Kills DR. X. And Saves Barbie after that they Got MARRied

Then Action Man Makes Barbie into Action Woman

Figure 14.1 (continued) Stephen's story: Barbie and Action Man.

Making choices

The introduction to a text for older readers, the graphic novel *Black Orchid* (Gaiman and McKean 1991), tells the reader:

> Like so many of the tales that make up our complex webwork of modern myths and contemporary entertainment, the tale you are about to read begins in violence. A woman – a super-hero crime-fighter known as Black Orchid – is tripped up by a crew of sophisticated crime-lords, just as she is about to penetrate their most closely guarded secrets. So far, so predictable. In the comics world, super-heroes are always discovered and threatened at crucial moments; indeed, it is how the hero overcomes his or her nemesis that too often imbues a comic book tale with not only its sense of plot or suspense, but also with its sense of mortal risk and moral triumph.
>
> But in this tale, something unanticipated happens. The man who has caught Black Orchid stands before her and says: 'Hey, you know something? I've read the comics … I'm not going to lock you up in the basement before interrogating you … then leave you alone to escape. That stuff is so dumb. But you know what I am going to do? I'm going to kill you. Now.' And then he does just what he has promised: he kills her – the woman who is the namesake of this book – in a brutal and unflinching manner.

This self-parodying set of subversions leads into a story combining an Adam's rib/*Pygmalion*-type story with quests into the underworld reminiscent of Eurydice or Babylonian myth. On the way it quotes from Gilbert and Sullivan, Frank Sinatra, Batman, Lou Reed, Alice in Wonderland … . The resolution is ambiguous, if hopeful. It is a complicated reading experience, which uses filmic technique, including a kind of voiceover, to make multiple and allusive meanings. This is not easy popular fiction escapism. The reader has to work hard to construct the narrative and to make sense of the morality offered.

Such stories encourage thought and imagination to coexist. They help young readers to confront oppositions and commonalities in power and in morality – not necessarily to reconcile those opposites but to acknowledge that they exist. While adults may fear the playful texts of popular culture, they nevertheless offer valuable experiences for learning the lessons adults want young readers to absorb. It isn't just a matter of 'being reasonable' as we grow older. Ursula Le Guin shows the importance of putting reason and fantasy side by side:

> In the telling of a story, reason is only a support system. It can only provide causal connections; it can extrapolate; it can judge what is likely, plausible, possible. All this is crucial to the invention of a good story, a sane fantasy, a sound piece of fiction. But reason by itself … cannot see that Elizabeth is, in fact, going to marry Darcy, and why. We cannot ask reason to take us across the gulfs of the absurd. Only the imagination can get us out of the

bind of the eternal present, inventing or hypothesising or pretending or discovering a way that reason can then follow into the infinity of options, a clue through the labyrinths of choice, a golden string, the story, leading us to the freedom that is properly human, the freedom to those whose minds can accept unreality.

(Le Guin 1989: 45)

I started with a question about the suitability of mythic tales for children. It seems clear that if children need to be helped to forge their understanding of morality in fantasy and to enact it in reality, then they need the chance to confront some of the harsh issues and to recognise that things don't necessarily end happy ever after. They need the imaginative space to enact the moral dilemmas faced by Pandora or the African serving men, and to weigh up the price of war. They need the chance to see people represented in different ways, exhibiting some common features as well as showing difference. They need the chance to become producers of their own fantasies in the stories they make for themselves and to talk about them and the choices as young people growing in interpretation. Myth can tolerate ambiguity; the stories encourage individual wrestling with complexity; they present the challenge of balancing the competing tensions of moral choices. Laurence Coupe puts it like this: 'it is the task of myth constantly to imply, but always to resist, completion' (1997: 197). Despite their perceived role as stories that teach, there are no easy moral messages to be got from myth.

Note

1   Stephen's story was written while I was working with a Year 5/6 class in a Cambridge school. I then talked at some length with Stephen about his Barbie story.

References

Bakhtin, M. (1981) *The Dialogic Imagination*, trans. C. Emerson and M. Holquist, Texas: University of Texas Press.
Coupe, L. (1997) *Myth*, London: Routledge.
Gaiman, N. and McKean, D. (1991) *Black Orchid*, New York: DC Comics.
Knappert, J. (1986) *Gods and Spirits from African Mythology*, London: Peter Lowe.
Kupfer, G.H. (1897) *Legends of Greece and Rome*, London: Harrap.
Le Guin, U. (1989) 'Some Thoughts on Narrative', *Dancing at the Edge of the World*, London: HarperCollins.
McCaughrean, G. (1992) *The Orchard Book of Greek Myths*, London, Orchard Books.
McDonnell, K. (1994) *Kid Culture: Children & Adults & Popular Culture*, Toronto: Second Story Press.
Perez Reverte, A. (1993) *The Dumas Club*, London: Harvill Press.
Robinson, A. and Curtis, R. (1988) *The King Who Killed the Minotaur*, London: Hodder and Stoughton.
Roy, A. (1997) *The God of Small Things*, London, Flamingo.

Afterword

Transitional transformations

Margaret Meek Spencer

In this book, teacher-scholars who understand the individual and social complexities of reading have opened up children's growth as readers. Approaching reading as different kinds of encounters with texts, they interpret the interactions of young minds with written language and semiotic displays, whatever they deem to be texts, then report what children *make* of reading in the company of authors, artists and other readers. The result is a rich pattern of descriptions of coming-to-know, including comments, play, drama, writing, and the growth of reading confidence and self-awareness. Clearly, meetings of children and texts are sites of transformations, metamorphoses of texts as well as readers, in a rapidly changing social scene of manners, ideational content and textual forms.

The emphasis in this collection of studies is on in-depth reading, the kind that makes the effort of continuing to read seem both worthwhile and a pleasure. In good company, young readers gradually come to see for themselves what reading is good for. Reading transforms readers, adults and children in different and unexpected ways. What readers read not only offers them information about actual events, people and things, but also proposes extensions, alternative views and versions of living. Adults give accounts of how the world is represented in books for children, treating some as 'real' and others as 'imaginary', yet recent studies show that this is too simple to be helpful. Even at a very early age, children do not confuse Rosie the hen with one they might see in a farmyard or on television (Lowe 1998). 'Consciousness', says Seamus Heaney, 'can be alive to two different and contradictory descriptions of reality and find a way of negotiating between them' (Heaney 1995: iii). Reading is one of the earliest of these negotiations where readers of fiction are in at least two places at once. The riches of this book lie in a gamut of evidence that children's early reading competences far outstrip limited descriptions of them. Whatever the future brings, we cannot give up the complexity of what we now know. Instead, we should be grateful for it. At the same time, we have to admit that some aspects of reading still elude us.

Most of my thinking about reading keeps coming back to the earliest questions I ever asked about it: What do I really do when I read? Why can't we be sure about what someone does when reading? What do we test when we test reading? It's like trying to explain thinking. One way through the maze is to listen to what children say about their encounters with books they enjoy, a privilege of grandmothers, whose conversations are less directive than classroom inquiries. Texts are the sites of transformations and transitions in children's reading, either potential or actual, because texts are new for young readers more often than they are for experienced adults. More particularly, however, those who write for the young know that they can *provoke* reading as well as promote it. They also know how to change it. Postmodernism in children's texts, as elsewhere, is about all kinds of change. As soon as children become independent readers, they move away from the kind of reading imposed by the limited texts of the first stages of learning to read, to discover texts they want to use, and own for the purposes of transformation.

Most of what follows is about changes related to reading and texts that interest me a great deal. When I have run myself in with some looking back, I propose to cast forward to what the National Curriculum calls 'challenging texts', the kind that children are expected to be willing and able to read when they change schools and are no longer beginners. To help me I have accomplices just at this stage.

Retrospective – to advance

In 1976, not long after the publication of the Bullock Report, A *Language for Life*, Aidan Warlow, Griselda Barton and I were collecting writings about children's reading in relation to critical approaches to children's books. Our intention was to assemble what we had found useful over a range of studies, not necessarily about teaching reading, but in pointing ways forward from the narrow, static, behaviourist view of learning to read exemplified by the teaching materials generally in use at that time and still, to a dominant extent, present in Bullock. Our conviction was that children's views of what reading was like were coloured, formed even, by the texts they were given to learn from. *The Cool Web* (Meek *et al.* 1977) offered (still offers) its readers a chance to weave their own text of children's reading from a collection of different kinds of evidence. We also wanted to show the parts played by a variety of texts in the complex patterning of children's reading growth. There is even a prototypical sketch of a genre theory.

We discovered a 'where' for the meeting of children and texts; a locus of the 'play' of imagination, in D.W. Winnicott's 'third area', the 'potential space between the inner psychic reality and the actual world in which the individual lives' (Meek *et al.* 1977: 102–3). I mention this in connection with the 'wheres' of this volume and also because James Britton described it in his article on fantasy in *The Cool Web* as 'the place where we are more ourselves'. At that time, most of the studies that now feature in the *International Companion Encyclopedia of Children's Literature* (Hunt 1996), and the reading debate we could have had much sooner than we did, were still in the future. Later, Karin Lesnik-Oberstein made extensive use of Winnicott's ideas in *Children's Literature: Criticism and the Fictional Child* (Lesnik-Oberstein 1994). That was a 'where' in the reader. There are also wheres in texts, and elsewhere.

What remains intact from that early attempt to present the depth and complexity of children's reading is Barbara Hardy's statement that 'narrative, like lyric or dance, is not to be regarded as an aesthetic invention used by artists to control, manipulate and order experience, but as a primary act of mind transferred to art from life' (Meek *et al.* 1977: 12). Over all the intervening years this has been asserted as incontrovertible by writers like Ursula Le Guin (1989) and a host of others. A most useful and thoughtful summary of narrative competences, including the relation of narrative to memory, is in chapter 6 of Carol Fox's *At the Very Edge of the Forest* (1993). Her great discovery was that, by the time they go to school, children incorporate both the words and the narrative tropes of texts read to them into storytelling of their own. They discover that, to make reading make sense, they have to become both the teller and the told (Scollon and Scollon 1981). This is the most important, untaught, early lesson. Children see themselves as readers before they can explain the nature of textual engagement. Nowadays, 2-year-olds play their way through books of pictures, performing reader-like actions demonstrated by adults before they bind themselves to the words. The difference is not in what they do, but in the fact that we have noticed that they can do some things sooner than we thought. The social and linguistic nature of reading is learned wherever textual messages seem important.

All these things are now in books, bibliographies and journal reports. In earlier times, when the details were emerging in the places that became the shared sites of various encounters, I discovered that informing ideas about children's reading have a vivid social reality in what children do and say about their reading. This was true even when young readers and I were discussing the most unreal fictions. Now, the ideas in *The Cool Web* about children's books and reading have undergone various changes, modifications and additions, as ideas must, but evidence about the transformation of young reader's ideas about reading, and transitions in their ability to do it well, still seem to originate at the point of engagement with a text. In a novel it is usually near the beginning of the narrative. Elsewhere, the evidence is much fuzzier. To track what happens after the beginning is quite difficult, but not impossible.

There is no longer (if there ever was) a straight, or strait, school road in reading from simple, unambiguous beginnings to acknowledged expertise. We tell each other that we are in the middle of the most profound changes in literacy since the invention of printing, so that what counts as *being* a *reader* is more difficult to define, and much more difficult to *test* (Harrison and Salinger 1998). (Are you a reader when you are not reading?) The material appearance of public writing changes continuously. Novelties, on paper, board or screen, in the street, on television or as photographic montage, are eye-catching designs, moments of significance, most of which are ephemeral. In contrast, every specialist discipline or topic, weighty with signification and significance that depends for its communication on print, offers abundant new information in a variety of formats and discourses. Even the most experienced readers have bald patches of illiteracy, texts where the notation as well as the subject matter is unfamiliar. We may know how reading works, but we still make mistakes in interpretations in unfamiliar contexts.

Because parents and teachers are still bound to see children's learning to read in a conventional manner as a fundamental part of their education, and thus of their life-chances, adult readers are apt to normalise textual changes and to ignore differences in what seems familiar. If we cannot understand a new advertisement immediately, we attribute our failure to the novelty of the product. Consequently, we fail to notice that transformed texts transform readers and reading. Peter Hollindale, writing about reading as the meeting of children and texts, points out that:

> between the author and the young reader there is a cultural and historical gap of at least half a generation, usually much more ... The conversation of minds between author and reader (relayed through its intermediate messengers, such as the narrator and protagonist), is different in nature from the conversation that takes place when the children's book is read by an adult.
>
> (Hollindale 1997: 12)

Recent transformations – the Internet and the World Wide Web are key examples – have given new descriptions. 'Browsing' is one such; an important, often underrated skill. New computerised browsing brings '*surface*' reading, radial eye movements that whip across a screen text, such as surgeons and picture restorers make when they examine X-rays and point to the bit that matters, or architects, engineers and others when they look at plans before they focus in on the point of interest. Reading now involves this rapid recognition of what is relevant, especially in quests for information. The balance between surface and superficial reading is a delicate one. Children begin skimming and scanning processes with picture books, television and videos. They pick out the details they recognise or want to know more about before they are able, or encouraged, to make a linear narrative or to understand a sequence of events from a succession of images. (The importance of a concept of print as something intrinsically linear has changed lately.) Because we use old words for these operations, we tend to think that the process is the same for beginners as for practised readers, who know what they can skip. This is the kind of assumption we may need to revise.

Although opinions may differ as to whether Bill Gates is a global benefactor or a new version of Big Brother, there is no doubt that communication technologies have extended the world's boundaries and compressed the universe into seconds, with accompanying photographs. Before they are adolescent, most young readers, whatever their views of reading or their interpretive competences, expect to have hands-on experience of some technological texts which move fast, transforming themselves at the touch of a key. But many of the same age group are also unwilling to see 'old' reading, which depends on the reader's practised skill in using language for learning, as anything other than a slow, unrewarding exercise. At this time of transition, the skilled conventional readers are making most progress with the new readings, hence public anxieties about the others.

Paradoxically, as a result of advances in computer and design technology, book production has been transformed in tenacious, polymorphous ways. Photographs, pictures and decorations take the space that was once reserved for words. Information texts for the young are designed to deliver the topic matter with the minimum of linear print. Book texts emulate the display of CD-ROM software. The present generation of teachers includes many who have grown up with modern picture books and who expect even better versions for their pupils in videos and other 'resources'. It's a long time since I saw a new topic in a curriculum subject being introduced by a book. A film does the job faster, more memorably, until revision time. Computerised publishing produces government curriculum material as soon and as often as there are changes in the frameworks of teaching. Screen reading will soon become common in all subjects. Children already know how to do it; teachers taught themselves when they knew they had to. At this transition time, we see children and teachers using computer texts and book texts simultaneously. We also know that access to new readings is neither universal nor equal.

Our eyes have to be on the future, yet we know that education has a strongly conservative effect. Historians suggest that transformational understandings about the world are slow to take hold. Umberto Eco says this is because each generation travels with the preconceived notions derived from cultural traditions. 'In a curious way, we travel knowing in advance what we are on the verge of discovering, because past reading has told us what we are supposed to discover' (1999: 54).

Forward

The texts I have chosen in order to look at the meetings they might have with their implied readers are part of a continuing inquiry into what constitutes a 'challenging' text for the inexperienced. The readers I have in mind are now past the early learning stage, able to choose for themselves, possibly making decisions about the kinds of books they prefer. In the lives of these readers, this is often at the point of transition from primary to secondary school; a time of 'ways not taken'. In reading, it may mean a serious foreshortening of pupils' chances to practise different kinds of reading.

Before we get to these readers, here's a short textual challenge. What do you make of this poem? What kind of attention are you prepared to give it? When you've read it, the poet will tell you what he had in mind when he composed it.

On the Question of Whether It's Possible to Sleep on a Train

Can I sleep on the train?
Can I sleep on the train?
Can I sleep?

On the train
On the train
On the train
On the train
Can I sleep?

On the train
On the train
On the train
On the train
I sleep.

This is one of a collection that Michael Rosen wrote so as to analyse his writing processes (Rosen 1997). He is watching himself doing it, so he becomes his first reader, meeting himself as a child in the text, or as a writer making a place for other readers to be in the text. His thinking about his thinking is not revealed to his intended readers of the poem, but to a panel of examiners reading his doctoral thesis on this topic. Here is a summary of a part of his commentary, by permission.

He considers the materiality of the poem: the paper, typing energy, the words as they take shape on the page, then examines the materiality of language as sound play, where the meaning of the words is of less account than 'pitch, tone, volume and implied volume, rhythm, percussion, cadence, unvoiced sounds, distortions of the expected that run counter to or in tune with the unfolding of meaning'. He maintains that children, discovering language and playing with it, meet its physical nature before its sense. The effect of the poem on the reader is, at that point, 'semantically weak'. Drawing attention to a number of things happening at once, he points out what often goes unnoticed when children are read to. Children's meetings with a text of this kind are usually discussed as 'early language play', but the poet has other plans. Did you register 'distortions of the expected'? Do you remember the text of poems that children couldn't understand although they liked the sound of them?

Rosen adds: 'My poem doesn't describe what trains do. I am saying, largely (but not entirely), with the sound of the words, "the rhythm of the train is hypnotic"'. We don't *know* directly what the young reader/listener makes of it as sound or meaning. The poet, himself a wanderer in trains, falls asleep.

At another point in the argument he is conducting with the well-read, Michael Rosen remembers his mother, Connie Rosen's, attachment to poetry (Connie wrote poetry, and also scripts for radio programmes about it):

She gave off a feeling that Yeats had affected her in ways that were beyond explaining to a child, or perhaps to anyone; that Yeats had said things to her that meant more to her than things that were said in everyday conversation, or indeed that anyone in the world had said to her … It was her private world and yet she, perhaps unknowingly, had passed on to me a sense that poetry had the potential to reach people in extraordinary, mysterious and powerful ways …

(Rosen 1997: 132)

Michael again: 'I remember her saying things like, "I need a poem that looks closely at an object."' I have made this detour to remind us that those who arrange the meetings of children and texts have a strong influence on these events. In old rhymes and modern wordplay, poetry has long been associated with early reading discoveries, partly because rereading verse is not an unusual thing to do. Later encounters are not simply repetitions of earlier ones, but new transformations of understanding while the words stay the same; importantly, perhaps, because verse is more quickly formed in the memory, together with the circumstances of its being heard or read.

The meeting of old and new, readers or texts, is a crucial site, a distinctive 'where' in transformations of reading. Older methods of teaching reading have to be adapted to new presentations, new kinds of telling, despite the insistence in some quarters that this is not so. In children's picture books, for example, the interaction of pictures and text are not taught as reading lessons, but they are learnt as such. Experienced readers simply count on being able to adapt their practised skills to new texts, but there is no guarantee that they are reading them for what they are. Children are not concerned to know how a new text differs from an old one unless the difference is alluded to. Nowadays, when writers make new versions of older stories, the entire text looks and sounds new to adults, but the older contents can be seen through the words of the new version by some readers. When adults read new versions of old texts they are often pleasantly surprised to uncover bits of meaning that had never occurred to them before. Here is Margaret Clark avoiding the 'preacherly tone' of the version of Aesop's *Tales* that spoilt the stories for her as a child. Behind the delicate economy of her version is a gentle irony that the young treat as a kind of confidential whisper:

A family of mice was being chased every day by a hungry cat. 'What are we going to do?' said Mother as they all sat around her one evening. Everyone had something to suggest, but the smallest mouse said, 'If we hang a bell round his neck, then we shall hear him coming and we'll have time to get out of his way.' All the mice squealed in excitement and told the smallest mouse how clever he was. Then the oldest mouse in the family spoke. 'That may *sound* a good idea,' he said, 'but tell me: which of you is brave enough to go up to the cat and hang a bell round his neck?' And why do you think none of them answered?

(Clark 1990: 14)

Some children are more at home than others with the enclosed nature of fables and parables, yet much modern writing is 'fabulation' in the sense that the words mean more than they say. So when the reteller moves closer to inexperienced readers by foregrounding what they know about the world – the ways of mice and cats, as here – then the meeting of reader and text emphasises the relation of the first sentence to the last. In this telling the point is swiftly made and, with it, two reading lessons: how the end changes the beginning, and the generalising force of the moral. The narrator also acknowledges the readers as those who know about certain kinds of foolishness. Readers then feel that they *have known* this, and that the writer also knows about them. Each generation needs such stories in the versions that make them relevant.

Many adults complain that children nowadays don't know the old tales, yet the National Curriculum put them on most book lists up to Key Stage 2 (age 11). To overcome this perceived lack, the editors of Scholastic books invited a number of well-known modern writers of children's books to tell a traditional tale as part of a series. The publishers designed the pages with decorated borders and typeface suitable for the inexperienced. Each teller was matched with an artist of note. The result so far is thirteen stories, robustly up-to-date, each bearing the stylistic hallmark of its reteller. To read them all is to feel the strong response of accomplished writers to 'make it work' for today's young readers. My 6-year-old apprentice latched on to the parts of *The Twelve Dancing Princesses* (1998), Anne Fine's contribution, through party-going. Dressing up, anticipation ('It's a bit like dancing class; all those shoes') and keeping parents in the dark were accepted as logical transformations, the way things go in this kind of tale. The conversations, 'doing the voices', were her best bit. She was in thrall to the telling throughout; the pace is judged to a quaver.

How, exactly, do you think children learn the *duration* of narrative events if not from the writer's poise of sentences? A nice detail in this story is the lightly touched individuality of all twelve princesses, a transformation begun by the author and completed by the reader. In the conference where many of the chapters in this book began as papers, Anne Fine attacked any attempt to 'dumb down' children's reading, thus demonstrating how seriously she confirms her readers' competences.

Most of the writers in the Scholastic series have brought closer together than usual the faerie aspects of the tales and modern social implications of certain details in the telling. The very clarity of the beginning of Henrietta Branford's *Hansel and Gretel* (1998) is subtly yet honestly menacing, with today's overtones of ill treatment. After the long fattening of Hansel and the growing anxiety, the children's triumph is swift and stunning. My admiration for the way Branford shows her readers how sentences work is unbounded. There is nothing here beyond the competence of a young reader's writing, but the details add up to something worse than loss: 'But when the moon came out there was no trail of crumbs. Ants had carried them off. Birds had pecked them up. Lumbering blackbeetles had clicked their pincers and gobbled them down. They were gone' (Branford 1998: 22). Every page has the same ringing clarity – nothing in this retelling is semantically or affectively beyond the reach of 7- or 8-year-olds. It's a perfect model for their writing, showing how the author lets the narrative carry feelings as well as actions and events.

In school, drama is an important key to the moves young readers make in interpretation of texts deemed by the National Curriculum to be 'challenging'. Enactment draws readers closer to the joining together of events and emotions in language. We need space and time to unpack this idea, beyond its association with difficulty, and the gaps in time, culture and language between writers and readers. Some picture books can become exotic play-scripts. The version of *The Emperor's New Clothes* by Naomi Lewis and Angela Barrett, a book of great beauty and subtle subversions, is one such. Here the reader sees beyond the words how the scoundrels carried on their deception As the weaving was 'done' at night, the gestures of the 'workers' are shown as silhouettes on blinds, to be seen from the street outside the palace. The Emperor's entire wardrobe and the fawning and faking of the courtiers are conveyed in subtly imaged detail of the *belle époque* in Monaco. In this version the character who blows the gaff is a little girl, who is perched on her father's shoulders to watch the procession where there is nothing to see. The book is a dramatic transformation of a story about illusions, surface appearances and deceit.

Other challenges

Even when they are willing to take chances with new authors and less familiar texts, readers need serendipities at certain times in their growth, especially in the matter of choosing which books to read. The transition from primary to secondary school upsets the routine of reading 'lessons' – reading progress is recorded less when it becomes an expected part of other learning. A number of pupils may quietly decide that reading is not their 'thing', often as the result of limited or unhappy experiences. Some are rescued by good teaching or increased confidence; others tread water for a year or so, then, for any of a score of reasons, catch up again in an area of interest. Boys are regarded as a special problem if they can read but don't. Independent, experienced readers move between confirming their earlier pleasures with more books by a favourite author, opportunistic sorties into the hinterland of magazines, or in peer-group coteries where books are passed round because they are 'cool'. At this stage, parents and teachers have to be tactful about making suggestions. Often they leave well alone.

What counts as a 'difficult' or 'challenging' text varies according to the reader's experience and expectations. When Allan Ahlberg, who has lightened most children's reading at some stage, demonstrates the *constructedness* of texts by showing how the books a writer has read beget the book she/he is writing. Readers of Ahlberg's *Better Brown Stories* (1995) may wonder why, in his acknowledgements, he not only mentions his good secretary, but also thanks Robert Louis Stevenson, Sir Arthur Conan Doyle, Somerset Maugham, Enid Blyton and Raymond Briggs for their help. It's a clue to the texts that lie behind Allan's text – he wants the readers to discover a different level of reading game-play where the reader has to do more of the work. This is a new set of transformations; a nudge from those in the know is helpful. Again, the balance is a delicate one. My reading companions spotted the Briggs and Blyton connections at once, then asked for clues about the others, saying they remembered *Each Peach Pear Plum*. Too much interpretive assistance and the reader flees, leaving the teacher (that is who is usually there) in sole possession of the text. Not enough help, and 'that kind of book' is simply written off. William Mayne, whose work I greatly admire, has suffered from rejections of his (apparently) tough first chapters. It's there he trains the reader, who is tugging at the sentences to race to '*what* happens'. Mayne seriously wants his readers to grow in reading, but not everyone will tolerate the uncertainties of showing rather than telling. How to guide a reader to the initial meeting with an author who does not have peer-group approval is really skilled pedagogy.

At this point, the problem of difficulty in reading arises again. Most children want books to be worth the effort of reading, but need encouragement to be patient. Some teachers don't let young readers learn to see worth as 'coming to terms' with what the author wants the reader to do, and so smooth the readers' path to the story without the necessary engagement with the first pages. Henrietta Branford's *Fire, Bed and Bone* (1997), for example, is a story told by a dog. By the end of the first page the skilled adult has 'placed' the narrator and moves on to piece together the evidence that locates the tale in the period of the Peasants' Revolt. The same page is a different experience for the less experienced reader, who wonders: Who is telling me this? What's happening? Who are these people? He or she has to weave the story from the words and from her/his inner construction of the scene, first to establish the narrator (against the run of experience), then to make the textual details into significant clues, not only to what happens, but also to the interpretation of what is at stake. It's a different kind of reading, trusting the author to make plain, from the dog's dramatic monologue, who's who and what counts. The trick is to keep going. My contention is that, given their experience of TV transformations, children should not have the text interpreted *for* them before being encouraged to engage with it directly. Writers now move their readers swiftly from one imaginative consciousness to the next, blurring the distinctions between reality and fantasy, as Philip Pullman does in his successful, serious trilogy, which has its roots in *Paradise Lost*, no less. Children 'get into' texts with the author's help, if we show them that is what readers do. What I am now seeing is a new growth of seriousness in writing for the young, a feeling that they must not only meet the texts and take responsibility for them, but also move, at this time, to a more generalised under-standing of the issues addressed. Here is an example from a story young readers are greatly enjoying, a really splendid narrative, J.K. Rowling's *Harry Potter and the Chamber of Secrets*. Transformation is the key theme.

The hero longs for the end of the school holidays:

> He missed Hogwarts so much it was like having a constant stomach ache. He missed the castle, with its secret passageways and ghosts, his lessons (though perhaps not Snape, the potions master), the post arriving by owl, eating banquets in the Great Hall, sleeping in his four-poster bed in the tower dormitory, visiting the gamekeeper Hagrid, in his cabin, in the grounds next to the forbidden forest and, especially, Quidditch, the most popular sport in the wizarding world (six goal-posts, four flying balls and fourteen players on broomsticks).
>
> All Harry's spellbooks, his wand, robes, cauldron and top-of-the-range Nimbus Two Thousand broomstick had been locked in a cupboard under the stairs by Uncle Vernon the instant Harry had come home. What did the Dursleys care if Harry lost his place on the house Quidditch team because he hadn't practised all summer? What was it to the Dursleys if Harry went back to school without any of his homework done? The Dursleys were what wizards call Muggles (not a drop of magical blood in their veins) and as far as they were concerned, having a wizard in the family was a matter of deepest shame. Uncle Vernon had even padlocked Harry's owl, Hedwig, inside her cage, to stop her carrying messages to anyone in the wizarding world.
>
> (Rowling 1998: 8–9)

The Gothic setting – 'a common convention to offset the suburban', says Terry Eagleton (1999: 2) – the conventions of school stories, baddies and goodies, everything derived from comics, cartoons, horror tales, magic of all kinds, crowd the fictive, carnivalistic world, where young wizards still have to abide by the rules, to learn the responsibilities of living in a world where the impossible is the norm. The author's own classical reading is the ground base of the narrative. It also provides a basilisk, a phoenix (where else would the young encounter them these days?), and a gift for naming the characters in terms of their func-tion, a tradition as old as fables. A diary at the heart of the mystery was written by an elderly wizard called Riddle. The professors profess what their names indi-cate; Malfoy, of potions, is the obvious no-gooder. The Gothic excess is both comic and deeply serious, after the fashion of true comedy. For all the surface app-earances of everything that young people enjoy and long for, real transformations are related to primary loyalties. Wizardly actions have consequences that wands and broomsticks cannot avert. Polyjuice Potion will work on condition that its users are prepared to run the risk of being transformed into someone else. Young readers can and should surf this book for the fun of it. But the kind of reading that Iser suggests is probably what it deserves: 'Reading, it could be said in a formulation of Gregory Bateson's, is like life itself, a game whose purpose is to discover the rules, in a process by which the rules perpetually change and always remain undiscoverable' (Iser 1991).

My next challenge is more perplexing. It's a book that young readers rarely choose for themselves. Adults are not sure which slot it fits into after reading the beginning:

> This man, he had no sort of name to waste breath on, he filled his mouth with drink. A swig and a slug before he had come through the door and like a horse at a trough at the wedding feast. Oh he would still be alive right enough but for the night he got drunk and his voice carried.
>
> 'Nails O' God! You dun mean thas, man!' he says. 'You dun mean to say he's thinking he's the first wi' her!'
>
> (Howker 1994: 1)

The story of *Martin Farrell*, a short novel by Janni Howker, is of a fierce family feud in the Debatable Land of the Scots–English border, in the hills, where the writ of neither country counted for much in the days of cattle rievers. They fought, hand to hand, for supremacy. Pride, greed, and revenge were more highly regarded than following the farmer's wooden plough. Without his knowing, the hero has birth ties to Armstrongs and Grahams. He fears both, and survives. The reader has to sort out the plot sequence from the telling voice of a scop-like narrator, who must keep clear of the action. It is an idiosyncratically composed text: short paragraphs, gaps, sharp utterances. The ghostly background is heavy with menace. This is the stuff of ballads, heritage business.

My experience suggests that young readers abandon texts they don't want to read. They cannot be forced to march through what they think is enemy territory. From time to time, however, it is worthwhile engaging those who think they are too short of breath to make the effort to surprise themselves. When I try to discover why some texts seem more difficult than others, I push away at something like this. My accomplices convince me that, if the story matters, comes to seem important, if the outcome of 'what happens' has significance in a wider, more general sense (e.g. what, exactly, is 'loyalty'), if it is worth talking about afterwards, then the needful effort of reading is part of the satisfaction of the meeting. A bridge has been crossed. *Martin Farrell* would make a good film; then 12-year-old boys would fall over each other to read it.

There is always a danger that children's reading may be too adult-led, too worthy, or unrelated to the painful transitions of foreshortened childhood or lengthened dependence in adolescence. *The Trokeville Way*, by Russell Hoban, seems at first a slow-moving story about a teenage boy who, after a fight with the school bully which left his senses strangely heightened, buys a landscape jigsaw puzzle from an ex-music-hall magician fallen on hard limes. In a trance-like state, he feels himself drawn into the picture, then into the lives of the former owner, the artist and the girl who is the object of his first romantic affections. As in *The Mouse and his Child*, but without the multilayered virtuosity of that text, we have an interesting blurring of reality and fantasy, as in significant daydreaming, where Hoban, making it all seem 'real', is probing the soft tissue of the hero's emotions and self-confrontation in a kind of inner speech. There are not many narratives that offer young males the chance for introspection as a part of the meeting. A suggested comparison is with Aidan Chambers' novels for older readers.

The examples I have offered so far, of meetings that imply transitions and transformations in reading, are all in the tradition of children's book as English literature. So, also, is this last example, but here the meeting is of a different kind. To pick up the thread of change, we cast back to the transformations of representations offered by new technologies in book production, so as to look at and read the true story of *Ethel and Ernest* (Briggs 1998). No English picture-book storyteller is more subversive, touching, profound and utterly funny than Raymond Briggs. Readers of all ages recognise and admire his comic-strip style, combining verbal and visual humour to upbraid the genteel surface niceties of middle-class manners with confrontational realism and fantastical characters: *Father* ('bloomin' ') *Christmas*, *The Snowman* and *The Man* are all young readers' favourites. *Ethel and Ernest*, a biographical narrative of Briggs' mother and father, is for any reader who wants to read it, of whatever age. Rendered with every ounce of Briggs' art in a fine book, in a smaller format than his usual wide-spread pages, it encapsulates the main events of this passing century as they brought about the transformations of social life of people (Briggs' parents) whom the blurb describes as 'decent' and 'ordinary', 'representative of us all'. I think it is an heroic tale: the inner life of the narrative is their coming to terms with transitions. As a meeting place of readers and text, it offers a challenge to traditional perceptions of reading, and an instance of dialogue with the future in the growing life of their only son, the artist author.

The opening three pages show the first meeting of the central characters over the days of a week in 1928. Ethel, a young working lady's maid, shakes her duster from the front window of a fine house just as Ernest cycles by in the rain. Two small views of the street show his skid marks. He passes again on Tuesday, but the encounter fails on Wednesday. The reader reads the meeting in the expressions of the characters. The only words on these pages are the days of the week and three speech bubbles – two on Wednesday: 'ETHEL! FOR HEAVEN'S SAKE! WHERE ARE YOU?' from somewhere out of sight, and the reply, 'Coming, Madam', from Ethel. On Thursday, her name has screech marks round it. On Saturday, a transformed, unexpected Ernest arrives with a bunch of flowers and invites Ethel to 'the pictures'. Nothing in this paraphrase conveys the effective subtleties of the pictures. Later, Ethel shows Ernest the house where she grew up and wonders why Ernest doesn't reciprocate. Now words do the work of describing what Ernest doesn't want Ethel to see:

Our street's full of diddacois and costermongers.

Horses and carts all down the road ...

Fruit and veg all over the place ...

Scrap iron, rag and bone men ...

There's three pubs ...

Blokes playing cards on the pavement ...

and there's horse-er-horse manure everywhere.

There's fights outside the pubs – women, too ...

The coppers won't go down there.

(Briggs 1998: 7)

In terms of information, reading to learn, this is one of the most accessible accounts of recent history. When my young associates had sorted their way through the narrative, they returned to the depth in the details especially about the Blitz, evacuation, nights in a shelter full of water, bombings and casualties – nothing in the grand heroic style but all the more telling for that. They spotted the arrival of new machinery, electric goods as points of change, they were sketchy about the politics but, on being helped to read aloud the arguments between the couple, and to see how they solved them, were soon off again into the more delicate bits of personal relations. Jacqueline Rose's conviction that origins, sex and death are compelling topics for young readers was well borne out. As I was following the poignant decline of the protagonists, they were upbeat about their son's progress, only later making connections between the last details of this book and others they already knew.

The meetings of readers and this text clearly held more meaning-making than I have been able to give account of here. The incidents are full of Briggs' multiple expressiveness – their actuality is never in doubt, yet every picture is suffused with imagination and love, and not a trace of sentimentality The presentation is a miracle of simultaneity; interpretations would take pages of prose to penetrate.

In simply recalling the encounters, not always long ones, when the books I've considered went from hand to hand, I realised the readings were already going, had already gone, through transitions and transformations in the readers. I had to let this series of meetings with the texts matierialise, and follow where they and the readers led me.

But, as I learnt long ago, it's even more complicated than that.

References

Ahlberg, A. (1995) *The Better Brown Stories*, ill. Fritz Wegner, London: Viking.

Branford, Henrietta (1997) *Fire, Bed and Bone* London: Walker Books.

——(1998) *Hansel and Gretel*, London: Scholastic.

Briggs, Raymond (1998) *Ethel and Ernest, a True Story*, London: Jonathan Cape.

Clark, Margaret (1990) *The Best of Aesop's Tales*, ill. Charlotte Voake, London: Walker Books.

Eagleton, Terry (1999) 'Allergic to Depths', review of Richard Davenport Hines' *Gothic: Four Hundred Years of Excess, Horror, Evil and Ruin*, *London Review of Books*, 18 March: 2–5.

Eco, Umberto (1999) *Serendipities: Language and Lunacy*, London, Weidenfeld and Nicolson.

Fine, Anne (1998) *The Twelve Dancing Princesses*, London: Scholastic.

Fox, Carol (1993) *At the Very Edge of the Forest: The Influence of Literature on Storytelling by Young Children*, London: Cassell.

Hardy, Barbara (1969) 'Towards a Poetics of Fiction', *Novel, a Form of Fiction*, Brown University. Reprinted in Meek, M., Warlow, A. and Barton, G. (eds) (1977), *The Cool Web: The Pattern of Children's Reading*, London: The Bodley Head.

Harrison, Colin and Salinger, Terry (eds) (1998) *Assessing Reading*, 2 vols, vol. 1 *International Perspectives on Reading Assessment*, London: Routledge.

Heaney, Seamus (1995) *The Redress of Poetry: Oxford Lectures*, London. Faber and Faber.

Hoban, Russell (1996) *The Trokeville Way*, London: Jonathan Cape.

Hollindale, Peter (1997) *Signs of Childness in Children's Books*, Stroud: The Thimble Press.

Howker, Janni (1994) *Martin Farrell*, London: Julia MacRae.

Hunt, Peter (ed.) (1996) *International Companion Encyclopedia of Children's Literature*, London: Routledge.

Iser, W. (1991) 'Das Fictive und das Imaginäre', quoted in Valentine Cunningham (1994) *In the Reading Gaol*, Oxford: Blackwell, p. 259.

Lesnick-Oberstein, K. (1994) *Children's Literature, Criticism and the Fictive Child*, Oxford: Oxford University Press.

Lewis, N. and Barrett, A. (1992) *The Emperor's New Clothes*, London: Scholastic.

Lowe, Virginia (1998) Is this a real story?: young children's concept of reality status of stories and pictures?, PhD thesis, Monash University, Victoria, Australia.

Meek, M., Warlow, A. and Barton, G. (eds) (1977) *The Cool Web: The Pattern of Children's Reading*, London: The Bodley Head.

Rosen, Michael (1997) 'A Materialist and Intertextual Examination of the Process of Writing a Work of Children's Literature', PhD thesis, University of North London.

Rowling, J.K. (1998) *Harry Potter and the Chamber of Mystery*, London: Bloomsbury.

Scollon, R. and Scollon, S. (1981) 'The Literate 2 Year-Old: The Fictionalization of Self', in special issue of *Advances in Discourse Processes*, vol. 8, 'Narrative, Literacy and Face in Inter-Ethnic Communication', Norwood, NJ: Ablex.

Index